Friends
Like These

For Greta
My best friend

And in memory of the
great and loved David McMahon

Danny Wallace

Friends Like These

With illustrations by
Daniel Wallace
Age 5

EBURY
PRESS

7 9 10 8 6

Published in 2008 by Ebury Press, an imprint of Ebury Publishing

A Random House Group Company

Copyright © Danny Wallace 2008

Danny Wallace has asserted his right to be identified as the author of this Work
in accordance with the Copyright, Designs and Patents Act 1988

The Random House Group Limited Reg. No. 954009

Addresses for companies within the Random House Group
can be found at www.randomhouse.co.uk

A CIP catalogue record for this book is available from the British Library

The Random House Group Limited supports The Forest
Stewardship Council (FSC), the leading international forest certification
organisation. All our titles that are printed on Greenpeace approved
FSC certified paper carry the FSC logo. Our paper procurement policy
can be found at www.rbooks.co.uk/environment

Mixed Sources
Product group from well-managed
forests and other controlled sources
www.fsc.org Cert no. TT-COC-2139
© 1996 Forest Stewardship Council

Printed in the UK by CPI Mackays, Chatham, ME5 8TD

ISBN 9780091896768

To buy books by your favourite authors and register for offers visit
www.rbooks.co.uk

'If a man has no tea in him, he is incapable of understanding truth and beauty.'
Japanese proverb

Prologue

'I think you should get a will,' said the man.

'A *will*?' I said. 'I'm only twenty-nine!'

'Doesn't matter. You're nearly thirty. Statistically, *most* people die above the age of thirty.'

'*Do* they?' I said, horrified.

'Statistically, yes. Do you own a house?'

'I've just bought one!' I said.

'A car?'

'Yes!'

'Do you have a wife?'

'Only a small one.'

'Doesn't matter. You should get a will.'

'Do *you* have a will?' I asked.

'No,' said the man. 'I'm only twenty-eight.'

This was just one of many similar conversations I would suddenly be having on my way to turning thirty, during a time in which I'd begun to question the way my life was going. I'm not saying I was unhappy – I wasn't, I was very happy – but I *was* beginning to feel *unnerved*.

Growing up is a strange thing to happen to anybody. And it does. To almost *everybody*. And for me, the way to cope with it became quite simple – to look back.

I was worried, when I wrote the following pages down, that you might not be all that interested in the people I met. That perhaps they might be too specific to me for them to matter to you. But then I realised – the more specific I was being, the more general everything was becoming… childhood, for example, and adolescence, and hopes and wishes, and friendship, and maturity... but if *they* don't strike any chords, there's a car chase and some ninjas for you, too.

The people you're about to meet are some of the people I grew up with, in ordinary schools, in ordinary places, in ordinary times. Wherever possible, and in the vast majority of cases, I've kept their names and details real – on those rare occasions where someone's asked me to change a name or detail, I've done so, and in one case in particular I've taken the decision myself, in the interests of privacy. Sometimes I've also had to move a date or event around a bit, but this is just so that you don't get bored and fall asleep too easily. I know what you're like.

Hey, wow – I've just noticed – what *excellent* shoes you're wearing. They really set off your eyes.

This, then, is the story of a summer in my life that came to sum up all the summers of my life, and perhaps prepared me a little for all the summers to come.

I still don't have a will, by the way. But I think I *did* find my way. See you in there.

Danny Wallace
Augsburger Strasse, Berlin, September 2007

Chapter One

In which we experience an earthquake...

There are moments in life when you come to question your actions. Moments of outstanding clarity and purest thought, when you look around you, you take in your environment, you work out what brought you here, and you decide that something is wrong.

For me, it was happening right now.

Right now, right this very *second*, in the middle of a harsh and sparse Japanese countryside, a little over a week before my thirtieth birthday, past a town I didn't know the name of, full of people whose names I couldn't pronounce.

My address book – a battered black address book with just twelve names in; an address book that had taken me around Britain, to America, Australia and now here – had proved useless this time.

It was four o'clock and I looked around me. I took in my environment. I worked out what brought me here. And I decided that something was wrong.

Here I was, standing in a rice field under a mountain in the afternoon sun, a Westerner in the far, far East, wearing grubby trainers, mud-flecked jeans and a T-shirt with the face of a small Japanese boy on it.

And I was lost.

I dug into my pocket and pulled out the document I'd brought with me.

I looked at it.

An Investigation on the Influence of Vitreous Slag Powders on Rheological Properties of Fresh Concrete

I stared at it for a moment, then put it away again. It wasn't helping.

But there – there, in the distance, just beyond a scattering of houses and a girl on a bike, I saw something. A hospital. A vast, bright white block. This was what I needed. *This* was what I had come for.

Because in that building – in that *hospital* – was a man I needed to meet. A man I had travelled ten thousand miles to shake hands with. A man who went to my school for six months in the 1980s, who I'd last seen twenty years ago in a McDonald's in the East Midlands, and who had absolutely no idea whatsoever that I was currently tramping through a Japanese rice field a quarter of a mile away to meet him. A man whose face I had on my T-shirt.

In the past few months I had met royalty. Rappers. A man who thinks he's solved time travel. I'd dressed as a giant white rabbit and I'd fought off a ninja.

And now... now I was going to meet Akira Matsui.

And I was going to meet Akira Matsui whether he liked it or not.

My decision to track down a Japanese man I hadn't seen since the days of Spokey Dokeys and B.A. Baracus, of Autobots and Optimus Prime, of aniseed balls and Raleigh Renegades, started with a text message, six months earlier. A text message telling me there was some important news. Important news I could only be told face to face.

I didn't know it then, but it was going to be quite a week for important news.

I'd moved house. Only a few miles on a map, but in London terms I had moved to a whole new world. No longer was I in the East End – an area I'd lived in for six years, where I'd become slowly and subtly used to the deafening thunder of the trains and the police sirens reminding you every few minutes that somewhere not too far away someone's been naughty. I was no longer living in the shadow of the council blocks which hid the sun from me four times a day but stood guard over me all the same. No longer a short walk from one of the nicest pubs in London, where Wag and Ian and I would spend long and lazy Sunday afternoons trying to flick peanuts into pint glasses or comparing notes on our important philosophies and ideas. Brick Lane, with its mile upon mile of curry houses, was now just out of convenient reach. Spitalfields Market, once round the corner, became somewhere we'd go *next* weekend, rather than this. And, perhaps most harrowingly, I was now no longer within Free Delivery range of Mr Wu's World of Meat. My world had been turned upside down.

I knew I'd miss it. And I was right. I missed it. I'm just not sure I *knew* I missed it.

For the time being, I'd been seduced. Seduced by a smart new area of north London. An area which was going places. An area where people did brunch, and drank lattes, and dined at Latvian restaurants, and drove long, silver cars, and wore Carhartt hoodies to make people think they were urban, and put everything apart from their house on the expense account. Where the men wore media glasses and the ladies wore skinny jeans and ate croissants and read the papers on a Sunday morning in a place with a battered leather couch before having a walk around middle-class antique stalls, with their thimbles and spoons. And everyone was married. Everyone! I liked it, but I found it laughable – this row upon row of cliché I had inadvertently stumbled into. What must they make of me here, I said one Sunday morning, over brunch, to Lizzie, my wife.

'What do you mean?' she said.

'I mean, what do you think they make of me here?' I giggled. 'Of *us*?'

Lizzie put down her newspaper, and I tore off another piece of croissant. I dipped it gingerly into my latte and raised my eyebrows. I was a bloody *maverick*.

'Who?'

'These married clichés,' I said. 'These thirtysomething media-glasses-wearing clichés in their Carhartt hoodies and their skinny jeans?'

'*You're* wearing a Carhartt hoodie,' said Lizzie, with a smile.

'Yes, *I'm* wearing a Carhartt hoodie, yes, but I imagine *I'm* doing it ironically. Anyway, I'm *urban*, aren't I?'

She wrinkled her nose.

'You're not *very* urban.'

'I'm urb-*ish*.'

'You're also nearly thirty and you're wearing media glasses.'

'These are *not* media glasses. These are merely glasses that are *shaped* like media glasses. At least I'm not wearing skinny jeans. I *could* be wearing skinny jeans! *Then* I'd be a cliché.'

'I'm wearing skinny jeans.'

'Yes. You are. That's true.'

I shifted around on the battered leather couch.

'Shall we have a walk around the antique stalls?'

'How do you ask for the bill in Latvian?'

The changes had started to happen without anyone noticing. But like the birds escaping the trees at the first fraction of a distant earthquake, the signs had been there, for anyone to pick up on, from the beginning. Just small things. Like the day I'd had to look up the number of a builder to do some work on our new little house. Looking up the number of a builder is the first step towards actually *employing* someone. I would be *in charge* of someone. A *man*. A *proper* man, with paint on his fingers and stubble on his chin. I'd be a boss. He'd probably call me his *gaffer*.

And then there was the morning Lizzie witnessed something terrifying.

'What are you *doing*?' she'd said, wide-eyed, as she watched me walking to the kitchen.

'I'm just taking this mug to the sink,' I'd said.

And then, as we realised what was happening – what that *signified* – how that was the *first time in my life* I had *ever* taken a mug to the sink within two days of finishing my tea – I stopped dead in my tracks and we both simply stared at each other in horror.

We had felt the first tremors of the earthquake. It was getting closer.

Soon, the evidence of impending adulthood began to pile up. The fridge was our early warning system. Gone were the Herta frankfurters and processed cheese of just a year or two before – replaced by skimmed milk, and hummus, and baby carrots, and fresh spinach. We'd gone organic, we were buying fairtrade, we had crisp white wine instead of cans of Stella. Clubs had become bars, nights down the pub had slowly morphed into intimate dinners with close friends. I ate low-fat pretzels with crushed rock salt where once Wotsits would have done. How had this happened? Was it the move? Or was it the fact that I was twenty-nine? On the brink of change? On the brink of finally, undeniably, irrefutably becoming… a man?

But I *wasn't* a man. I was a boy. I had a silly job, for starters. A job I'd entered into quite without meaning to, through a slightly odd set of circumstances. A job which gets strange looks. A job I'm slightly embarrassed to tell you about. A job which changed title every time I completed a new piece of work, but which, at the moment at least, you could sort of describe as 'very minor television personality' if you were being kind, and 'quiz show host' if you were not.

I told you it was silly.

Since I'd started popping up on shows, asking questions and providing answers, my friends had started to think of me as someone good to get on a pub quiz team – despite the fact that I have never in my life won a pub quiz. People texted me questions set by trivia machines in burger bars, hoping I'd help save their last two quid by telling them who in 1970 was signed by Hull City to become one of the youngest-ever managers in football history. Cabbies asked me to settle bets. I'd become recognisable on the streets, but only to people who thought they'd gone to school with me or met me at a wedding, or actually *had* gone to school with me or met me at a wedding. I was *especially* recognisable to *them*.

But it was fun. It was a different me, though. I had to pretend to be confident and in control and knowledgeable, but I felt a little like a fraud. Sometimes I wondered if I knew who the real me was. But still, it left me with a great deal of down-time. Down-time like this summer. I knew in the spring I'd be tackling a big new project, so for now I was happy bumbling about, writing the odd piece for a newspaper or magazine to keep the bills paid, seeing Wag and Ian when I could, and trying somehow to convince myself I was able to handle DIY. It was time I should have been investing wisely, to be honest. And yet I was doing nothing to stop this constant slide into domesticity…

So for weeks the rumble got louder. We'd started buying fresh bread. We'd visited a farmers' market and bought some olives, despite the fact that very few local farmers have ever actually farmed an olive. I wanted to talk to Lizzie about what was happening, but she seemed so comfortable, so at ease with it all, so in her element, that it never seemed the right time. She brought home display cushions. She bought some sticks which she stuck in a jar and convinced me were a 'dramatic focal point' for our living room. She bought the box set of Krzysztof Kieslowski's critically acclaimed *Trois Couleurs* trilogy, which she assured me would explore the French Revolutionary ideals of freedom, equality and brotherhood and their relevance to the contemporary world, and I'd smiled and hidden the copy of *Kung Fu Soccer* I'd bought that afternoon in HMV.

But these were all foreshocks... mere tremors before the main event. The day the earthquake threatened its arrival proper was the day my phone, sitting above the very epicentre of it all, jolted violently around the table, in controlled, measured spasms. Either there really *was* an earthquake, or I'd had a text.

Come round to ours on Friday night! It's a book launch! And we've got something we'd love to ask you...

It was from our friends Stefan and Georgia. Two names which prove, even more than a casual dunk of a croissant in a latte, that we were now operating in a whole different world. Were we still in the East End, I have no doubt that that text would have been from Blind Eric and Jimmy the Lips, inviting us out to throw traffic cones at cars.

The Friday arrived the way Fridays do, and we'd gone along to their vast Highbury mansion to find that Stefan, a chef, had prepared an elaborate spread of unusual dishes. It was all in aid of his latest cookbook, and felt very fancy and posh and middle class. Now, Stefan is a man who likes his food slightly odd. I know this because I once ate some soup at his house and on the third spoonful discovered a severed fish head staring back at me. He is yet to offer an after-dinner counselling service, but it can only be a matter of time before the authorities make it a legal requirement. So, as a joke, I'd brought along a Pot Noodle, 'just in case there's anything I don't like!'. Stefan laughed and I laughed and Lizzie laughed. I can be quite funny sometimes. But then he looked a little offended and put it in a cupboard.

I opened a beer and found the food.

In front of me was a plate of odd meat. Stefan joined me with a fine wine in hand.

'What's this?' I said, pointing at the dish.

'That's donkey sausage,' said Stefan.

'Oh,' I said. 'And this?'

'That is herring sperm.'

'Right. Good. Herring sperm,' I said. 'Where did you find that?'

'Up a herring,' said Stefan. 'We've also got some crickets for later. I picked them up in Beijing.'

'You have to be so careful these days,' I said, but it seemed from his expression that Stefan had actually picked them up on purpose.

Half an hour later, in the crowded garden, Lizzie was being kicked by a small child called Owen, and I was finishing my Pot Noodle.

'Georgia said they'd be over in a minute to ask us that question,' said Lizzie. 'I wonder what it is?'

Owen had started to kick *me* now. I tried my best to ignore him.

'I dunno,' I said, shrugging. 'Maybe he wants to know where I source my excellent Pot Noodles. Or maybe…'

And then I looked down and noticed that Owen was rubbing a donkey sausage into my shoes.

'Christ. Hold this…' I said to Lizzie, who had never held a Pot Noodle in her life before. She looked at it and pulled a face that was completely new to me, but which I imagine must have been one of wonder and intrigue. I don't want to make you jealous, but life with me is full of magical new experiences like holding Pot Noodles.

I got a pen and paper out.

'What are you up to?'

'I'm going to get rid of *this* little numbnut.'

I probably shouldn't use words like 'numbnut' in front of five-year-old boys.

I wrote a message on the paper and gave it to Owen, who was laughing and pointing at my shoes.

'Give this to your daddy,' I said.

Owen beamed at me. He'd been given a job. A job, by a grown-up! Me! I was his gaffer! This was precisely the same innocent beam of gratitude I could expect from the builders. He scuttled off to find his dad, pushing past Stefan and Georgia, who were walking towards us with big smiles and rosy cheeks.

'Listen, guys,' said Georgia. 'Time for the question. We were just wondering... and you can say no if you want to... but would you two possibly consider being... well...'

She paused, and looked to Stefan.

'Being what?' I asked.

'Godparents,' said Stefan.

There was a silence.

My mouth dropped open.

And I realised.

Somewhere deep inside me, the earthquake had finally hit.

Godparents! Responsibility! Adulthood!

Forget buying focaccia instead of Hovis! Forget buying wheels of brie instead of Dairylea Dunkers! This was the moment! *This* was grown-up! How had I not seen this coming? How had I been lulled into this? How could anyone see me as someone worthy of being a godparent?

We had just registered on the Richter scale.

All this had happened in a tenth of a second.

I looked over their shoulders. Poppy, their six-month-old daughter, was asleep on the sofa, a picture of calm and beauty. So tiny, and so frail, and so precious...

'We... what, *us*?' I said, in disbelief, and not a little panic.

Stefan's smile started to fade, but Lizzie jumped in.

'We'd love to,' said Lizzie, who is excellent in almost every situation, her job in PR helping her to put a distracting spin on my rather surprised reaction. 'We'd *love* to be Poppy's godparents.'

Stefan and Georgia nodded, then smiled. And then Lizzie smiled. And then I pulled a face which I hoped was one of confidence and adulthood – a face that said, 'yes, of course I am capable of looking after your child and rearing it should anything render you unable to do so yourself!', but which doubtless actually looked like I'd just trapped something I needed in my zipper.

And then we all hugged.

Stefan and Georgia walked away, arm in arm, under some kind of impression that they had just made a wise parenting move. As they went, I realised with a sigh that during the hug I had managed to smear some Chicken & Mushroom Pot Noodle down the back of Stefan's shirt.

I grabbed Lizzie's arm.

'Jesus, Lizzie, this is it!' I whispered. 'This is how they get you!'

'Who?'

'The grown-ups! It's like a club. We've been *selected*.'

'You *are* a grown-up.'

'I'm not! I'm a child! A boy! I've been faking everything else so far! I didn't understand a bloody *word* of those DVDs. I watched *Kung Fu Soccer* when you went to bed! Sometimes when you're out I buy Wotsits! The other day I went on eBay and looked at Scalextrics!'

Lizzie smiled and touched my arm.

'You're twenty-nine years old!' she said. 'I'm pretty sure you would've got into the club one day. And there's no crime in the eBay thing – everyone looks back when they hit thirty…'

'But this is *automatic* entry! This is responsibility! Am I ready for this? I need more time! And what do you mean, "when" they hit thirty? I'm still in my twenties!'

'You'll be thirty in six months,' she said. 'But yes, you've got time…'

She smiled, soothingly, not realising she'd just added to the terror.

'I'm here to help you, baby. You're *ready* for adulthood…'

It sounded reassuring. The trouble was, when she'd said 'you're ready for adulthood', she'd said it in the way that mothers tell small children they're 'ready to use the *big* pot'. It rather took the edge off the whole 'adulthood' thing.

And then I heard the rumble.

The rumble of anger, and danger, and fear.

It wasn't the earthquake. It was an aftershock. It was…

'WHO GAVE YOU THIS?'

It was loud and aggressive and instantly I knew – it was Owen's dad.

'Oh Christ,' I said.

We looked over the crowd, to the French windows. Owen's dad, with a copy of Stefan's book and a glass of something that looked rather strong, was leaning over his son, demanding more information.

'OWEN – WHO HAS DONE THIS TO YOU?'

'Shit,' said Lizzie. 'What did you write?'

I was panicking now.

'It was a joke!' I said. 'It wasn't meant in a bad way! He was rubbing donkey sausage in my shoes!'

Owen was now looking out into the garden, into the crowd, trying to pick us out, while his father flung Stefan's book to one side and tried to do the same...

'What did you *write*?'

I tried to think. What had I written? My mind was racing.

'I think he really thinks Owen wrote that note!' I said, terrified.

'Why would he believe Owen wrote that?'

'Wrote *what*?'

'He's going to see us in a second!'

'What did you *write*?'

I had to come clean.

'I wrote, "Dear Daddy, they have been feeding me booze. I am pissed off my tiny tits."'

Lizzie looked horrified. She went into crisis-management mode.

'Just keep still and don't look over at him,' she said, and so consequently we both instantly turned and looked straight at Owen. He locked eyes with us and his little arm shot forward to point us out. His dad's face turned to one of thunderous fury. There was rage in his eyes and violence on his mind. Stefan and Georgia had heard the bellowing and were now upon him, calming him down and asking what the problem was. Owen broke free and ran towards us.

'This isn't looking very good,' I said.

'No, it's not looking too good at all,' said Lizzie.

'What do we do now?' I asked.

'I'm not really sure,' said Lizzie.

We looked back towards Owen's dad, who was now pointing us out and whisper-shouting at Stefan.

'I think it'll be okay,' said Lizzie. 'Stefan will simply explain the situation and how we would never give a five-year-old booze, and—'

We looked down at Owen. He was standing at the buffet with a glass of red wine in his hand.

'*Whose wine is that?*' I cried.

'I think that's *mine*!' said Lizzie, her face suddenly white with terror. 'I only put it down when we all hugged!'

'OWEN! YOU PUT THAT DOWN! YOU PUT THAT DOWN RIGHT NOW!'

Owen looked at me and smiled. Although Lizzie would later claim he did not, I *swear* to you it looked like he mouthed the word 'numbnut' at me.

Lizzie started to walk towards him, but I pulled her back.

'Leave it! Don't go anywhere near him! It'll look like you gave it to him!'

Stefan was calming Owen's dad, but Georgia was quick off the mark, replacing the wine with orange juice. But his dad hadn't finished.

'WHO ARE THEY?' he demanded. Everyone looked round. 'THOSE PEOPLE HAVE BEEN GIVING MY CHILD ALCO-HOL!'

Lizzie and I suddenly found very interesting things in the garden to turn and point at.

'I think maybe we should go,' whispered Lizzie.

'Yes, I think maybe we should,' I whispered back.

'How do we get out?' she said.

'I think we should simply walk past them with our heads held high,' I said. 'And try to convey a sense in our general demeanour that as responsible adults we would never feed a child alcohol.'

And so we turned, and we passed them, and it was only when we were in the hallway on the final stretch that we heard, from the garden, and in a tone of disbelief and anger that lives with me to this day, the words: 'POPPY'S FUCKING *GODPARENTS*??'

One minute I had been welcomed into the adult world, the next I had proved beyond all doubt that I just wasn't ready for it. But I *had* to be ready for it. I had to at least *pretend*. I knew something was wrong. I knew something didn't feel quite right. But I didn't know what it was. And not knowing what it was really didn't help me understand how to make it better.

Lizzie let me buy a packet of Wotsits on the way home and I ate them on the bus. I told myself I would be fine, so long as I never stopped eating Wotsits.

A week or two later, I got a text from Ian.

And that was how it all started.

Wedesday 2nd November.

This morning I looked out of the window and saw a post van. Coming to get the post

✓ *
neat.

Chapter Two

In which we learn that
nobody moves to Chislehurst...

Like its sender, the text had been fairly simple.

I have important news. We must meet up.

I had been in the queue at the Post Office when it came through. Someone had just coughed on the back of my neck and a large woman was arguing with her dog. I'd texted back immediately.

All right then!

I began to wonder what Ian's important news could be as I edged closer to the front of the queue. I like it when people tell me they have important news. It makes me think they're considering invading a country, or they've discovered the whereabouts of an ancient scroll that will save all humanity. He texted back, mentioning neither scrolls nor invasions. Perhaps he was being watched. We agreed to meet in an hour's time at a pub near me.

'Next, please...' said the man behind the counter.

I handed him the slip of paper that had arrived through my postbox that morning. He disappeared for a few moments and came back with a large and mysterious box.

The day just kept getting more exciting.

*

'Hello?'

'Mum?'

'Yes! Who's that?'

'Your only son.'

A pause.

'Daniel?'

To be fair, I'd only given her one clue.

'Yes, it's Daniel!'

'Hello, wee bean!'

My mum has a way of inventing names for me that have never before been said to anyone. Her strong Swiss accent somehow makes them sound quite sensible, and she says them with such confidence you wouldn't be surprised if heads of state used the same terms when addressing each other at conventions. She doesn't allow herself to be constrained by words that actually exist, either, creating new ones out of the ether or inserting strange Swiss German nouns. In the past few weeks alone, I have been greeted as Pomplesnicker, BimpleWicker and Bobbely. I got off lightly. My dad's had thirty-five *years* of Minkeybips and Toodlebear. I'm not even sure if he knows his first name any more. I'm not even sure if I do.

'Mum, did you just send me a massive box?'

'Oh *no*!' she said. 'Was it *too* massive?'

She also has a knack of thinking everything is a potential disaster.

'No, it's just the *right kind* of massive,' I reassured her. 'But what's in it?'

'Just some things we thought you might need. You know. We're having a clearout at home, and we didn't want to throw this stuff out, and we thought it might be handy.'

'What kind of stuff?'

'Oh, you know. Old things we found in the loft.'

I'll be honest – 'old things we found in the loft' didn't scream 'handy'. Suddenly, opening a massive box – ordinarily a deeply exciting moment – was something I didn't mind putting off for now. So I thanked her, and promised I'd go through it all later, and somehow managed to lug it all the way to the pub to meet Ian.

It had been a recent discovery, this pub. It had pot pourri in the toilets and a sausage of the week.

I liked it here. Everyone in it seemed to be very comfortable in their skin. They belonged here. And I wanted to belong, just like them.

Once the shock of the events of Stefan and Georgia's party had died down, I'd realised the only way to deal with what was happening was to let it. To succumb to its inevitable, brutal force. To allow myself to be swept along on the crest of this magnolia-coloured, basil-scented wave. I'd just have to accept it. Stefan and Georgia thought I was ready. Lizzie thought I was ready. Which meant: I was probably ready. And so, in the week or two before meeting up with Ian, I'd simply got on with things.

Ian had looked suspicious when I finally saw him walk in. He didn't recognise me at first because I was hidden slightly by my copy of the *Guardian*. I called out his name, and three or four other men also reading the *Guardian* lowered their copies to look at him. They were all wearing similar glasses to me. Ian looked at them, and then at me, rolled his eyes and sat himself down.

'So!' I said. 'Important news!'

'Important news calls for important pints,' said Ian.

'They only do bottles here,' I said.

Ian shook his head, solemnly, and I went to get them in.

When I got back, Ian was staring at my massive box.

'So what's in it?' said Ian, poking at it with his finger, as if that would somehow tell him.

'Handy things,' I said.

'Gloves?' said Ian.

'Handy as in useful. I don't know. *Maybe* gloves. My mum sent it.'

'How about the bag?'

He indicated the plastic bag next to it. This is Ian's version of small talk. He'd be going through my pockets next. I opened the bag and showed him.

'What in the name of *God* are *they*?' he said, peering in. 'What in the name of *God* have you brought to the pub?'

'They're coasters!' I said, delighted. 'I just bought them!'

'Hide them!' he said. 'Someone will *see* us. And please tell me they're for Lizzie.'

'No. They're mine. Well, *ours*. I bought them. They depict various different industrial scenes through the ages.'

'I can see that. Who are you? Your mum? Why've you bought coasters?'

'If we put them in the living room, they will offset the display cushions perfectly.'

'Right. You have *display* cushions?'

'We have two display cushions.'

'Do you sit on them?'

I put my finger in the air.

'They're not for bottoms. They're for display purposes only.'

Ian put his beer down and studied me carefully. He seemed a little annoyed with me. There was a silence. And then finally he said, 'So how are you, anyway?'

'I'm fine,' I said. 'I'm fine. And you?'

'Very well.'

But he was still looking at me, suspiciously.

There was another silence. This was odd. Usually we never found it hard to talk.

I looked out of the windows, desperate for inspiration. Some children were kicking a cone. It reminded me of something I'd just read in the paper.

'League tables!' I said.

'Football?' said Ian, confused.

'No, the schools one,' I said. 'According to the latest schools league tables, the schools around here are well above average. Although others are apparently *below* average. I think that means they average out.'

'So the schools around here are average?'

I nodded, eagerly.

'You are a deeply interesting man.'

I smiled a smile of gratitude. And then I realised he was being sarcastic and tried to subtly change it into a smile of annoyance, but it just looked weird. Ian sat back in his chair and exhaled, heavily.

'Okay,' he said. 'That's it. My news can wait. Let's deal with the matter at hand. What in the name of all that is right and proper has happened to you?'

I blinked.

'How do you mean?'

'You've bought some coasters! You've got *display cushions*! You have made reference to an area's *schooling*!'

'It doesn't mean anything, Ian,' I shrugged, hiding the fact that I knew perfectly well it did. 'And the cushions are just a little cosmetic flourish.'

'*Cosmetic flourish*? What's cosmetic flourish?'

I thought about it. What *was* cosmetic flourish? And what was I doing *talking* about cosmetic flourish?

'I don't know,' I said. 'I saw it on *Property Ladder*.'

Ian shook his head in disbelief.

'You've gone all old!'

'No, I haven't!' I said, defensively. 'And if I have, you have as well! We're not getting any younger, Ian!'

I made a wise face and took a sip of my beer. I looked at the bottle and made a satisfied 'Aah' sound. Ian put his head in his hands.

'I have seen this happen before, my friend. I have seen this happen before and it's dangerous.'

'Seen what happen? What's dangerous?'

'This. You. Now. Approaching thirty. So-called "growing up". Buying things no normal man would ever want to buy. Making "Aah" sounds. Using words like "flourish". It's happening to you, Dan. You're becoming one of Them.'

'One of *who*?'

'*Them*!'

'The New World Order?'

'No. The thirty-year-old married man who's lost all sight of his sense of self! Look around you. Are we in the Royal Inn?'

'No.'

'No. We're *not* in the Royal Inn, are we? We're not in the same pub we've drunk in for the past who-knows-how-many-years. We're in some weird gastropub in north London with ironic photographs on the wall, drinking Taiwanese lager. Look! Look at that sign! They have a sausage of the week, for Christ's sake! A sausage *of the week*! And it's not even a *proper* sausage!'

'Lamb, mint and apricot is *not* an unusual sausage. It's very in right now.'

'How do you even *know* what sausages are "in" right now?'

'They do a newsletter.'

Ian sighed and took a sip of his pint.

'Do you remember Micky Thomas?' he said.

'No,' I said.

'Exactly. *No one* remembers Micky Thomas. Because when Micky Thomas hit thirty, he bought a Volkswagen Polo and some Premium Bonds. *You're* Micky Thomas!'

I was suddenly very frightened indeed.

'I don't want to be Micky Thomas!' I said. 'I don't *remember* Micky Thomas! Why don't I remember Micky Thomas?!'

'Actually I'm not sure you ever met him. But the point remains, men like Micky Thomas disappear all the time. They're good men. Fine men. But they catch this… this *disease*. This *need* to wear brogues and discuss congestion charging. They wear jeans with elasticated waists. And then, one day' – he clicked his fingers, theatrically – 'they're gone.'

'We have to find them!' I said. 'We have to find these elasticated men!'

'Some claim to have seen them,' said Ian, staring into the middle distance. 'Some say if you get up at just the right time on a Sunday morning, you can still see these lost souls wandering around IKEA, or in the linen section of John Lewis. But I think those are just stories to frighten the children.'

'But what if it's happening to me, Ian? I don't want to be one of those lost souls! I want to be young and carefree and stick twos-up to the Establishment! I want to go backpacking and do riots!'

'It nearly happened to me,' said Ian, heavily, and then, with real gravitas: 'I even bought a juicer.'

I remembered that. He'd drunk nothing but carrot juice for six days and his elbows turned yellow.

'I managed to pull it back from the brink,' said Ian. 'That's what you have to do. Before you become a Stepford Man.'

I realised I had to be honest with Ian. Yes, he'd seen the coasters… but the coasters were *nothing*.

'What if it's too late?' I said, panicked and nervy. 'What if I've already *become* one of Them? Just the other day… Christ, I can't believe I'm going to tell you this…'

Ian closed his eyes again and waved me on.

'I saw a girl walking through town. I could see her midriff, and...'

His eyes suddenly opened. He leaned forward, keen to know more, but this was almost too awful to say.

'... and I *tutted*, Ian. I bloody *tutted*!'

'You *tutted*?'

He was outraged. This was worse than he thought.

'It was *cold*, Ian!'

'You *tutted* at a *lady's midriff*!'

'Magic FM said it was likely to get worse later on in the afternoon. I hoped that my tutting might act as a subtle warning of the forecast ahead.'

Ian shot back into his seat and put his hands up.

'*Magic FM*? You were *listening* to *Magic FM*?'

'They do all the hits from the seventies, eighties, and the best of today, Ian! It's not my fault, it's just so feelgood.'

Ian looked terrified.

'Bloody hell, Dan – stop talking like this! I was only mucking about!'

'The other night we had pitta and hummus and I even asked for some more hummus!'

'Dan, you're scaring me, please...'

'I can swear in Latvian, Ian! Bezdeet! *Bezdeet*!'

'Sssh...'

'I like my pine nuts *lightly toasted*, Ian!'

'*Dan*...'

'I ate a herring's sperm! I *ate a herring's sperm*!'

'Stop *talking* this way!'

I slammed my hands over my mouth. I had to stop these demons escaping! Ian was right – this *was* happening to me! This was happening to me and it wasn't natural!

Slowly, I removed my hands from my mouth and we calmed ourselves.

Ian was first to talk. He had a plan.

'We're going to find a proper pub, Dan. A proper one, that serves proper beer, and we're going to sort this out.'

I nodded, sadly. Ian drained his Taiwanese lager and banged the glass down, like a man full of life and youth and vibrancy.

I looked at him.

'You should use a coaster,' I said. 'You're going to mark the table.'

'Y'see,' said Ian, opening the Wotsits. 'The thing about your married, thirty-year-old man, living in north London, is that he's lost his way. That's all. Simple as that. He's let himself be seduced by the Habitat catalogue. He's probably got "Sunday clothes". He's lost sight of the important things in life. By all means have a scatter pillow, Dan, but never forget your roots.'

'Display cushion. And you're right, I know. It just all happened so fast. It feels like my twenties have whizzed by. I've gone from pound-a-pint nights to christenings, and I have no idea how.'

'Look at these fellas, here,' he said, pointing around the pub. 'That old fella in the corner...'

He nodded towards an old man with a cap on. He was rolling some tobacco and coughing over his hands.

'Do you think he's got any scatter cushions? Do you think he's popping home for a ciabatta? No. And yet he looks perfectly happy, doesn't he?'

We both looked at him. He coughed some more and then started talking to a fly.

'The point is, he's stayed true to himself. That's what you need to do. Stay true to your roots. Otherwise, *that*...' – we both looked again at the old man talking to the fly – 'will only ever be a *pipe* dream.'

I was full of gratitude to Ian. He was a good friend. I was lucky with my friends. I had the coolest wife in the world, a wife whose laid-back Australian ways would mean that coasters were a lifestyle choice, not a legal requirement. And then there was Wag – a musician on the verge of greatness. A man with a heart of gold. And Ian – radio presenter and man about town. A man who also had a heart of gold – and elbows to match. A man I'd been through so much with. A man who stood shoulder to shoulder with me, no matter the problem. A man who was always there.

I relied on these guys. I guess as you get a little older, your social group becomes a little more focused. A little more honed. And with it, a little more reliable. Trusted. *Needed*. As people drift away, or move off, or get married, have kids, emigrate, or whatever it is they do where you're from, you're lucky to hang on to the people you do. I realised this as I looked at Ian.

'Thanks, Ian. I'll do as you say. And I'll talk to Lizzie. I'll suggest a numerical limit on the amount of scented candles in the house. She'll understand. Maybe I needn't rush into adulthood. It's the World Cup soon. And I've made a decision. One that I think will combat all the changes of late.'

Ian looked quizzical. But I knew I'd sorted this problem out.

'Me and you and Wag will watch the World Cup at the *Royal Inn*. In the East End. As God intended.'

There was a pause where he should have said 'Yes we will!' and then clashed glasses with me and drunk to my health. But he didn't. He said, 'Ah.'

'Ah?' I said.

'Ah,' he said. 'Yeah. Ah.'

'What do you mean, "Ah"?'

'I forgot. My news.'

'What's your news?' I said, suddenly nervous. News that begins with an 'Ah' is invariably bad news. Like 'Ah. I broke it', or 'Ah. I see pirates'. I nodded Ian on.

'So what is it?'

He took a deep breath.

'I'm moving away.'

I was stunned.

'You're... you're what?'

'I'm moving away. There comes a time when you have to just... move away.'

What? This wasn't possible.

'This is a bit bloody sudden!'

'The loss of spontaneity leads to the death of the man.'

'Eh?'

'I'm like the Littlest Hobo, Dan – now I've sorted out your problem, I've got to keep moving on.'

'But… where *to*, Ian? Please say it's round here!'

Ian smiled, proudly.

'To Chislehurst.'

'*Chislehurst*?'

Why the hell was he moving to *Chislehurst*? Who spontaneously moves to *Chislehurst*?

'Oh, it's *brilliant* in Chislehurst,' said Ian. 'I took one look at Chislehurst, and said, right, I'm moving to Chislehurst.'

'You *can't* move to Chislehurst! *No one* moves to Chislehurst!'

'I *have* to move to Chislehurst. In fact, I'm *moving* to Chislehurst. I put my flat up for sale, someone bought it the next day. I'm moving to Chislehurst!'

He raised his glass and instinctively I clinked it. But then I realised I didn't want to and put my glass straight down again.

'But you said you hated Chislehurst! You had that bad experience there! The one you don't like to talk about!'

'I have moved on, Dan. Sometimes, to be at peace with what's coming up, you have to be in touch with what's already happened. And I am now at peace with Chislehurst. Plus, London's just a bit… *stabby* right now.'

'*Stabby*?'

'Yeah. And… *bomby*.'

'But… is this forever?'

'At least until Christmas, Dan. I will rent in Chislehurst and then I will look once again at the situation and decide whether Chislehurst is indeed the future.'

'But… but what am I going to do? Chislehurst is *miles* away!'

'You'll be fine. I'll still be about from time to time. But I'll mainly be in Chislehurst.'

I shook my head in disbelief.

'But there's nothing to do in Chislehurst!'

Ian looked offended.

'They have an internet café in Chislehurst now.'

I couldn't quite take it in. Ian was inexplicably moving to Chislehurst. I tried one last move.

'But what about all our plans?'

He frowned.

'We don't *have* any plans.'

Christ – he was right!

'Anyway,' he said, 'Wag's only over in Hackney. That's *minutes* away. Although I'd be careful, because Hackney is *particularly* stabby at this time of year. But you can continue your journey of self-rediscovery with him. Just keep away from sausages of the week, okay? That's when they've *got* you!'

My head was spinning. There was so much to take in.

'To Chislehurst!' said Ian, raising his glass. And then he shook his head in wonder. 'How's *that* for excellent news?'

'Now, how's *this* for excellent news,' said Wag, on the phone. I'd called him for reassurance, and to share the day's strange events. I was slightly out of breath, having tried to run home with the massive box in my arms.

'Before you tell me this excellent news,' I said, 'please, Wag – tell me you're not moving to Chislehurst.'

'What? No one moves to Chislehurst!'

'I *know* no one moves to Chislehurst! But *Ian's* moving to Chislehurst!'

'Forever?'

'At least until Christmas!'

I took a sip of my tea as Wag did the necessary computations.

'But… why's he moving to *Chislehurst*?'

Phew. This was what I needed. Someone who shared an appreciation of the lunacy of a situation like someone moving to Chislehurst.

'It is inexplicable,' I said, shrugging dramatically. 'Not even *he* can explic it.'

'How do these things happen?' said Wag, and I was full of warmth towards him. Yeah, so we wouldn't have Ian this summer. But *we'd* hang out. *We'd* have fun.

'So,' I said, sitting down on the box. 'It looks like we'll only need two seats down the Royal Inn for the World Cup…'

'Yeah,' said Wag, slowly, and then: 'Ah...'

My eyes widened. They were now touching my ears.

'What do you mean, "Ah"?'

Silence.

'Wag, Ian said "Ah" just before he told me he was moving to Chislehurst! He said "Ah" just before he told me *his* excellent news... People say "ah" just before they see *pirates*, Wag...'

'Well... and I'm sure you'll be happy for me about this... we're going on tour!'

'Who?' I said, confused. 'Me and you?'

'No – me and the band! It's going to be brilliant!'

I tried to remain calm. This was not a problem. This was probably miles off yet. This was probably in the new year, or maybe even the year after...

'We start next week!'

'Next *week*? How... how long for?'

'Six months! With the possibility that it might be extended!'

I took a deep breath and tried to relax. It was probably a tour of provincial arts theatres. Or London pubs! It was probably just a tour of London pubs!

'But you'll still be around in the evenings, won't you?'

'It's a World Tour... Russia, the US, Australia...'

I was speechless. Wag wasn't.

'I've gotta go – I've got more people to tell!'

'Wag! Wait! I have to tell you something!'

I didn't know what to say. I just didn't want him to go. He was my pal and now he was going to be gone for six months! Six months at *least*!

I *had* to say something!

'What is it?'

Come on, Dan! Convince him that rock and roll is the devil's music! Convince him the baby Jesus frowns upon his ways!

But all I could think of to say was...

'The other day I ate a herring's sperm.'

There was a silence. And then Wag sounded truly delighted for me.

'That is *excellent* news! It's all happening, eh? I told you – this is our year! Hey, listen, I've got a call on the other line, I think it's the tour manager...'

He had a tour manager? When did he get a tour manager? When had all this happened? Was I too busy sitting on display cushions and eating hummus to notice that my two best pals had moved on without me? Were we all, in our own ways, growing up?

I started to say goodbye, but he'd already hung up.

I put the phone down and sat on the sofa, heavily. It was all too much to take. In the space of a day I had lost both Ian and Wag for an entire summer. My two pals. Gone. Just like that. With no warning whatsoever. And just when I needed them most. Just when I needed them to keep me on the straight and narrow. To remind me of who I used to be, before lattes and brunches and Latvian swearing.

I knew I was being selfish. I knew that, for both of them, there could have been no better news. But their happiness made me panic all the more. Wag had probably already bought a tour van and a new plectrum. And Ian – Ian was probably already at the Chislehurst Arms, making new friends, sneering at 'the rat race' and drinking bitters with names like Old Badger Tits or the Snooty Poodle. He was probably editing the parish newsletter, and writing furious editorials about out-of-town superstores and proposed bypasses, and going foxhunting in a ludicrous top hat. What a wanker. How *dare* he go foxhunting in a ludicrous top hat?

And then – an irrational and unwelcome thought hit me. What if this was somehow the end of our friendship? What if we were now destined to grow apart? After all – men who have display cushions can't be friends with rock stars. And everyone knows once someone moves out of London you never see them again. They turn into Micky Thomases! This could be the end of an era!

It was not an entirely unfamiliar scenario to me. I'd moved around a lot as a kid. Moved cities, moved schools. Always made a pact with my then best friends that this wouldn't change anything, that absence meant nothing, that we'd always hang out. But we'd never quite been able to stick to that pact. The damage was always done – people make a habit of moving on. Now I was older, though – living in an era of portable phones and MySpace and YourSpace and electronic messaging services – surely that would make a difference? We were no longer at the mercy of our parents' jobs, after all. And it wasn't as if anyone was disappearing anywhere, particularly. Provided Wag's tour was a crushing failure, he'd be back in the winter. *That* was something to hope for. And hey – maybe Ian's house would burn down!

I got up and mooched around the house. It was all slightly depressing. There was still so much work to do. Boxes to unpack. Sockets to fix. Walls to paint. I stood and stared, transfixed, at a fruit bowl. I shook my head. How did it come to this? How did it come to me owning a fruit bowl?

But there… there on the wall. A picture. In a brushed-aluminium frame. Lizzie. My wife. I smiled.

You see? It wasn't so bad being grown-up. Being grown-up meant I had Lizzie. My one constant. The one reliable thing in my life. *She'd* be there for me. *She* wasn't going to join a rock band, or move to Chislehurst. This could be a special summer for us. Our first summer as a married couple. We could go for walks in the park, or build kites and fly them about a bit. We could borrow a dog. Life would be good. Life would be *great*. Because I'd be with Lizzie.

And as if to confirm this, I suddenly heard the keys in the door.

Lizzie! She was home! I was disproportionately excited.

'Hello!' I yelled.

'Hello!' she yelled back, before wandering through the door and throwing her keys down on the sofa.

'It's been a very odd day,' I said, hugging her.

'For me as well,' she said. 'Oh. I see you've received a massive box.'

'I have,' I said.

'What's in it?'

I shrugged.

'Handy stuff.'

'It must be quite a lot of handy stuff…'

I smiled, opened a cupboard door and pushed the box in.

And when I turned round, Lizzie was holding something up in the air. She made a little *ta-da!* noise. It was a bottle. A large, green bottle. With a large, white label.

'*Champagne?*' I said.

She kissed me on the cheek, and then smiled.

'I have some *excellent* news...'

Monday 12th September.

My Friends are leaving
~~leviing~~ leaving

(their) Mooving house.

They are moving

Chapter Three

In which we learn the sad fact that sometimes,
it's not possible to be friends forever...

'I need three cards,' I told the lady behind the counter. 'Each of them celebratory, but each of them balanced by a subtle tinge of regret.'

The lady had a think about it.

'That's quite a specific request,' she said. 'Can you be more general?'

'No,' I said. 'But I *can* be *even more* specific. One of my requirements is a card for someone who is moving to Chislehurst. Do you have a card for someone who is moving to Chislehurst?'

She looked around her, at the stock, and put her hands on her hips.

'Well, we have *sympathy* cards,' she said, and we both laughed for a very long time indeed. Probably too long, because the man in the queue behind me made a grumpy noise and shuffled about a bit.

'But seriously,' I said. 'Do you have anything like that?'

She shook her head.

'It's a niche market,' she explained. 'Nobody moves to Chislehurst.'

The next morning and I was reflecting on the night before. Lizzie's excellent news had indeed been excellent. She'd been offered a job. A new job. A job on the publicity team of the nation's favourite reality show. The same show she finds herself addicted to whenever it's on the telly. It was *perfect* for her. She would be *paid* to indulge an obsession. I could only imagine what that must be like. And I was happy for her.

'But it's going to be tough,' she'd said. 'They'd want me at the studio a lot, and it's all the way out in Borehamwood...'

I had waved these concerns away, like a magnanimous king telling a peasant he could keep an onion.

'... and I'd have to work at weekends, and late nights, too. They're already talking about me staying in a hotel for a lot of it...'

I'd tried to wave these concerns away, too, but the wave kind of stopped midway.

'Really?' I'd said. 'Well, that's...'

'I don't *have* to take it, baby... especially as we've just moved, and with Wag and Ian being away...'

'Don't you worry about Wag and Ian being away. They are both men, following their dreams. They will be back when it all goes wrong.'

Lizzie had laughed.

'But I worry about you. You're so tight with those two.'

'I have other friends.'

'Yes, but they're mainly children you play online at Xbox.'

'Some of them are very mature.'

'Who did I hear you calling a pipsqueak last night?'

'The Bald Assassin. And I called him a nitwit. He always creeps up on me and hits me in the back of the head on Call of Duty. Anyway, I'll be fine – I'll just call someone and hang out.'

'Yeah, you could always call *someone*, but Wag and Ian, well... they *understand* you.'

'What's not to understand? I am very understandable.'

'I just mean, they *get* you.'

'*You* get me.'

'But I'm going to be away so much...'

'I'll be fine. I'm nearly *thirty*.'

'That's what I worry about.'

'I'm not going to be lonely. I've got Sky+, an Xbox and broadband.'

'Nerd. There's always Friends Reunited...'

I'd pulled a face which said 'the cheek!' and we'd laughed.

'Look,' she'd said, 'I'll only take the job if—'

'Lizzie. You *have* to take the job. I will be personally offended if you do *not* take the job.'

'Really?'

'Really.'

I'd smiled the smile of a confident and in-control late twenty-something.

But inside, I was thinking, *oh, bollocks...*

Lizzie started work on the new job almost immediately. A PR buzz around the show was already starting. Who were the new contestants? What would happen to them? How would things change? I smiled as I sat on the sofa, reading the excitement in the *Mirror*, and felt proud that my missus was doing so well. She was involved in something *intriguing*. And *I* was, too. After all, in about twenty minutes, *Street Crime UK* would be on, and there was time to make a toasted sandwich before that.

But then the bell rang. And I remembered. It was eleven o'clock on Tuesday morning. And at eleven o'clock on Tuesday morning, I would succumb to the inevitable, and become a man.

If this was going to happen, it was going to happen *on my terms*. It was time to seize the day.

'Mr Wallace?'

'Yes?' I said, proudly, opening the door.

'I'm Paul – you called me about your guttering?'

'Come in!' I said.

So this was it. This was the moment I became a *boss*! I'd chosen Paul out of the Yellow Pages because his advert had said:

To be or not to be! – well, you did ask for a quote!!!

I'll be honest. Now that I've written it down, it seems to have lost a fair amount of its humour. But at the time I remember thinking it was good that he had displayed a sense of fun about his work, as guttering can be a very serious business. People have died just thinking about it.

'Are you that bloke off the telly?' said Paul, and I said yes and smiled. I'd thought perhaps he was going to say he liked my stuff, but he just scowled at me and said, 'Right.'

'The guttering's round here,' I said, hoping my intricate knowledge of where the guttering was would impress him. 'It's on the outside of the house.'

'Right – let's have a look at her.'

Shit. I should have referred to the guttering as female. Why did I call it 'it'? Why didn't I call her 'her'? I was failing already.

'Yep,' I said, pointing at it. 'That's her. That's… our lady.'

'Oooof,' said Paul, shaking his head. 'I can tell already, she's in a bit of a state.'

Now, I knew from hours of watching *House of Horrors* and *Rogue Traders* that this was *exactly* what men like Paul were *supposed* to say. But I was under pressure, and all I could manage was, 'Is she? That's sad.'

'Let me get my ladder,' said Paul, and, because I was the boss, I did.

Forty minutes and a cup of tea later and Paul was off. He'd be back on Monday, he said, and so long as I paid 80 per cent of the money upfront it'd all be sorted out quickly and easily. I'd done as he'd asked, and looked forward to seeing him then.

'Can I leave my ladder here?' he said.

'Don't you worry,' I said, 'I'll take care of the little lady.'

And he'd looked at me a bit oddly.

I felt like I'd really achieved something, and walked back through the house, wondering if that was enough work to justify knocking off for the day. After all, I'd made someone a cup of tea *and* patronised a ladder.

I flicked on the telly. *Street Crime UK* was halfway through. A policeman was telling a youth to get off a wall. A caption told me this had happened in Birmingham in 2003. Somehow, this made things less exciting. Knowing that several years before, a policeman many miles away had asked a child to get off a wall wasn't really something I felt I could relay to strangers in an interesting manner. And so I switched the telly off and wandered around the house.

There was still much do to, DIY-wise. Sockets needed replacing. Walls needed plastering. The toilet needed a new seat. I stood and looked at it all for a bit. I whistled through my teeth like I'd seen builders do, and then scratched my head, because I'd once seen the bloke off *Brush Strokes* do this, and it had seemed pretty cool.

I sighed, and realised I could either whistle while staring at a toilet, or do what Lizzie had said – and *call* someone.

I reached for my phone and texted Wag.

Hey. A farewell drink?

And then I texted Ian.

Hey. A farewell drink?

And then I stared at the toilet again. It did nothing of interest. It just sat there. And I just stood there.

A few moments later, my phone beep-beeped. It was Wag.

Hey! Can't! At the American Embassy getting visas! Rock on!

I nodded, solemnly. He'd be off soon. I looked at the toilet again.

A minute passed.

My phone beep-beeped. It was Ian.

Sorry, Dan – sorting out removal dates. Chislehurst here I come!

I sighed. This wasn't fair. Everyone was doing something incredibly exciting. Or moving to Chislehurst. And what was *I* doing? I was whistling at toilets or watching kids up walls. My friends were moving on without me. Getting on without me. Doing things without me. I was reduced to thinking about sockets and wiring and wallpaper.

But I knew how to cope with it. I would simply get on with things. I resolved to sort out the sockets.

'Damn you, the Bald Assassin! DAMN YOU!'

It was half an hour later and the Bald Assassin was beating me at Call of Duty. I'd been hiding by a window with my sniper scope trained on the window I was certain *he* was hiding behind, when he snuck into my secret lair and bashed me on the back of the head with his rifle butt. He was always sneaking into my secret lairs and bashing me on the back of the head with his rifle butt. It was the most annoying manoeuvre he could possibly pull off. It showed that while *I* needed guns and grenades and binoculars and little maps, all *he* needed was a small piece of wood. And it didn't matter where I hid, either. Behind walls. Under tables. On roofs. In bushes. Somehow, the Bald Assassin knew my every move.

I heard the Bald Assassin laugh through my headset. It was the laugh of the skilled and in control. The Bald Assassin and I never used our microphones to talk to one another. It had gone beyond that. We'd simply scowl at each other, secretly, and then mumble our goodbyes at the end of the game.

'Bye,' I mumbled. And I switched the Xbox off. Bloody Bald Assassin. Outside, the sky had darkened, and a dull grey light had overtaken the city. Small specks of rain had started to fall, forcing London into a hush as workers and tourists and everyone else stopped hurrying about and just stayed where they were instead. Soon the rain became heavier and the trees outside took the brunt; whole branches waving at me as the shower became a storm.

I thought about switching the Xbox on again, but the place was a state and there were still all those boxes to unpack. And so, with a sigh, I walked to the spare room where most of them lay. I found some scissors and opened a box at random. DVDs. Ah well. That was easy. I'd sort them later. I opened another. Paperwork. Well, that would require filing expertise, and somewhere to file them all. Later.

And then I saw a third box. Smaller than the others, but still rather large. Especially if you had to carry it home from the Post Office, like I'd done.

The box from my parents.

Intrigued – and because I still had a pair of scissors in my hands – I sliced through the parcel tape and flipped back the lid.

And what I saw confused me for a second.

There were letters. And videos. And photographs. And, more than anything… *memories*. It appeared to contain the contents of my childhood. A few schoolbooks, the scrapbook I'd kept when I was ten (when I'd wittily Tippexed out the 'S' to turn it into a crapbook), and letter after letter after letter.

I smiled, and laughed, and started to pick through the stuff. I found badges, first: an *I AM 7* badge. A Tufty Club badge. My Dennis the Menace Fan Club badge. And then certificates: my Silver Cycling Proficiency certificate, which took me straight back to the playground at Holywell Junior School and the day we took the test. I'd done it on my brand new off-white Raleigh Renegade, and passed with flying colours... mainly because all you had to be able to do to gain your Silver was not fall off. Mind you, it can't have been *that* easy. Ian Holmes failed, and *he'd* arrived on a tricycle.

And here... here was another one. Another something I hadn't seen in *years*... my FIRST PLACE certificate in the North Leicestershire Schools Swimming Association Under-Tens Boys Breaststroke competition. First place! I remembered how proud I'd been. You probably remember the day yourself, because it was all *anyone* on my street was talking about, so as you'll know, that was the day I became the fastest nine-year-old in Leicestershire! Well, in *north* Leicestershire. At breaststroke.

But they were just *details*. The 18th of March 1986 was the day I became a *winner*! Yeah, so it probably remains the only race I have ever won in my life, on land, sea or air, but I thought back to the magical day I'd had to stand up in school assembly to accept my certificate; an experience marred only by the fact that someone official had gotten my name wrong, and when I looked at it, it did not read DANIEL WALLACE, but P. WALLS instead. This offended me as much as a *speller* as it did as a winner. They hadn't even given me a new certificate. Just stuck a small white sticker over the front and written my proper name in biro. They wouldn't have done that at the Olympics, so why they should do it at Holywell Junior School is anyone's guess.

I dug deep into the box and pulled out more stuff. A sticker with a footballer on it. Some copies of *Fast Forward* magazine. And photos – dozens of old photos. Photos of me as a kid. Photos of me with my friends. Photos of where we lived, and what we did, and of all the fun we had.

I spread everything out on the floor, and started to pick through it, so much of it firing off memories and triggering thoughts I hadn't had in decades. Here was a picture of me dressed as a tiny soldier, in the days where all I'd wanted was to be a stunt-man like Lee Majors and have Howling Mad Murdoch as my best friend. Here was one from my first day at school in Dundee, complete with blazer and tie, as was the law in Scotland for four-year-olds. That was also the day my mum, in the panic of new ex-perience, had forgotten to give me my first-ever packed lunch. The teachers, insisting that I eat something, had taken me to the canteen and bought me a plate of strange, unfamiliar food. I had never seen a boiled carrot before. It had been in front of me for two, maybe three seconds, staring back at me like a bald orange finger. Nerves took over. I couldn't eat that! What was it? Where was my mum? Where was my mum's *food*? My body did the only sensible thing it could. It vomited on Scott Butcher's lap. He didn't seem to mind, and we became great friends. It is the only time I have made a friend this way. If you try it as a grown-up, on a crowded tube train, say, or at a wedding, people tend to frown upon you.

From Dundee we'd moved to Loughborough, and here was a picture of Mum and Dad and a seven-year-old me standing in front of our new house, looking all proud. My arrival in the East Midlands had caused quite a stir. For a start, as Ian would soon doubtless find with Chislehurst, no one had ever moved *to* Loughborough before. Added to that, the thick Dundonian accent I'd grown up with in Scotland caused worry and concern among my new neighbours and friends. No one had ever heard anything like it. A few people put forward the theory that perhaps I had been dropped on my head as a baby. Most horribly, when the school play came around, I was given the part of the amusing weatherman, mainly due to the fact that the Scottish weatherman Ian McCaskill was at the height of his broadcasting fame. The rehearsal went well. People laughed in the right places. But on the night, I would recite my lines to a hall packed with silent, horrified, open-mouthed faces. There was an audible gasp. A woman in the front row made a sympathetic face, as if to tell me how brave she thought I was, coming out here in public with such a terrible condition. At least one person held my mother by the arm, and told her how much she admired her for all she must have been through. 'I don't know how you cope,' she'd said, and my mother, not understanding, just smiled and said yes. The next night I was demoted, and put on as a mute, English footballer. And two or three months later, my accent turned English too.

It was strange. The last time I'd seen these places, I'd been *in* them. And now they were just flat, slightly discoloured photos. In a box. In my adulthood. Suddenly, my years in Loughborough had become real again. I remembered the day Dad took me to Woolworths and bought me Way of the Exploding Fist for our brand new BBC B Microprocessor with dot matrix printing capabilities. I remembered opening up a Griffin Savers account at the Midland Bank with a deposit of £1.25 – and then withdrawing the entire amount the next day to buy 'Dancing On The Ceiling' by Lionel Richie – mainly because I'd seen the video and thought it might *actually* help me dance on the ceiling. And I remembered my friends. I remembered my friends more than anything.

Especially when I picked up a smooth and sleek black book, which I'd somehow overlooked until now… I recognised it instantly. This had been my address book. But a *special* address book. My grandma had given it to me on one of my visits to Switzerland, and I'd been inordinately proud of it. The edge of each page was red, and the paper gave a brilliant shine to whatever names I wrote in it. I would take the details of only the most important people I knew, and painstakingly add them in the best handwriting I could muster… including stickers and doodles for effect. And now here it was once more.

I opened it, excitedly, and started to flick through…

The names hit me one by one…

ANIL TAILOR!

MICHAEL AMODIO!

Remember them? I did!

CAMERON DEWA!

SIMON GIBSON!

Cameron! The Fijian kid! And Simon! The scruffy one!

PETER GIBSON!
CHRISTOPHER GUIRREAN!

Peter! And *Chris*! My first-ever best friend from my days in Dundee!

And they just kept coming... the names, and the memories. Twelve in total, in an address book I intended to update regularly but only ever really updated every year or two, or when Mum and Dad had decided it was time to up and move on... but these guys had meant a lot to me. They *must've*, to have made it into the Book...

I smiled, and laughed, and flicked through it again.

Twelve names. Twelve great names.

AKIRA MATSUI!

The Japanese kid who'd come to our school! He was brilliant!

LAUREN MEDCALFE!

Wow – a name I hadn't thought of in *forever*.

Where were these guys now? What were they up to? Were they happy? A thought suddenly struck me. *They'd* all be about to turn thirty too. How were *they* dealing with it? Did they feel like me? Like they... weren't quite *ready*?

I closed the book and looked out of the window. The storm had stopped some time earlier, but the day had given up the fight and evening was knocking on the door. I looked at my watch. Lizzie wouldn't be home for hours. But I was in such a good mood, now... I wanted to go out. *Call* someone. *Do* something. Tell them about finding the Book. Ask them about *their* childhood friends.

But who?

Things didn't *used* to be like this. The Book proved that much. The Book was from the days when everything was exciting and new and friends were pretty much all anyone cared about. I used to have a wealth of them; people I could call on a whim and see in a *moment*. Who'd populate the parks, playgrounds, streets and benches of this fine country. What had happened? Where had we all gone? We used to be able to spend *days* together, not just *minutes*. We never had to *arrange* anything, just *turn up*. Never fix a date, or shift a meeting, or consult the diary. Never 'make time' or 'reschedule', or 'no-can-do' or 'raincheck'. Friends came first – or *used* to come first – so what had happened? Why wasn't I with a friend right *now*?

Yeah, we all grow up. We all get busy. But we *all* need friends.

I *would* meet with a friend today. I had *plenty* of friends. I *knew* I did. They were right here, inside my poncey little BlackBerry. I clicked on 'Address Book'. I started at the 'A's.

Adam.

Yes! Adam! I could call Adam! Adam would do just fine! I called Adam. I waited for the ring tone. His number had been disconnected.

Okay. Not Adam.

I scrolled down. The 'B's. Ben. No, he moved to Spain. Another Ben. Didn't he move, too? On I scrolled.

C.

Carl. CARL! I hit Call.

Call Carl, I thought. That was quite funny. I laughed to myself. A second passed.

'Hello?'

'Carl! I thought I'd call Carl!'

I laughed.

Carl didn't.

I continued.

'So where are you?'

'I'm in Manchester. Where I live.'

'Okay!'

I hung up and scrolled down faster, furiously trying to find some-one – *anyone* – who might want to see a Wallace...

H, I, J, K...

Kyle! Kyle! Yes! *Kyle*!

Wait a second. I met him in Uganda.

L! M! N!

Neil! What about Neil! Or Noel! Neil or Noel? The choice was too difficult. I went on instinct. I dialled Neil.

It rang. No answer.

I scrolled on...

O!

I know *no one* whose name begins with O.

P!

I know *too many* people whose names begin with P.

Q!

I know *one person* whose name begins with Q, and he's a nincompoop.

R!

Yes! Rob! What about Rob? ROB! I hit Call and leaned against the wall.

'Yo yo yo! Rob here. I'm not around at the minute. Why not leave a message and I'll get right back to you?'

The beep did its beep and I couldn't help myself.

'ROB IT'S DANNY HOW ABOUT WE HANG OUT DANNY WALLACE I MEAN GIVE ME A CALL LET'S GO FOR A DRINK I'M FREE RIGHT NOW CALL ME I AM WAITING!'

I paused for a second, couldn't think what else to say, and hung up.

A moment passed.

I reflected on whether I might have seemed a little over-keen.

I put the phone in my pocket.

Who the fuck was Rob again?

Lizzie got home at around half past nine that night. She looked tired.

'How was work?' I said.

'Busy,' she said. 'Really very busy indeed.'

My BlackBerry was on the floor. I looked at it. It was still on 'Address Book'. There was no tiny yellow envelope. No little red light. I had no messages.

Lizzie looked to her left and clocked something.

'There appears to be a large ladder in the hallway,' she said.

'She's retractable,' I said.

'"She"?'

'It's what we say.'

'"We"?'

'Us in the trade. We tend to refer to things as women. I think it makes us feel more manly.'

Lizzie smiled.

'How was your day?'

'Oh... you know. Pretty full on. I looked at the toilet for a while and on *Street Crime UK* there was this kid on a wall.'

Lizzie looked impressed.

'But also... I opened that box. The one Mum sent.'

'The one full of handy things?'

'Yeah... turns out none of them were all that handy. But they were... *interesting*. Stuff from my childhood. Photos and stuff.'

Lizzie's eyes lit up.

'Get them!'

'And who's that?' asked Lizzie.

We were sitting on the floor eating fajitas.

'That's Anil Tailor,' I said. 'His mum used to force-feed me curries. Not that I complained. Although I was once sick in a neighbour's bin because of it.'

'Why's he dressed as a cowboy?'

'It was Wild West day at school.'

'And you haven't seen him since you were a kid?'

'Actually, Anil's about the only one I *have* seen. Just once. For an hour or two. He'd stumbled across my name on the internet and got in touch.'

'What was that like?'

'It was a bit weird because he was still dressed as a cowboy.'

'*Really?*'

'No. But it was good despite that. I was passing through Yorkshire where he was living. He's an architect now. And we met up and hung out and it was fun.'

And it *had* been. And even though we'd decided and promised and sworn we'd definitely do it again, the moment had seemed to pass. I had to be in London. He had to be in Huddersfield. I suppose we could have met halfway, but halfway would have been Peterborough, and meeting in Peterborough would have taken a friendship of epic proportions. We'd said, as kids, that we'd be friends forever – but time and distance and life somehow got in the way. I suppose as adults you learn the simple and sad fact that sometimes it's just not possible to *be* friends forever.

'Who's Andy?' she said, leafing through a bundle of letters. 'He liked writing you letters, didn't he?'

'Andy "Clementine" Clements, yeah. But I'm not sure I ever replied much. I feel slightly guilty now.'

'He *does* keep asking why you haven't written back. Never mind. I'm sure he's over it now.'

I hoped so. Why hadn't I kept in touch? I guess it seems friendship is something you just have to keep working at. Because if you don't, one day you'll stop getting letters.

'All this stuff is great,' said Lizzie, studying an article from the *Loughborough Echo* about me winning a conker championship aged nine. 'And it turns out you were good at conkers! Imagine how proud that makes me as a wife.'

'Don't tell your friends about the conkers, as it's not fair on them.'

'What else were you good at in school?'

'Mainly spelling,' I said.

'Spelling?' she said. 'I'm better at spelling than you...'

'I'll have you know I am an *excellent* speller,' I said. 'I can spell *all* the words in the sentence I have just said. And that one.'

I was glad Lizzie liked seeing this stuff. Touched that I'd found someone who took an interest in things. I thought about showing her the address book, and telling her about how it'd made me think about life, and growing up, and about whether the friends in the book were feeling the same way I was... but I couldn't quite bring myself to do it. I didn't want her to think that lawnmowers and display cushions and brushed aluminium frames were making me worry about what I was becoming. And I didn't get the chance, anyway, because moments later she said, 'So... shall we have a woman of wine?'

'A *woman* of wine?'

'Yeah. A "glass" of wine. I'm just trying that manly thing out.'

'I'm not sure that's how it works. You can't just call everything a woman. It's more subtle than that. It's a grammar honed over generations of sexist tradesmen. But yes, let's have a woman of wine...'

*

We were on our second woman and Lizzie was telling me about her day.

'The weirdest thing is, the people on the show, they're not even allowed to tell their friends,' she said. 'Their *friends*! Imagine going into that house and not being allowed to tell your friends. And then when these people come out, they'll be like this completely different person. What must *that* be like?'

'I dunno,' I said, shaking my head and finishing my glass. 'It's weird.'

'Months must seem like *years* in there,' she said. 'I wouldn't do it. Not for all the tea in China.'

'Is that the prize this year? How does China feel about that?'

'They're very angry,' she said.

We smiled. And then she stifled a yawn.

'You go to bed,' I said.

'Yeah. I have to be in early. Are you coming?'

'In a bit.'

Lizzie got up from the sofa and rubbed her eyes.

'You know,' she said, 'I'm a little worried about you.'

I made a confused face.

'Will you be okay?' she said.

I nodded, as confidently as I could.

'Yeah,' she said, moving away. 'I know you will. You'll find *some* way to amuse yourself.'

I smiled.

'See some mates,' she said, clicking the door shut.

And I smiled again. But this time, it seemed sad.

I listened to her walk down the stairs, and stared at the ceiling while she brushed her teeth, thinking about the old days.

I flicked through the address book one last time, and noticed that on one of the pages near the back, I'd written something in an excited, blue scrawl...

Friends Forever!!!...

And then I closed my eyes.

*

A couple of hours later and I was asleep on the sofa. Something woke me up. I looked around to see that *The Mint* was on ITV. Brian Dowling was being very excited. I have no idea about what, but being Brian Dowling, it could have been almost anything. Maybe someone had some shoes on, or perhaps he'd noticed a pen. I squinted, and then looked at the clock. It was half past midnight. And then, it happened again.

Bzz. Bzz. Bzz.

My pocket was vibrating.
A message.

Danny! Neil here! Blimey! Long time no see! I got a missed call from you! Would call but thought you might be asleep. Listen – it's my thirtieth on Monday – would be great to see you after so long!

And that was the second text that would help to change everything.

Tuesday 24th May
I am going to go to a birth
day party on Sunday

Chapter Four

In which we learn that growing up is less worrying when you realise that *eveyone's* doing it...

I was slightly annoyed as I stepped off the bus at Primrose Hill and tried to find the pub. Not because it was a balmy summer's night and I was already quite sweaty. Not because I'd had to stand most of the way on a crowded bus while a man kept hitting me in the face with his paper and standing on my feet. But because my ultimate nemesis, the Bald Assassin, had once more managed to best me, as I hid behind a small garden wall, my sights trained upon the only door he could *possibly* have been hiding behind. I had laughed the laugh of the finally victorious. I felt merciless to his plight. I had a full complement of grenades, a sniper scope, machine gun, three smoke bombs, a pistol and the best position possible. I had every exit covered and all I needed to do was wait. And yet moments later he'd managed to somehow sneak up behind me and slap me on the back of the head. To make matters worse, he'd run away giggling straight after and didn't seem able to stop.

'Well done,' I'd said into my nerdy headset, moodily moving to switch the Xbox off, and noticing I'd still done nothing about that socket.

'Thanks!' I heard him say, just as the screen went blank. To hear his voice annoyed me even more. Either he was a eunuch, or he was about twelve.

I decided he must be a eunuch.

But now my annoyance faded as I found the pub – a vast and sprawling place, covered by ivy and with huge, polished windows.

What would the Bald Assassin be doing now? Probably his homework. Whereas I, a *man*, was going to the pub on a summer's evening to meet a friend I hadn't seen since the Bald Assassin would've been the Baby-faced Killer.

Neil.

'Neil! Happy birthday!'

'Hello, mate! Blimey! How are you?'

Neil hadn't changed one bit. I'd first met him when I'd started at the BBC as a trainee radio producer. He'd started just weeks before, making trails for Radio 4 dramas and the like, and we'd ended up sharing a table in the much-maligned BBC canteen. We'd emailed each other that day, and he'd taken me under his wing, showing me around Broadcasting House, introducing me to the tape library, pointing out where the best coffee machines were, and which sandwiches not to buy. Since I'd left, we'd talked about meeting up, but never quite made it happen. Until now.

'Are all these people here for you?' I asked, amazed.

I looked around. The place was *rammed*. There were balloons. Banners. Small posters of Neil with 'I Am 30!' written underneath. And some very happy people indeed.

'Yeah... good turnout, eh? Nothing better than a big bunch of mates taking over a pub... let me introduce you around!'

And so he introduced me around.

I met Tom, who now works with Neil. Tom wants to write a book for children about a lamb and a turtle who don't get on.

I met Dan, who *used* to work with Neil. Dan likes dancing but says he's got three left feet. He most enjoys the samba.

I met Fiona, with whom Neil was at university. Fiona once met Rosie O'Donnell, and has an interest in Grenada.

I met Al, who travelled round Australia on his gap year with Neil. They once had a fight over a bagel in Adelaide, and once kissed the same girl without knowing it.

I met Joanne and Ben, who went to school with Neil. He used to cheat at his maths exams and sent a valentine to his history teacher.

And I met Simon, who'd grown up next door to Neil, had

started school the same day as him, had known him all his life, despite different high schools, gap years, universities, girlfriends, moves to London... and Simon had a story for every day of Neil's life. I instantly thought of *my* first best friend. Chris Guirrean. How different things could've been if I'd stayed in Dundee, stayed at that school, stayed *in touch*. Maybe I'd be going to *Chris's* thirtieth, just as Simon was at Neil's.

Each person I met seemed to have known Neil that little bit longer than the last. And with each story they told me, I understood Neil a little bit more. Each tale was delivered with affection and kindness and love. I looked over at him. He was gratefully accepting another pint from another friend, and holding court, and introducing strangers to friends they hadn't met yet. I felt bad. All *I* could really tell these people about Neil was that I liked him, and that he'd once shown me where the best coffee machine in the BBC was. As stories go, it's not like there'd be a fight over the film rights.

'So,' I said to Simon. 'You'll be turning thirty soon as well, then?'

'Next month,' said Simon. 'I'm looking forward to it.'

'You're looking *forward* to it? But do you feel... ready?'

'For what?'

'For... you know... being a... *man*.'

'We're all moving forward. All growing up. Most of the people in this room are the same age as us. People Neil went to school with, or uni with. Everyone in this room's either just turned thirty or is about to. Makes it seem less worrying, doesn't it, when you know *everyone's* doing it...'

Suddenly, from somewhere behind me, someone started singing 'Happy Birthday', and within moments the whole room was cheering and whooping before, on one of the big tellies on the wall, a video kicked in...

The title came up... **30 Years of Neil Findlay**!

Neil's girlfriend, Beth, had put together a special video presentation charting Neil's life.

The music began... the Wham! Rap...

And there we saw him... a baby... then as a little boy... picture after picture, bits of old cine film and videotape, edited together as a record of his life.

'That's me!' said Simon, pointing at a small boy looking grumpy next to a tiny Neil. 'That's me right there!'

I smiled, and laughed, and the crowd cheered as the pictures of Neil moved onto his gawky, teenage years to the strains of 'The Power of Love' by Huey Lewis and the News. Neil with big glasses on. Neil with his sleeves rolled up trying to look cool. Neil and his first girlfriend, Rebecca, who was here tonight and whom everyone cheered and pointed at.

Then there was Neil in Australia with Al. Neil on the day he met Beth. Neil at the BBC. Neil passed out on a bench.

And then Neil – the *real* Neil – was standing on a chair, taking the applause, before quietening everyone down to say a few words...

'All I want to say,' he said, looking genuinely emotional, 'is that you're the best bunch of friends a bloke could have. And friends really are the most important thing you can have... so *thank you*. Not just for coming. But for being my friends.'

And the crowd went wild.

I arrived home late that night, starving, and slightly confused about life.

On the one hand, I was happy: I hadn't known Neil as well as anyone else there, but I'd been welcomed into his world – and into his circle of friends – with great grace.

But on the other hand, it had made me think.

Everyone there had seemed so relaxed about things. So happy to be leaving their twenties and entering their thirties. It had seemed much more of an adventure to them than I'd thought it could be. Like they were all in it together. But it was easy for Neil. He had those people around him all the time. People he'd grown up with. People who'd watched him stumble and trip and fall through the earlier years. People who knew him not just for what he was, but for how he *became* what he was.

It was something I wasn't sure I had.

Yeah, so things were magnified right now, because of Ian leaving London, and Wag leaving the country, but still... I couldn't help but feel there was something else that was... *missing*, somehow.

The lights were out as I walked into the house. I needed food. Chips. Or pizza. Or a packet of Wotsits.

On the stairs was a small message from Lizzie.

Hey baby
Got in late, but getting up early... gone to bed already.
Left you a plate in the kitchen.
Love,
Lx

Aw.

Some things about growing up are great. My tummy rumbled in appreciation. But there was something else I wanted to do first. Something that Lizzie had joked about, but which now seemed almost... sensible. And strangely urgent.

I edged my way past the ladder in the hallway and sidled up to my computer. I turned it on and typed in a web address.

Friends Reunited.

I'd last been on the site maybe four or five years earlier, when I'd left the following profile:

Hello. There is something you should know. At school I was obsessed with you. That obsession has only grown with time. Three years ago I began to follow you around. I am actually standing behind you as you read this.

I hadn't really know what else to write at the time. Finding old friends hadn't really been a priority – it had been a laugh, a fad – and I'd thought this would suffice for the time being. But as I tapped in my usual password and username, it seemed Friends Reunited disagreed...

Your account has been removed because you have posted abusive or misleading information.

Eh? I couldn't believe it. I had been *banned* from Friends Reunited!

Who gets *banned* from Friends Reunited? Banned! For being 'abusive'! Or 'misleading'! And which one was it, anyway? What if it had been neither? What if I really *had* been some kind of crazy-faced stalker, who'd engineered it so that the object of his affection would be reading that profile just as he appeared from behind the curtains? Eh? *Then* they'd be sorry!

I grumpily created a new account and started to click my way around, feeling slightly dirty thanks to Friends Reunited's unfounded allegations of abuse and mistrust. I found my way to my first two schools...

Park Place Primary School, Dundee: where I first vomited on Scott Butcher's lap. I'm not sure why I wrote 'first' there; it's not like it happened more than once. It would have been a pretty odd hobby.

Holywell Junior School, Loughborough: where I was mistaken for P. WALLS and which later burnt down. Two incidents which I must assure you are completely unconnected.

I was to be disappointed. I'd expected a treasure trove of old names – names that would tug at the heartstrings and redden the cheeks. But none of the big guns were on there. None of the major players. None of my *gang*.

How had Neil done it? How had Neil managed to keep hold of everyone?

Sure, there was Lucy Redmond. But Lucy Redmond stank of chips and used to beat people up.

Mmm. Chips.

Just a few more minutes...

And anyway, who'd want to be reunited with old chippy-fists Redmond? Plus, her uncle once stabbed a man. (I may or may not have changed her name.)

And so I moved on to Ralph Allen School, and then Garendon, but it was the same story. My gang seemed to be a gang that didn't want to be found. There were interesting diversions, of course. People I remembered, or half-remembered, or *thought* I remembered. People who were reaching out to their pasts, and saying hello, and filling you in on twenty years in just one or two simple sentences. Whole lives summed up in twelve words or less...

... I'm now dad to Harvey and working in web design...

... I got married in September to Jon, we are very happy...

But where there was celebration, there were also some that hinted at... something *else*. Dreams gone wrong. Or opportunities missed. Or regrets just realised. Or simply the fear of being forgotten...

... Bought a house. Too young. Had a kid. Too young. Get in touch and let's remember better times...

... Hi. Does anyone remember me? Pleeeeeease email me if you do...

... Would love anyone who remembers me to get in touch... oh, and if anyone needs a wedding dress, I've got one for sale. Worn once, never used...

Some were married. Some already divorced. Some had kids. Some talked only of work. And the first girl I ever kissed had just come out as a lesbian. I was happy for her. Although I couldn't help but feel slightly responsible.

But down through those long lists of names, on page after page, I saw no Cameron Dewa. No Akira Matsui. And no Christopher Guirrean.

I was just having a strange sense of homesickness for the past. All I really wanted was to see whether these people were okay; whether they were still having fun; whether they were still out there. Just knowing would've been enough.

I thought about what Neil's friend Simon had said tonight, about growing up, about growing older. '*Makes it seem less worrying, doesn't it, when you know* everyone's *doing it...*'

I thought back to Christopher Guirrean. To our first day at school. We had bonded instantly, best friends from the first moment we laid eyes upon each other. For me, he summed up an entire part of my life. A part that had evaporated the minute we'd clambered into our canary-yellow Morris Ital and driven out of Dundee. And as I searched the site, and searched it some more, I realised Chris was nowhere to be seen. Nowhere to be *found*.

Still. Maybe *he'd* find *me* one day.

Maybe *he* was going through the same thing *I* was.

It made sense. We were the same age. Always had been. From the same place. Always had been. Maybe right now, Christopher was on a computer, somewhere, too...

Or maybe he was eating chips.

God, I was hungry.

Quickly, I entered a new profile onto Friends Reunited.

Hi. It's Daniel here. Daniel Wallace. I'm just updating my address book. Get in touch!

I didn't quite know what else to type. Just updating my address book seemed a good enough excuse. I logged out, and typed a few names into Google. But nothing really startling came up. A Chris Guirrean who was about forty years too old to be mine. An Akira Matsui who was about twenty years too young. I sighed. Ah well. It couldn't have been *that* easy. But at least now I'd made an effort to be found. I'd put my fingerprint out there and invited people to get in touch. I'd *done* something.

And anyway, I thought, what was I so worried about? I was just in a weird place, was all, during a time of change. I wandered into the kitchen and noticed that Lizzie had indeed left me a plate. It was covered in tinfoil, and I filled a glass with water, grabbed a knife and fork and took it all to the living room.

Thing is, I thought, I'd been right last time. I should just be more accepting of the way my life was going. Embrace the sockets that needed mending. Buy *more* brushed aluminium frames, not less. *Display* my display cushions. Light a scented candle and put *extra* cumin and basil and coriander on my sun-dried tomato focaccia.

I sat down on the sofa, feeling marginally better about the whole experience, took a sip of my water and took the tinfoil off my plate.

And then I just stared at it.

It was a lamb, mint and apricot sausage. A sausage of the week. I had been *bought* a *sausage of the week*! There was mash, too, though, and I suppose mash is a bit like chips, so maybe I could just pretend this was sausage and chips... but the mash was a bed of *minted* mash with a *hint* of rosemary and port *jus...*

It was the most grown-up post-pub meal possible.

I looked at my tap water, half expecting it to be *sparkling.*

What would *Ian* say?

And then I *remembered* what Ian had said...

'*They have an internet café in Chislehurst now.*'

No, not that. The thing about being at peace...

'*Sometimes, to be at peace with what's coming up, you have to be in touch with what's already happened.*'

He was right!

He was *so* right!

Yeah, so he'd been talking about Chislehurst at the time, but the point remained. That was why Neil and his mates were so laid-back. That was why turning thirty for him was a night of joy, and friend-ship, and memories. I suddenly thought about *my* thirtieth. What would *I* do? Where would *my* mates be? Wag would probably still be on tour. Ian would probably be in that internet café. It'd just be me, with four display cushions and a sausage of the week.

Maybe I needed to do what Ian had inadvertently suggested... maybe I needed to be in touch with what had already happened. Subconsciously, I'd already started tonight... I thought back to what I'd written on the web...

Hi. It's Daniel here. Daniel Wallace. I'm just updating my address book. Get in touch!

I put the plate down and bounded to the corner of the room, where the contents of the box that Lizzie and I had been going through still lay... and there, on the top of the pile...

... was my old address book.

Just updating my address book, I thought. *That's all. Just updat-ing it.*

I flicked it open to page one.

A.

Anil.

Wild West Day at school.

His mum's curries.

That night in Yorkshire, which we'd always said we'd do again, but never ever did...

Friends Forever.

I picked up my phone. Did I still have his number? It'd been years. I'd changed phones at least twice since then.

I checked.

No luck.

But wait.

I ran downstairs, rifled through my desk, until I found it – an old SIM card from an old phone...

I unfastened the back of my BlackBerry, and jammed the SIM card in...

I turned it back on...

Waiting...

Waiting...

It *worked*.

I hit Address Book.

I hit A.

And there it was...

ANIL.

I paused for a second.

I pressed Dial.

Minutes later, I sat down, and smiled. I had a *plan*. Something to do. With no idea of where it would lead, or what would happen, or how it had come to this. But this was fun, I thought. *I'm just updating my address book.*

I picked up my sausage with my fingers and chewed the end off. The way sausages are *supposed* to be eaten.

And then something else caught my eye.

I looked at the pile of pictures, and papers, and at the big bundle of letters, all tied together with a red elastic band.

December 19th, 1988

Dear Daniel,

Hello – It's is Andy here!

At the weekend I went up to Invercarie with Brian and Auntie Anne. Brian bought a new Frisbee. We went to get a Chinese take-away and as we stopped outside one about twenty kids appeared from nowhere and filled the shop so we had to find another one.

I haven't had a reply to my last letter yet so I must guess that you are really really busy again! Plus you never answer my questions!

I would have written earlier but couldn't, this is due to the fact that I was waiting to get a new printer ribbon for my computer and the only place I can get one is Leicester.

I've got a new desk!!!!

Not sure you know what's happening in Neighbours, but today Henry went to work in New Zealand and it was a traditional Neighbours leaving scene showing Bromwin thinking about all the good time's, and Madge was crying.

HAHA! Remember when we locked Emma Robert's in the cupboard at school?

I hope you write back soon!

Andy

June 6th, 2006

Andy 'Clementine' Clements!

Hello! It's Daniel here!

I'm so sorry it's taken me around eighteen years to get back to you, but things have been very hectic here.

I am now a married man who is nearly thirty.

Congratulations on the new desk! And how is the new printer ribbon? Yes, it was fun locking that girl in a cupboard.

Andy, I recently found all your old letters in a big box my parents sent me. I have been reminded of all the fun we had; fun I'd completely and utterly forgotten about.

From reading them again, it seems like I didn't reply much. I'm sorry.

But better late than never. Please rest assured I will answer all the questions you had for me, and give my advice where I can.

Your pal,

Daniel

P.S. I hope you have stopped locking girls in cupboards. I am trying to cut down, but it is just so hard once you have the taste for it.

NORTH LEICESTERSHIRE SCHOOLS'
SWIMMING ASSOCIATION

GALA AWARD

THIS CERTIFICATE

**has been awarded by the Committee
of the North Leicestershire
School's Swimming Association**

to _David Walker_

for FIRST PLACE in the _Under Tens Boys Breaststroke_
at North Leicestershire Schools' Swimming Gala

Chairman _S. A. Hutchell_ *Secretary* _Brian Owens._ *Date* _18th March, 1986._

Chapter Five

In which we learn that Daniel has lost his youthful menace...

The train pulled into Loughborough on a fine and sunny Saturday lunchtime and I hopped cheerfully out.

I'd rushed to the internet and booked the ticket the very same night I'd managed to find Anil's number. He was heading back home that weekend to see his parents and had immediately invited me to stay. I'd had no hesitation in saying yes. I'd known, there and then, that this would be *fun*.

The next morning, of course, I'd considered the potential awkwardness of it. Of spending a weekend revisiting things that I'd never thought I'd need or want to revisit. But what if this was exactly what I needed? What if all I needed was a quick blast from the past to be able to move on?

And anyway – this was a one-off. A salute to times gone by. All I was doing was updating my address book. Making an effort. *Doing* something. Seeing a friend.

The station hadn't changed one bit in the sixteen years since I'd last seen it. And I mean not *one* bit. But then, as I'd find out, nothing much *did* change in Loughborough. I'd managed to spend six happy years here. Happy years of not much more than cycling about, and running around. Of mild, leafy summers and mild, never-all-that-chilly winters and mild, conker-filled autumns... which reminded me of something...

CONKED OUT!

Delayed by other events, the annual conker championship at Holywell Primary School, Loughborough, between finalists Timothy Sismey and Daniel Wallace was declared a draw when, after thirty 'strikes' each, both boys had registered the same number of hits.

Impressive enough. But even *more* impressive... one witness described the event as 'eye-popping'. Oh yeah. And I'll tell you what: it *had* been eye-popping. An eye-popping finale to a *legendary* competition. But the truth was – and this breaks my heart – Timothy Sismey had *won* that year; not drawn. My prize conker, Brutus – discovered under a bush, as if a gift from God – had been splintered and scattered across the school hall, in full view of more than two hundred excited children, their tiny fists punching the air, as the classic face-off they'd been waiting weeks to witness had finally ended. The annual conker competition was the highlight of our year – trained for in every playtime and on the slow walk home after school. Dozens had entered, but only the brave and talented few had made it through to the finals. This year had not been without controversy. Luke Trehearne had been banned after rumours had surfaced that his dad had been secretly varnishing his conkers. Which is a rumour that twenty years later could land you jail time. But now, here we were – me versus Sismey. My conker nemesis. The battle of the 1980s. And Sismey... had *triumphed*.

I had accepted my defeat with grace. We had both been given a box of Toffifee bought from a garage as prizes. Tim, as the winner, received a 24-pack. Mine contained a mere eight. But I never really got over it. His victory over me was made all the worse by the *Echo*'s inaccurate coverage of the event. 'Congratulations!' family friends would say when they saw me. 'I read about the conker championship.' I would then have to tell them that they were mistaken, that Timothy Sismey was the real victor, that I had come a mere second. And in that moment I would see their respect and admiration for me dwindle, so I'd tell them about the swimming gala, but I just knew as they walked away that they were thinking, 'I'm *sure* P. Walls won that...' Since then, I'd kept largely quiet about the whole thing.

Incidentally, you might be surprised that the *Loughborough Echo* decided to report on what now, more than twenty years later, seems a little less important than it did then. But this is the *Loughborough Echo*, where no story is too small. These are four completely genuine headlines from the *Loughborough Echo*, which all ran in the *same edition*, this year:

STRANGER STARED AT BY LOCALS

This was the news that a stranger had been spotted in town, and that some locals had stared at him.

TOWN NEARLY HAD TRAMS

This was the news that someone had just found out that Loughborough had once nearly had trams, but then in the end hadn't.

MOTH CAPTURED ON FILM

This was the news that someone had taken a picture of a moth in their back garden. It was accompanied by a picture of a moth. It remains unclear whether this was the same moth that had been seen in the garden, but the eyewitness does go to some lengths to explain that he had seen a moth the *previous* year, although that was in the *front* garden.

And finally, my favourite:

NO ONE INJURED IN ACCIDENT

No one injured in an accident! Alert Larry King! And all of these incredible events occurring in just one week in the Bronx of the East Midlands – Loughborough! Suddenly, I am surprised that news of a conker match between two children was not at the time deemed worthy of a souvenir pull-out section.

I folded the article back up, put it in my pocket, and wandered out of the station. And there, standing by the entrance, under the big sign saying LOUGHBOROUGH, was the man I'd come to see.

Anil Tailor.

We jumped into a sparkling, mint-green Mini and Anil revved it up. 'It's my sister-in-law's. You know Sunil got married? I'm an uncle now!'

Jesus. An uncle. Anil didn't look old enough to be an uncle. Mind you, he hardly looked old enough to be a *nephew*. When I'd seen him in Huddersfield that time, he'd looked every bit the man. He'd shaved his head and he was wearing smart clothes; the successful young architect about town. But today – today he looked like the boy I used to know. I'm not saying he was wearing tiny velour running shorts and a Ninja Turtles top, like the old days – but there was something in his eyes. And something in the fact that here we were, together again. A kind of childish glee.

'So to what do I owe the pleasure?' asked Anil.

'I just realised it'd been so long,' I said. 'I mean, I know we saw each other that time in Yorkshire, but...'

'Hey – check it out!' he said, pointing at the coach ahead of us. The sign on the back read WALKER COACHES.

'Remember Andrew Walker from school?'

'Yeah?' I said.

'That's one of his coaches!'

Blimey. So Andrew Walker was now Loughborough's premiere coach magnate. He probably had a red leather chair and smoked cigars. I still thought of him as the kid whose stink bomb accidentally went off in his pocket during assembly one day. He was also the first of us to admit that he got funny feelings when he saw Sue Ellen from *Dallas* in the shower.

'What about the other guys? Do you know anything about them?' I asked.

'Remember Richard De Rito?'

'Yeah. His dad ran the Mazda dealership. He had a different car every month. His dad told us it was because he was in the witness protection programme.'

'Well, he's married now. And Louisa Needham – she's married too. To a Guy.'

'A guy?'

'No – a Guy. A guy called Guy.'

'She was the first girl I ever sent a valentine to. She used to be obsessed with Shakin' Stevens. I wonder if Guy looks like Shakin' Stevens – that would certainly mean Louisa's life had worked out as planned. I used to hang around her house. I used to play Jet Set Willy in her brother's room.'

Anil shot me a concerned look.

'What's Jet Set Willy?' he said.

'A game,' I said.

Another concerned look.

'What *kind* of game?'

'A *computer* game.'

He looked relieved.

'I never played that. Thank God it's a *computer* game. You hear *stories* about people's childhoods... hey, remember Michael Amodio?'

'Of *course* I remember Michael Amodio!'

He was, after all, the second name in the Book.

'He's still in Loughborough. We should surprise him!'

I thought about it. Would that be weird?

Yeah.

But sod it...

'We *definitely* should!'

I was beaming. This would be *fun*. Plus, I'd be updating *two* addresses in my address book. Two for the price of one! Not that that was what this was all about. No, no. This was just a today thing. An excuse to do something random and youthful and not at all grown-up.

We passed a sign saying TOWN CENTRE.

'Let's drive that way so you can get your bearings...'

And so we did. We drove past Geoff's Toys, which amazingly hadn't shut down yet, despite seemingly *always* having a sale on. We passed Charnwood Music, where my mum had signed me up to an ill-fated series of guitar lessons with a man named Roger. Roger had been a lovely teacher, with one bizarrely long thumbnail which was useful for guitar-work but absolutely terrifying when you shook his hand. Things had gone well at first, but we'd had an argument one day when it became clear he was teaching me 'Twinkle Twinkle Little Star' instead of 'Thriller' as I'd insisted. And there was the Curzon cinema. I thought back to my ninth birthday, when my mum had treated me and half a dozen friends to see the new action film in town – *Red Sonja*. Sadly, it wasn't until the film had started that anyone realised that the Curzon had put the wrong audience rating up. Someone had placed a PG where a 15 should have been, and my mum was too embarrassed to move us, as we all just sat there, wide-eyed and mildly traumatised, as heads flew across the screen, swords cut through faces and blood spurted violently from sockets where arms had once been. Oh, and then Brigitte Nielsen gave Arnold Schwarzenegger a 'special hug', at which point Mum tried to distract us all by dropping a pound on the floor and shouting 'Scramble!'

And there – on the corner. McDonald's. Now that may not sound like a big thing to you, but the arrival of McDonald's in Loughborough was absolutely one of the defining moments of the late 1980s. Even bloody *Moscow* got one before we did. Up until '87, we'd simply had a Wimpy, where you had to share your table with grannies drinking tea, and you had to eat with a knife and fork and use paper serviettes. Despite this, it was a regular Saturday afternoon hangout. Even Gary, the DJ who ran the roller disco in the Leisure Centre, ate there sometimes. Gary was the coolest guy in Loughborough. Possibly even the coolest guy in the whole of the North Leicestershire area. He was probably about twenty, and he wore white jeans and Hawaiian shirts and had blond highlights and he *knew my name*. He'd sometimes say hello to me in the Wimpy, which made me feel incredibly grown-up. He was Loughborough's George Michael, *and* he had a *girlfriend*. Which made him way cooler than George Michael, who, to be honest, never seemed to be able to meet the right girl.

And for a while at least, all I wanted in the world was to be like Gary. All I wanted was to grow up and run a weekly two-hour roller disco in a regional leisure centre for children. Only now do I realise he probably worked in Kwik-Fit the rest of the time. Anyway, one day in the Wimpy after Gary had climbed into his electric-blue Ford

Capri and shot away, we looked up and were amazed to see a huge, red banner being put up outside the town hall... we rushed out and read it.

COMING SOON TO LOUGHBOROUGH...
McDONALD'S!

We had stood and stared at it, in stunned, silent awe – me and Andy 'Clementine' Clements. We couldn't believe it. *We* had been *chosen*! *We* were to get a *McDonald's*! We may have hugged at this point.

The day it opened, we were first in the queue. Neither of us could handle a Big Mac – in those days we couldn't even finish a can of Coke – but the fries and the chicken nuggets and the barbecue sauce were a taste *sensation*. And on its opening day, you got to meet Ronald McDonald himself! He'd come over specially for the opening – he must've looked ridiculous on the plane – and in what I could only assume was an attempt to fit in, he'd even adopted a gruff, local accent. He was calling people 'me duck' and hiding his American roots and he seemed to know his way around town already! I even heard him grumbling to his mate about the one-way system! I wanted to shake his hand; to thank him for what was *surely* the finest cuisine the world had ever known. I wanted to know how he'd done it; how a simple clown with a ragtag group of friends had founded one of the global sensations of the 1980s. But I never got the chance. The last time I saw him was when he was being driven away in a yellow transit van with a fag hanging out of his mouth. It was quite an occasion, having Ronald McDonald in town – the only other celebrity I saw in Loughborough was Barbara Windsor, the day she opened the Asda on the high street, when I'd decided my new hobby was autograph collecting. You might remember me appearing in the local newspaper expressing my delight.

But soon, McDonald's was a firm part of our Saturday afternoons – as established as the Woolworths pick 'n' mix counter and a walk around the market, marvelling at the stolen Liverpool tops and knock-off *A-Team* duvet covers.

The A-Team had been my *particular* childhood passion. It was all

I cared about for quite some time. I'd written to *Jim'll Fix It*, of course, asking if perhaps he could fix it for me to have Dwight Schultz, Mr T, George Peppard and *especially* Dirk Benedict get in a chopper and pop round to 63 Spinney Hill Drive for the week… and yet somehow it seemed Jimmy Savile was far happier to grant the wishes of children who wanted to know how a *tyre factory* worked than piling the A-Team into a chopper and sending them 40,000 miles across the world. I couldn't understand it. Meeting the A-Team was *much* better television than a visit to a *tyre* factory. It was almost like *Jim'll Fix It* was cheap TV.

'The Wimpy's still there,' I said, and Anil nodded, as amazed as *I* was.

'Shall we go see your old house?'

So we drove down Forest Road, and up towards Spinney Hill Drive – the road I'd lived on and cycled down for so many years. We parked up outside the house and stared at it. It looked a lot smaller than it used to. They'd put up a basketball net, and a new window in the roof, but they weren't fooling anyone – the house had shrunk. They had a car painted one of those weird colours – the kind of sparkly aquamarine you occasionally see and assume must have been bought after a short-sighted man had purchased an issue of *AutoTrader* with printing problems.

But it was weird that someone else was living there now. Sleeping in my room. Hanging out in my garden. Eating in my kitchen.

'What was that room, again?' said Anil, pointing at the one closest to us.

'That was my dad's study,' I said. 'And where the computer was.'

My dad's an academic. A professor of German studies. Our move from Dundee to Loughborough had been from university to university. Our next moves would be, too.

'I never went in your dad's study.'

'You *must've*! Surely! You must've played Way of the Exploding Fist on the BBC B in there.'

He shook his head, sadly.

'Nope.'

Crikey. He'd never played Way of the Exploding Fist. He'd

never played Jet Set Willy. I was beginning to identify serious holes in Anil's youth.

The house backed onto university grounds, and growing up, me and my friends had always sneaked on in order to get chased by the security guards. It was fun. We were tiny kids – they were fat old men in dirty blue vans. In our heads, we were doing the most daring thing imaginable, stepping out into enemy territory. We'd hide behind trees, or in bushes, to try and avoid the all-seeing-eyes of the bad guys, who were right up there with the KGB and CIA in terms of organisation and power. And when we *were* seen, when those dusty vans awkwardly mounted the kerb to give chase across a field, their exhaust pipes rattling and trailing the ground, there was nothing more exhilarating than the collective cry of 'PEG IT!' and the mad rush home.

Suddenly, it was all very tempting again.

'Why don't we sneak on to the university?' I said. 'We might get chased!'

'We're nearly thirty, Dan. We're older than the students. The guards will probably think we're *lecturers.*'

The idea instantly lost some of its appeal. Christ. We were *old*. We were *too old* to look suspicious. How *depressing* to look so *unsuspicious*. What had happened to our youthful menace?

And then we noticed a curtain twitch and a middle-aged lady staring back at us with what looked like real concern in her eyes.

I waved, as if to say 'Hi! I used to live here!', but then realised we were essentially two grown men parked outside her house staring at her property. And now I was waving at her, as if to say 'Hi! Me and my Asian friend are going to rob you!'

'PEG IT!' I shouted, and we did.

Anil lived down by the little row of shops, just next to a small and tatty green we used to play football on. Everything looked exactly the same. A little greener, with better-tended gardens, but just the same. The newsagent still had the same name above it – A. MISTRY. I had always hoped that A. MISTRY had solved crimes in his spare time, and that running a small newsagent's was his eccentric passion, like Inspector Morse and classical music, but it turned out that he was just a newsagent. Life is full of little disappointments. Outside, there was a group of kids, swapping stickers and sweets, just as we'd done, right there, at that age.

'I wonder what stickers they're swapping,' I said.

'Germany 2006. World Cup stickers,' said Anil, with some degree of authority in his voice.

'The last time *I* did that it was Mexico '86.'

'Did you complete the album?'

'No,' I said. 'I think I needed a Hungarian. I never managed to finish those things. Never managed to finish a hobby.'

'Never?'

'Not when I was a kid. How about you? You used to do karate, didn't you?'

'Yeah... I kind of stuck with that.'

Anil got his keys out and opened up the door to the family home. And there she was – Mrs Tailor. She looked exactly the same. Loughborough must be magic. Or maybe your memories just don't get old – even when you meet them in the flesh.

'Daniel!' she said. 'How are you? Sit down! I saw you on TV recently.'

'Did you?' I said.

'You were a bit odd.'

'Oh.'

'Would you like a drink? I have been making masala dosa! I hope you are ready to eat.'

And then the smell hit me – the glorious smell of Mrs Tailor's masala dosa! Instantly, any memories I had of being sick in a neighbour's bin were gone. I pointed my finger in the air, to make me look important.

'I am *ready*!' I said.

And with that, Mrs Tailor sprang into action, darting back into the kitchen where I heard plates clattering and drawers being opened. Within seconds I was sitting in front of the kind of feast I'd last witnessed twenty years before, with dips, and chutneys, and spices, and sauces, and the first of the masala dosa... pancakes filled with vegetables prepared in a fresh coconut sauce. I eagerly tore my dosa apart, while Mrs Tailor looked on, proudly. I felt so welcome, as I looked around the room.

'I see what you mean about the karate,' I said. When I'd left Loughborough, Anil had only just begun his karate lessons. Apparently, it had gone quite well after that. We were surrounded by literally hundreds of trophies, and certificates, and medals, and a picture of the day Anil got his black belt, during which he had decided to sport an unusually wispy moustache. The kind every teenage boy cultivated the first chance they got. The kind that took between eight and ten months to grow.

'*You* did karate as well, didn't you?' he said.

'It kind of went the way of my other hobbies,' I said. Hobbies really weren't my thing. I'd try my hardest, and be *desperate* to stick with them, but after a while boredom would get the better of me and whatever hobby I'd been passionate about a week before would find its way to the back of another cupboard. I think I managed to collect about eighteen different postcards of passenger jets before realising I had no interest whatsoever in large aircraft. My dalliance with autograph-collecting faded after meeting Barbara Windsor – the last one I got was Emlyn Hughes when I saw him in a shopping centre promoting a new line of Hi-Tec trainers. They'd run out of proper signed photos and I'd had to make do with a photocopy someone had done in the back office of InterSport. And at eleven, I'd given up stamp collecting after suddenly realising one morning that there was no way I was *ever* going to be able to collect them *all*.

But karate, I remember thinking... karate would be *different*. Karate would *last*, and be my lifelong passion. Like every other kid in town, I'd just seen *The Karate Kid II*, and was insisting people call me Daniel-San – just as I'd insisted my dad call me Indy after watching *Raiders of the Lost Ark* for the fourth time. Films of the 1980s had that effect on me; had Loughborough Leisure Centre had the insight to offer courses on Ghostbusting, I'd have been first to sign up. And when it came to the noble art of *ka-ra-teh*, it wasn't just me and Anil. Michael Amodio also shared the passion.

Each week we'd make our way out to some industrial estate

where a man with a handlebar moustache and a maroon Jaguar would charge us £2 to stand in a bright room with a dozen older kids and punch the air. My first day didn't go terribly well. The instructor had told us of the importance of stretching, and so, for twenty minutes, we had all tried to touch our toes, reach for the skies, and do all manner of other stretches I had never, ever found the need to do. My body became more and more relaxed as we lay on the floor, arms above us, trying our best to warm up.

'Right! That'll do!' shouted the instructor, whose name, I have just remembered, was George.

We all started to clamber to our feet. But something happened. Something I just did not see coming. Something *terrible*.

I made a small involuntary parping sound.

I froze.

My eyes widened.

My face went hot.

Had anyone heard?

Did anyone know?

'WHO WAS THAT?' shouted George.

Yes, apparently they did.

'THIS ROOM IS A PLACE OF DISCIPLINE!'

I could feel Michael Amodio edging away from me to my right.

'WHO WAS THAT?'

This was awful! It was *clearly* me! Everyone around me knew – and if they didn't a few moments ago, it was becoming more obvious by the second! But what should I do? Should I admit to it? This room was a place of discipline, damn it! But it wasn't my fault! My body just wasn't used to such manoeuvres!

George stared at us all. He was furious. Absolutely *furious*. Christ – what had I done? I had insulted thousands of years of Japanese heritage! I could keep quiet... but this man... this man was an *authority figure*... and what if this was some kind of ancient *test*?

I slowly put my hand up. My eyes remained on the floor.

George sighed, heavily.

'One of the *new* kids...' he said. 'Trust me, you are *not* going to be trouble for long.'

I didn't *want* to be trouble! The parp was a parp against my will!

'Down and give me twenty.'

And so began the beginning of the end.

I finished off my first masala dosa and looked at Anil.

'My karate career was quite short-lived,' I said.

'What belt are you?'

'White with red tips.'

'Okay. The first belt.'

'How many people reach the first belt?'

'Basically anyone above the age of five.'

I could live with that. At least I'd be able to take a four-year-old in a fight. How many people can say *that*?

Suddenly, Mrs Tailor was there again. She dumped another masala dosa on my plate and then scuttled off to make more.

This was great. This was like being nine again. I was staying over at someone's mum's house! For the first time in *years*! I was having a *sleepover*!

'I think karate runs in our family, somehow,' said Anil. 'My brother's got his own dojo. He's the current World Kyokushinkai Kata Champion.'

'That's amazing,' I said, although I wasn't really sure what Kyokushinkai was. It could have been just jumping, for all I knew. I marvelled at the trophies once more. All *I* had to show for my karate career was a small plastic card which showed I was up to date with my £2 payments. Maybe if I'd stuck with it, like Anil and Sunil, *I'd* be the current World Kyokushinkai Kata Champion. Maybe *I'd* be a world champion at just jumping about.

The problem with *my* karate, I think, was that I was just too imaginative with my moves. George, and indeed the entire karate governing body, was quite hung up on every move being performed perfectly, just because that was 'the way it had been done for thousands of years'. He didn't understand that perhaps I was trying to move the genre on a little. My moves were unusual, sometimes improvised, with flailing limbs and a refusal to be constricted by the boundaries presented by the karate mats. This was *street* karate – the street in question being Sesame Street, where no one was ever in danger of getting hurt.

Well, apart from me.

My final lesson took place one rainy Wednesday night. Michael Amodio had inexplicably failed to turn up. I had no partner to practise with. So George took his place. He towered above me, as he lined everyone up to face each other.

'This,' he said, turning towards me and measuring the distance between us with his arm, 'is what I want you all to do. The straightforward strike may seem simple, but it is a thing of great power and requires immense discipline and control. Do not simply hit out. Know your move. Feel it *before* it happens.'

He took a step back and lowered himself, like a tiger about to pounce.

'And then...'

He drew his arm back.

'LIKE THE PYTHON!'

He shot forward with a small scream and punched me straight in the face.

I span right round, and then fell backwards into the wall.

There was a confused silence.

An embarrassed cough from somewhere.

A forty-year-old man with a handlebar moustache had just started a fight with a small boy.

'Oh,' said George. 'We should work on your block.'

I was on the fourth masala dosa and I was feeling it.

The pressure to eat them had been great enough in the 1980s. Now, because so many years had passed, and because I'd come all the way from London, the pressure was even greater. I didn't want to let Mrs Tailor down. But I had just eaten the equivalent of a month's worth of curry, and there seemed to be no sign of her letting up. The more I ate, the brighter the fire in her eyes became. She was becoming addicted to my eating; determined I should continue. I began to feel slightly afraid. What would snap first? My manners or my belt?

'More on the way!' she shouted from the kitchen. 'Keep eating!'

Anil was keen to talk about the old days and what we should do that afternoon. I was finding it harder to talk. Every bite seemed to fill another area that had never been filled before. I was convinced I now had very fat toes.

'We should take a walk down to the old school,' said Anil, who, as far as I could tell, was still on his first serving. 'And then we could walk up and see that old tree – the *magic* tree!'

Now, I *wanted* to see the magic tree again. Contrary to its name, there had been virtually nothing actually *magic* about it, so far as we could tell. It was just an old tree we used to sit under and read comics. We'd stopped going after being told that the local bully – a terrifying kid called Tez – had bought some rope and hanged a woman off it. We believed every word of that story, despite the fact that Tez was only about twelve at the time and no one else had ever heard anything about it. Either Tez had been an incredibly powerful child with a tight grip on not just the police, but also the local media, or someone had made the whole thing up. Either option seemed hard to believe, so I guess we'll never know.

'And then we could head into town!' he said.

I was trying to respond but with a stomach full of curry my responses were slow. In my head I was simply trying to think of ways to turn another serving down. Wait! I could just put my knife and fork on the plate! In the tried-and-tested position which means 'I couldn't *possibly* eat any more'. That was good – that was *polite*! I just had to finish this last mouthful off...

'And we need to surprise Mikey...' he said, and I nodded, now noticing just how much I was sweating. But Christ – what was *this*?

I now sensed a presence over my shoulder. No! It was Mrs Tailor! I turned, slightly, and out of the corner of my eye I could see she was holding a pan. A pan with another steaming masala dosa in it. She was getting ready to lunge in with it! It was huge! I couldn't handle that! I couldn't handle *another*!

I just had to be grown-up about this. I was nearly *thirty*, for God's sake! I couldn't be bullied by a friend's mother! I had to be strong! I turned to her...

'Mrs Tailor, these have been *delicious*, but I—'

'ONE MORE!' she shouted. 'ONE MORE!'

I instantly became a frightened child. Mrs Tailor's voice had gotten much, much louder.

'I'm not sure I—'

'ONE MORE! COME ON!' she yelled. 'WHAT'S WRONG WITH YOU?'

I couldn't believe it. She *actually* said, 'WHAT'S WRONG WITH YOU?'

I had to get out of this! This could kill me! What would the doctors tell my parents? 'It appears your son was 85 per cent curry!' They'd have to bury me in one of those aluminium containers with the cardboard lids!

'JUST! ONE! MORE!' she shouted.

I put my hand up to signal that she had to stop, that this *had* to end, but I'd inadvertently given Anil's mother a clear path to my plate... she saw the weakness and darted forward... I tried to stop her but my arm was too slow...

And then – boom. It was on my plate.

George had been right. I needed to work on my block.

Mrs Tailor cackled.

That's right – *cackled*.

I stared at my fresh plate of curry. If this had been a cartoon, one of my buttons would've popped and landed in a fishbowl.

'I'll get some more going,' she said, running off to the kitchen.

I looked Anil straight in the eye.

'The last time I had six masala dosa,' I said, 'I was sick in a neighbour's bin.'

It seemed to do the trick.

'Mum!' he shouted. 'We have to go now! We have to go and surprise Michael Amodio!'

'I am making more!' she shouted back.

Anil looked at me and smiled.

And then he mouthed the words, 'Peg it!'

It was exciting, standing outside Michael's house. He lives on the other side of Loughborough now, near a B&Q, not too far from the station. I realised I'd have felt a little odd being here on my own, turning up out of the blue to say hello to someone I hadn't seen since I was a kid... but Anil was here. It felt more like a celebration than anything. I tried to think of the last time I'd seen Michael, but I couldn't remember. There hadn't been any goodbye, any see-you-soon – I think one day we'd just been playing, the next I'd packed up and gone... but I was suddenly worried. What if he didn't remember me? What if he didn't want to see me? But then I reminded myself – all I was doing was updating my address book.

I turned to Anil.

'Shall I?' I said.

He nodded, and leaned back on the Mini.

I knocked on the door.

A moment later there was a figure behind the glass.

The door was unlocked.

And there stood a man.

He had Michael Amodio's face. But he was a *man*.

'Michael?' I said.

'Jesus Christ! Come in!'

Chapter Six

In which we learn that quite often, the truth is rubbish...

'I'd have cleaned up if I'd known you were coming round!' said Michael, bringing three cups of tea into the living room. I was pleased to see he hadn't changed much. We were surrounded by Xbox discs and Stallone DVDs. 'And I'd have done something with my hair...'

He pointed to the side of his head. There was a large patch of hair missing.

'I saw you on telly,' he said.

'Oh!' I said.

'You were a bit odd. I suppose you have people to do your hair nowadays, do you?'

'It wouldn't look like this if I did,' I said.

'Problem is, I tried to cut my hair last night with an electric razor. It didn't work quite as well as I'd hoped.'

I pulled up the sleeve of my shirt and showed him a small, straight burn.

'I noticed my shirt was a bit creased the other day,' I said. 'I tried to iron it while I was still wearing it.'

Michael shook his head.

'It's tricky being a grown-up, isn't it?' he said. 'You're just expected to *guess* your way through. No one teaches you these things at school...'

It was then that I realised perhaps we'd have been better off at a *special* school.

'So how are you?' he said, his face full of warmth. 'And what are you doing here?'

'I'm just updating my address book,' I said, and he pulled an odd face. 'Also, I gave Anil a call, and he said he was coming to Loughborough, and... well... it just sounded like a good idea...'

I didn't tell him about the Box. I didn't tell him about feeling like I was growing up too fast, stepping into adulthood before I was ready, hoping that finding my roots and revisiting my childhood might let me extend my stay. It was better to keep things innocent for now.

Michael had been one of my very best friends as a kid. We'd had real fun, me and him. But despite that, he'd always been quite subdued. Quite quiet. Sometimes he'd disappear for a while. But here he was, I thought. Right in front of me.

Just then someone started to walk down the stairs.

'Danny, this is Nikol, my girlfriend. She's from the Czech Republic. She's the girl I'm going to marry... She's a belly dancer!'

'You're engaged!' I said, delighted. 'To a belly dancer!'

'Well, no, not yet... but one day.'

Nikol and I shook hands and said hello, and she sat down next to Michael. She had long hair, right down to her waist, and it was obviously she adored him. And Michael had been working out. He'd gone from six-stone weakling to the kind of guy you'd think twice about messing with.

'I'm a chef now, at the university.'

'Loughborough University?'

The same place we'd all spent our youth creeping on to to try and get chased by security guards! Mikey was now part of the Establishment!

'Do the guards still chase you?'

'Not as much nowadays, if I'm honest. But whenever I see them, I think back to those days. But I've not been there long.'

'What did you do before?'

'I was in the army,' he said. 'I didn't enjoy it much.'

'Really?' I said. 'The *army*?'

It just didn't seem to fit with the quiet, softly spoken kid I used to hang out with. Michael had been through quite a bit as a child. He'd kept it all in, and just got on with life. His was a sensitive soul. I was surprised at his career choice.

'I enjoyed it for a while. But I ended up injuring my back in training while I was running up a hill. I had to stop training altogether. And that... well... that made me see a different side to the army. You don't mind being shouted at while you're training, but then... then it all just got a bit much. And as someone in his mid-twenties, I thought, is this really what I want to do with my life?'

'Getting shouted at by burly men?'

'It's... it's worse than that,' he said, and Nikol squeezed his hand. 'And it's very difficult to get out of. I've seen things I really didn't want to see... I know things I'd rather not...'

And then he told me one or two of those things. And trust me: *you* don't want to know them either. I felt sad. Getting into your twenties was always about making your own choices, to me. Mikey had nearly lost that power, in one way or the other. But then he brightened up.

'Still, the CS gas was fun.'

'Eh?'

'They spray it in your face. It's really funny.'

'*Funny?*'

'Yeah,' he said, with no hint of irony or sarcasm. 'They spray it in your face and you start coughing and crying, but afterwards it's hilarious. Everyone's rolling around in pain, trying not to rub water on their face because that intensifies the pain...'

'It sounds... great,' I said.

'I much prefer what I'm doing now. I'm a chef at the university. It gets tiring, but what job doesn't? And if I hadn't started there, I'd never have met Nikol.'

Nikol smiled. Mikey kissed her on the forehead.

'And I learnt stuff in the army. A bit of self-defence doesn't hurt.'

Not unless the self-defence in question involves you being smacked in the face by a forty-year-old called George.

'Do you remember that day you didn't turn up for karate, and I got whacked in the face?'

'Oh yeah!' said Mikey. 'I felt a bit guilty about that. But my dad had rented *Cobra* on video and I wanted to see it. Sorry about that. Hey – do you remember that Japanese kid at school?'

Yes. I did.

'Akira *Matsui*!'

'When was the last time you heard that name?' said Anil, and I *knew*: it was just a couple of days before, when I'd seen it in the Book and whispered it in awe...

'I remember when I'd just seen *The Karate Kid*,' said Mikey, 'and I thought it would be a good idea to welcome Akira to the school by imitating the Deadly Crane Kick from the end of the film. But I accidentally followed through and kicked him in the head and he fell to the floor. I felt so guilty afterwards. I think he thought I was an evil ninja. Or a racist.'

Akira Matsui had come to Loughborough with his family and been placed in our school for a short while. The only link any of us had with Japan was Mr Miyagi, and we'd employed all the wisdom we'd learnt from the films to make Akira feel welcome. On his first day, I'd run up to him and counted up to five in Japanese, very loudly, in his face. He had been terrified. Anil would shout 'Wax on! Wax off!' at him, in the hope of somehow making a *connection*. And then, apparently, Michael had kicked him in the head. Which I suppose was a *real* connection. As welcomes go, there have been better. But when Akira recovered, we all became firm friends. We had just three foreigners in our school. Akira, a Greek kid called Spiros, and... I suddenly remembered someone... someone from the Book... someone *important*...

'You've just reminded me of someone else,' I said, excited. 'Cameron Dewa! Remember him?'

Anil piped up.

'The albino?' he said.

'The Fijian,' I said.

'I knew it was something like that.'

'I wonder where *he* is now,' I said.

'Probably Fiji,' said Michael, and we all agreed that that was quite a sensible answer.

'And what about Simon Gibson?' I asked. 'Remember how excited we all were when we saw McDonald's was coming to town? I wonder how he is?'

Michael's hand shot in the air.

'He's back!' he said.

Anil looked puzzled.

'Last I heard he was working in Aberdeen,' he said. 'No, Birmingham. At a Toby Carvery.'

'They moved him – he's manager of the Toby Carvery in Colwick.'

'Where's *Colwick*?' I asked.

'Just outside Nottingham,' said Anil.

'But that's...'

'*Close*,' said Mikey.

I looked at Anil. I raised my eyebrows. He shrugged and nodded.

We would go and find Simon Gibson. A third name from my address book. A third name to be updated.

'Mikey, listen,' I said. 'What are you up to later on?'

'Nothing,' said Michael.

And then I uttered a phrase that I'd never said to either Anil or Mikey in my entire life before.

'Shall we go to the pub?'

We were going to meet later on that evening in the centre of Loughborough to catch up some more and fill each other in on what we'd been up to. It felt good to see Mikey again; like I'd recaptured something. Revisited somewhere I thought I'd lost.

And as we were leaving, I remembered something.

'How's the family?' I said. 'How's your brother?'

'He's a policeman now,' said Michael.

'Cool,' I said.

'Yeah. He gave up the stripping.'

'The *stripping*?'

'Yeah. He was a stripper for a long while. He was in a male stripping group called Natural Born Thrillers. They were very successful. They went to Greece and everything. But he gave it up after there was a riot in Middlesbrough when sixty drunk old women went mental when he was late on stage. I think he decided enough was enough after that.'

I didn't really know what to do with that information.

'Listen, Dan...' said Mikey, suddenly. 'And, Anil, too... listen... this is... I don't know how to put it...'

Anil and I both looked at Michael. He wanted to tell us something. We didn't know what. We couldn't even be sure *Mikey* did. And then he waved it away and looked to the floor.

'It's... I'll tell you later...' he said.

And I nodded, and we hugged, because we *would* see each other later. We could see each other whenever we *liked*, now.

And then Anil and I jumped into the sparkling, revved-up Mini and set off.

I was excited.

We were going to find Simon Gibson.

In the late 1980s in middle England, the Toby Carvery was the height of exclusive dining. Not only did they offer quality meats at reasonable prices, but if you were a dedicated visitor to 'Tobies', you could also buy individual Toby jugs – mass-manufactured clay jugs in the shape of a grotesque man's face, which, if you had enough of them on your mantelpiece, could instantly knock thousands of pounds off the value of your property. Apart from the jugs, grown-ups would unfailingly make reference to two things when they talked of a Toby – the fact that you couldn't go back for second helpings, and the invariably excellent parking facilities.

And now I was returning to that cosy, clay world.

The sky was darkened by storm clouds as we pulled off the motorway to arrive in Colwick, a few miles to the north of Nottingham, along the River Trent. Anil and I had been swapping anecdotes about growing up; catching up on the things we didn't know about each other. Then we had seen it there before us: the mighty Toby Carvery Colwick. It ruled the area, like a castle on a mountain: a powerful brick square standing guard over the round-about and the dual carriageway beyond.

Inside, it was glowing. It looked busy in there. Weeks later, I would find the following on the internet. A review from a regular punter, keen to spread the word of Colwick's number one Toby Carvery:

I have been to this establishment twice. On both occasions I took a disabled person in a wheelchair. I had the chicken and bacon wraps both times and so did he. They were cooked to perfection. You can help yourself to as much veg and potatoes as you want but you can't go back for seconds which is a disadvantage.

It also has a decent-sized car park.

I hope that helps.

'Shall we go in?' I said.

'Definitely,' said Anil.

We parked the Mini in the excellent car park and approached the front entrance. The rain had started now, and the Toby Carvery took on the kind of warm and inviting glow you see in films set in Victorian times. Through the windows you could see families enjoying themselves – a wooden bar, and red carpets and attentive staff running to and fro.

We were welcomed by a girl in official Toby Carvery clothing.

'I demand to see the manager!' I said, which I had intended to say in an amusing voice but which had seemed to terrify the girl.

'Oh! Um...'

'We're old friends,' explained Anil, and I realised I should have said that. But it didn't matter, because there, just by the bar, I saw him...

'There he is!' I said. 'There's *Simon Gibson!*'

Simon Gibson had certainly grown up. In the old days, he'd been the scruffy kid at school, with a cheeky face and a fringe that always needed an inch taken off it. He'd worn the same tracksuit every day of the summer holidays and even though he had trainers, he'd always worn his school shoes, until the soles had been peeling off, like in a Charlie Chaplin film. His brother had called him fat – my mum had reassured him he was 'pleasantly plump', which I think in the end might have done more damage – but the puppy fat had gone, and now here he was – smart. Suited. In control. He was clearly sorting out some kind of problem, but doing it with a smile. He glanced over at us, didn't quite take us in, and then looked again, harder.

'I don't believe it!' he said.

*

Simon was rightly proud of his work at the Toby.

'We run a tight ship here,' he said. 'We have a laugh, but we get the work done, which is important.'

We were sitting at the special table in the corner – the one only members of staff get to sit at.

'We take a hefty sum each year, do three and a half thousand dinners a week. About twenty-five staff. But we *do* have fun.'

'That's brilliant, mate,' I said, genuinely impressed with how big it all sounded. 'How about at home?'

'Oh, I'm married now. To Claire. She's amazing. The best thing I ever did was marry Claire. She's so easygoing. There are only two rules she sets me – no other women, no other men. Other than that, I'm as free as free can be.'

'We're going out a bit later on in Loughborough with Michael Amodio,' said Anil. 'Are you coming out?'

'Right...' said Simon, thinking. 'I might have to run it by the wife.'

Luckily, Claire works at the Toby Carvery as well, and Simon dashed off to ask permission.

'We're with Simon Gibson!' I said, to Anil. 'He's a whole new man! He's in *charge* of all this!'

It seemed a far cry from the Simon of old. It was great.

Moments later, he was back.

'Right. I have permission. But I can't be out too late. Claire's said she'll get a lift to Loughborough later on and drive me back in our car. Listen – I only live round the corner. I should put a different shirt on. Come round – you can see my baby!'

'You've got a *baby*?' I said.

Simon had *definitely* grown up.

Simon whipped the white rubber sheet away and said, 'There she is! My baby! My pride and joy!'

We stood there, staring at a classic white MG – clearly the result of a boyhood ambition successfully realised.

'She's beautiful!' said Anil, and I kicked myself as I remembered that I too should refer to cars as female.

'What a lovely old woman!' I said.

'I'd always wanted one of these,' he said, proudly. 'Of course, we've still got the Ford Fusion. Got to have a sensible car, too. But this... this is my baby. Hundred pounds a year insurance, no tax.'

I made an impressed face using my eyebrows and lips. I never know what to say when people tell me about their car insurance.

'Anyway, I'll get my shirt... come inside, meet the dog...'

Simon's front room was as cosy as the carvery, with soft lamps and large sofas, and photos of his wedding scattered about the place. And, most noticeably, a large and enthusiastic dog who clearly hadn't seen anyone all day.

'What's the dog called?' I shouted to Simon, as it tried its best to pop its paws inside my mouth and nose.

'Pepsi!' he shouted.

Ah. I got it.

'You always did like Pepsi & Shirley. Is that who she's named after?'

'She's named after the drink,' he said. 'The drink of "Pepsi".'

I felt a bit silly asking that. Maybe it was just me who'd become momentarily hung up on those days. Simon had so far seemed a little further on down the track of accepting adulthood than me. Yes, he was settled, like me, but he'd taken it *further*. He had a proper job with 'manager' in the title. He had a *dog*. And he'd even bought his midlife crisis car – about fifteen years before he'd needed to. He was embracing his move into the world of the thirtysomething with gusto and grace. He wasn't looking back. He wasn't looking to the past. He wasn't hung up on things that were once important to him, like...

Hang about.

What was *this*?

'Simon! What's this? On your wall.'

'What's what?' said Simon, coming down the stairs with a smart shirt on.

'This!'

I pointed at it.

'Ah...' he said. 'That, my friend, is a sealed, framed original *Back to the Future III* movie poster, signed by Michael J. Fox, along with cells from the actual film.'

My God. This was like 1980s *treasure*.

'Now *that* is impressive,' said Anil.

'The fact that it's signed?' said Simon.

'The fact that your wife lets you hang it up in the living room.'

'I told you,' he said, putting his finger in the air. 'No other women. No other men. The rest is up to me. Right. I'd better just feed the dog or Claire will go *mental*.'

Simon took Pepsi into the kitchen and for a moment Anil and I simply stood in front of the poster and stared at its action-packed beauty. We were the post-*Star Wars* generation. For us, *Back to the Future* was probably the defining movie trilogy of our lives. It was the reason I'd got a skateboard for my tenth birthday – a skateboard I'd had to carry around everywhere because the wheels didn't work properly. But that didn't matter. Because from that day forth, I was no longer Indy. I was no longer Daniel-San. I wasn't even Dr Venkman. I was *McFly*. McFly with a knackered skateboard, but McFly nevertheless.

'There's actually more of a reason I've got that,' said Simon, closing the door to the kitchen. 'I'll tell you down the pub.'

Anil and I both nodded. As if just *having* it wasn't reason enough.

'Right!' said Simon, holding up his car keys. 'To the Fusion!'

We drove in convoy back to Loughborough – me and Anil in the Mini, Simon in his silver Ford Fusion people carrier.

'Isn't it funny that Simon's got a Ford Fusion people carrier?' I said. 'It's the new Simon. If it was still the old Simon, it'd be a Ford Cortina with no hubcaps.'

'If it was the old Simon, it'd be a nine-year-old boy driving a car,' said Anil. 'But it's funny seeing him drive. It's funny how we've all been separated, but all gone through some of the same things. Learning to drive, getting our first cars...'

'Your first heartbreak. The day you move out of home. Kissing a lady.'

'You've kissed a lady?'

'Once.'

But I knew what Anil meant. You always imagine you grow up with your mates. But you grow up anyway. There are some processes we all go through no matter what. Processes far more fundamental, of course, than just learning to drive or moving out of home. Processes that define you, and just you, but which define everyone else as well.

'The past is just as important as the present,' said Anil, wisely. 'It's like... if there's a wrong in your past, you might as well try and right it. Like in that telly show. That's why the past is still there. You can always go back to it.'

I took a moment to think about what Anil had said.

'Anyway, what was her name?'

'Who?' I said, lost in my thoughts.

'The lady you kissed.'

'Oh. Um...'

'See, I *knew* you were lying...'

'Our first pint!' I said, and we clinked glasses.

'To old friends,' said Mikey, and I thought back to the doodle in my address book.

It was a wonderful moment. A moment I couldn't have predicted just a couple of days before. A moment that meant something.

Here I was, sitting outside a pub in Loughborough, with Anil Tailor, Michael Amodio and Simon Gibson. The old crew. The old gang. Back together. Three of the first names in my address book. Reunited.

Instantly, the chat began... we talked relentlessly about the times we'd had, and the things we remembered, and the things we remembered about *each other*. We compared notes, and filled each other in, and laughed and joked.

'Thing I remember about you, Dan,' said Simon. 'Always very good at spelling.'

'Yes! Thank you!'

I made a mental note to remind Lizzie of this when I got home.

This was warm, and fun, and felt important, somehow. Like a meeting had been inevitable; like nothing had ever changed.

We discovered that Simon's dad was indeed – as we had predicted at the time but which Simon had furiously denied – the only man in Loughborough to have bought a Betamax video. That Anil was the one who changed the lyrics of 'He's Got The Whole World In His Hands' to 'He's Got The Whole World In His Pants' the morning we all had to stay behind in assembly and apologise to Jesus.

We talked about the day our primary school burnt down – 'I'd left 60p in my drawer at school *and* some MicroMachines,' said Simon. 'I'll never see *them* again.'

And then I changed the subject. Changed it to something I'd been wanting to ask since I'd first seen the boys again. But how to phrase it? How to phrase a question that means so much? That contains so much angst, and worry, and paranoia?

'Can I ask you all something?' I said, slowly. 'Has anyone else here...'

I still didn't know quite how to put it.

'What?' said Anil.

'Has anyone else here,' I said, '... started listening to Magic FM?'

There were coy looks around the table. No one made eye contact. No one seemed keen to speak. Was I the only one worried about growing up? Growing old? Turning thirty?

And then Mikey coughed once, softly, and spoke...

'I wouldn't say I was a *regular* listener,' he said.

'So you *do* listen to it?' I said.

'Sometimes it's on in the background,' said Simon.

Maybe I wasn't alone!

'But have you ever listened on *purpose*?'

He went a bit red.

'It's just so *feelgood*,' said Anil. 'They do *all* the hits.'

Thank God. Thank God it wasn't just me. Here we were, four nearly men, each sharing a terrible admission of guilt. Maybe this was perfectly natural. Maybe this was just part of the process. I suddenly felt such warmth towards my friends. Okay. I hadn't seen them in the best part of twenty years. But we were all the same age; we'd gone through the same things in different ways. We'd continue to for the rest of our lives, even if we never met again.

It made me realise there would *always* be a connection.

Simon was explaining how he'd entered the world of carvery management.

'I started off working at the one in Loughborough... the one down by Forest Gate? I worked there for a while and then the offer of a job up in Aberdeen came up, so off I went. Then Birmingham, where I met Claire, and then off I went to Colwick. Although they're opening up a new one in Banbury next year which me and Claire might have to go off and start...'

'And how about the rest of the time? Any hobbies?'

'Well, with the car, the dog and the wife, all my time is taken up, really...'

'There must be *something* you enjoy doing...'

'It's such a lot of work, y'see...'

'*No* hobbies?'

Simon shook his head.

I guess that was the thing about growing up. Responsibility takes over. Hobbies can easily become a thing of the past. Sure, we'd all had time to collect stickers and learn the guitar and go BMXing when we were kids... but those days were done. And Simon didn't seem to mind one bit. Of the four of us, he was the most grown-up. The most at ease. The most *sensible*.

But then he said...

'Oh! There is *one* thing...'

'What's that?' I said. Maybe he was still collecting Micro-Machines, or he'd remembered that he quite enjoys Doritos.

'Well, for the past few years,' he said, 'I have been working on my own independent theory of time travel.'

I looked at him. I blinked a couple of times.

'You've been what?'

He took a sip of his pint.

'I've been working on my own independent theory of time travel.'

Mikey and Anil were talking about something else. I felt Simon's statement warranted an interruption.

'Fellas... did *you* know Simon's been working on his own independent theory of time travel?' I asked, amazed.

'Your own independent theory of time travel?' said Michael.

'My own independent theory of time travel,' said Simon. 'I think I've basically cracked it.'

'You've *cracked* it?' I said, stunned. 'You've cracked *time travel*?'

'Basically, yes,' he said. 'And string theory as well, although that was just a by-product, I didn't *mean* to crack that.'

'You've cracked *string theory*? So it's no longer a theory? It's string... *fact*?'

I imagine we were the only people in the *whole pub* having this conversation.

'It's the simplest thing in the world,' said Simon. 'It really is.'

'You can't just say that,' I said, outraged. 'Tell us how time travel works! I want to know how time travel works!'

If Simon's theory was true, perhaps there was still a chance for me – perhaps I could still be McFly!

'It's all about dimensions and thinking laterally,' he said. 'Think of time as a clock or date... are you doing that?'

I nodded.

'Right. Don't. It's nonsense. No. Time... is a map.'

He said this in quite a magical way, as if everything had suddenly become clear. But I'll be honest: it hadn't.

'Think about Einstein's theory of relativity, think about every element that works... you can mark time, you see, so if you work out the velocities that move the earth round the sun then you can easily map where time is going to be, and where it's been. It's all about where the earth is *going* to be. We think of it as here and now, but...'

And I just stared at him while his mouth moved and words like 'relativity', 'wormhole' and 'galaxy' popped out.

I was amazed. Since leaving school, Simon Gibson had managed several Toby Carveries *and* solved time travel! Of course, I had no real proof of this incredible claim whatsoever, but he certainly knew some long words, and more often than not, that's enough for me.

'And like I say, this theory also proves wormhole. But you know' – he shook his head like a tired and beaten man – '*you* try telling Hawking this stuff…'

'Have *you* tried telling Hawking that?' I asked. 'Because if you faxed him on Toby Carvery-headed notepaper, there's a chance he might not have read it!'

Just then, we were joined by Michael's girlfriend, Nikol. We all said hello and were as polite as we could be, but it's difficult to focus on airs and graces when someone's just told you they've solved time travel. But Nikol represented a fresh perspective.

'Simon's solved time travel,' I said.

'Just now?' she asked, in her thick Czech accent.

'No – it took a few years,' I explained.

She looked unimpressed with the length of time it had taken Simon to crack one of life's eternal mysteries. I should have told her he had a dog to look after as well. If Einstein had had a dog, or a local carvery to run, he'd have got a lot less done. And you'd probably always find hair in the soup.

'Hey,' said Anil, and we all turned to listen. 'I guess now Simon's warmed you up with a bit of weirdness, it's okay for me to join in…'

'What was weird about that?' asked Simon, genuinely confused.

'You've solved time travel!' I said.

Anil waved this away and began to speak.

'Now, like I say, this is weird, but… the other day, in Huddersfield, I was on my way home from work. I don't know why, but I took a different route from normal. I was waiting for a bus to pull out at a junction, and I was sort of lost in my thoughts…'

But Simon solved time travel! was all I could think.

'And then I saw this bloke coming out of a pub. He looked like a Sikh guy, with a beard but no turban on, and when he saw me, he sort of saluted at me. I thought he was saluting at someone behind me, and so I checked, but there was no one there…'

He wasn't even any good at maths!

'And then when I look back round he's right there – right next to my window. He knocks on it, and asks me to wind it down. So I do…'

And this is where Anil caught my attention. Because I suddenly realised what he was saying *was* weird. Because what he was saying – or at least a variation of it – had once happened to *me*...

'... so this stranger, he says to me, "You're worried."'

'That's odd,' said Simon, which just goes to show *how* odd it must have been.

'It *was* odd. But it gets odder. He says to me, "You're wondering whether you should stay in your current job, or move somewhere else." And I *had* been. I'd just been thinking that. I was thinking, should I stay here in Huddersfield, or should I move to London, or Chicago...'

I noticed Nikol leaning in slightly. She was fascinated.

'... and then he says, "Show me your hand," so I show him my hand, and he says, "No. The one you *write* with." So I showed him the other one, and he said, "Some important things will happen to you soon. On a Saturday next month, you will meet with an old friend, and have a happy time.'

We all looked at each other, slightly dumbstruck.

'"... and this will lead you to opportunities away from your current job."'

'Oh,' someone said.

'"... and then, after that, something important will occur between you and someone with the initials E.J."'

'So who's E.J.?' asked Simon.

'Elton John!' said Michael. 'It could be Elton John! Something important is going to occur between you and Elton John!'

'My ex-girlfriend's initials are E.J.,' said Anil, and we all realised that made far more sense. 'This guy, he was speaking in Punjabi but I understood most of it, and it was just... *unusual*...'

And it was. A very similar thing had happened to me a couple of years before. I'd been going through an odd time, staying in, not doing much, and a stranger had muttered a few words that had struck a similar chord... and that stranger had been right. What's more, my stranger had *also* been Asian. *Also* had a beard. It sent a chill down my spine. Since I'd started telling people about it, I'd heard similar stories of similar experiences happening all over the world, but this was the first time it had happened to a *friend*. I was about to say so, when Nikol suddenly and confidently uttered a sentence I don't think anyone had been fully expecting.

'My grandmother is gypsy witch.'

I'm not sure *you'd* been expecting that, either.

'She is every day collecting wood in the park. She lives in the town now but she used to live in forest. I would run for years in bare feets around the forest and seeing no one for three or four months. I know about these things...'

I looked at Mikey. He closed his eyes and nodded.

'The left hand is the past. The right hand is about what is gonna really happen in the future if you can make your own destiny.'

We all looked at our hands. As if somehow any of us would suddenly spot our destiny nestling between two fingers and a mole.

'A mate of hers read my veins once,' said Mikey, and we all said 'Oh' like that was the most normal thing in the world.

'What I mean,' said Nikol, 'is perhaps this man, he knows what he is saying. Perhaps he is telling you your destiny is in your hand.'

Anil thought about it.

'Well, he was right about the meeting old friends bit,' he said. 'And it's been good, hasn't it? I mean, it's so easy to forget about the past. It's wrong to do that, and you should always right a wrong. I mean, you leave home, you go to uni or whatever, you concentrate on new people, your whole world is new. And then, when that dies down and those people drift off and start having kids and whatever, you start thinking about the people that came before. And sometimes you realise that they're the ones that matter. They were part of your early life, your real life, before you knew who you were or started pretending to be someone you weren't...'

We'd all been listening to Anil, rapt. He'd suddenly become quite wise.

'So... all I'm saying is...'

He held his glass up.

'Cheers!'

We moved on soon after. The boys gave me a tour of Loughborough at night. We bar-hopped, and pub-crawled, and made our way to a club. And then, at one point, Mikey pulled me to one side.

'I wanted to say something,' he said. 'But now's not the right time. Are you around tomorrow?'

And we arranged a meeting.

'Danny!' shouted Anil, interrupting us. 'Simon's solved the riddle of the Sphinx!'

'*What*?' I said.

'Have I *hell*!' said Simon. 'That's *impossible*!'

And we laughed our tiny tits off.

It was genuinely sad when Simon had to go.

'I shouldn't be late for Claire,' he said, and we hugged and said our goodbyes.

'We'll have to meet up again soon,' I said.

'Definitely,' said Simon. But there was something about our goodbye that made me think it could be our last. I didn't want that to happen. But I didn't quite know what to say. So I didn't say anything, and just let him walk away. But not before he'd said, 'You know, this *could* have been awkward. It gets more awkward the longer you leave it, I think. But it's *rewarding*, too...'

I knew exactly what Simon meant. This whole Saturday had been great fun; much more fun than I'd *thought* it could be. I was with old friends; people who'd seen me grow up, and trip, and stumble, and embarrass myself. I looked at Anil and Mikey in front of me, and I remembered all the fun we'd had.

This had been a *good* idea.

Anil and I got in at 2am.

There was a note from Anil's mum.

I HAVE MADE THIS VEGETABLE CURRY.
YOU BETTER EAT IT OR ELSE.

We got some forks out and silently got to work.

The next morning – after several servings of Mrs Tailor's spicy North Indian breakfast pancakes – Anil and I met Mikey in the car park of the Toby Carvery in Loughborough. Simon would've been *proud*.

It really was an *excellent* car park.

'Listen... all I wanted to say last night,' said Mikey. 'But which for some reason I couldn't... was *thanks*.'

'*Thanks*?' I said.

'For what?' asked Anil, standing underneath the Toby Carvery sign.

'When I was a kid, sometimes I wasn't around all that much,' said Mikey. 'I could've been a better friend. There were just... there were hard times...'

Anil and I didn't quite know what to say. Being kids, we hadn't really *known* about the hard times. All we'd known about were the *happy* times. The mucking-about times. The aniseed-ball and cartoon-time times. I guess it's only when you're an adult that you know what a childhood can be.

Mikey hadn't finished.

'This has sort of been like banishing a demon, for me, this weekend. I don't want to get too heavy... but I've always thought I could've been a better friend as a kid. Not just to you, but to *all* the people I cared about back then. And now maybe I *can*.'

And we hugged.

Because maybe we *all* could.

At the station, Anil had something on his mind.

'Can I ask you something?' he said, while I packed away the substantial curry-based lunch Mrs Tailor had made me for the journey. 'What made you decide to ring me? What made you decide to come here this weekend?'

'Oh – you know. I'm basically just updating my address book.'

Anil didn't seem convinced.

So I thought about it.

'The past, I suppose. I'd forgotten about all the good times. And then I opened up a box. And there it was.'

Anil nodded, thoughtfully.

'Nice metaphor,' he said. 'The Box of Life. Sometimes we're too keen to put a lid on it.'

I shook my head.

'No,' I said. 'An *actual* box. I opened up an *actual box* and there was all this stuff from the past, and I'd been worried about what I was turning *into*, and that perhaps I'd forgotten what I *was*, and we talked about Loughborough, and... well. It was a nice weekend. It was a *great* weekend.'

It was somehow less impressive than the metaphor Anil had imagined I'd wisely come up with, but it was the truth, and sometimes the truth is rubbish.

'It *was* a great weekend. It's a pity some of the others couldn't have been here, too.'

'Like who?'

'I dunno. Peter Gibson.'

Peter Gibson. Another name from the Book. Another address in need of updating.

'Yeah, Peter...'

'He was always drawing, wasn't he? And he had that massive train set, too...'

We both turned to see my train approaching.

Anil looked misty-eyed for a second.

'I wonder where everyone is,' he said. 'You know. Not just Peter Gibson, or that albino kid. But the others. When you think about it, they could be *anywhere*.'

We both turned and looked at the big map behind us. But then we turned back again, because it was a map of Leicestershire and, as such, not particularly inspiring.

But I smiled.

Because I *had* thought about what Anil was saying.

And on the train home, I'd think about nothing else.

July 26th, 2006

Dear Andy

Many thanks for your letter of February 4th, 1989, and once again, apologies it has taken nearly twenty years to get back to you.

I hope your school project on leaves is now out of the way. It would have been a real pressure to have that hanging over your head throughout the nineties and into the noughties, so I trust you're all done, and you can move on with your life. If not, for God's sake hand it in or you'll get marked down.

I am pleased you saw a dog.

You asked how things are going for me... well, they're going well. I went back to Loughborough for the weekend, and met up with Anil and Mikey and Simon. They are all well. Anil is an architect, Mikey is a chef, and Simon's solved time travel. Perhaps you are now an expert on leaves. Or dogs! That would be exciting.

I hope your pizza was good. What toppings did you have? Please try and remember, as it is good to have the full picture on these things.

Daniel

P.S. I'm aiming for a friend named Peter Gibson next, I think... I'll keep you updated...

Chapter Seven

In which we learn that where there are acronyms, there is hope (WTAATIH)

My letter to Andy Clements had been one of great hope and optimism. I didn't know whether he still lived in the same place. I didn't know if he'd remember me, or ever thought about me, or even if he did and he had, he'd want to reply. Maybe he was a doctor, or a lawyer, or a stuntman, or a thief. Maybe he was no longer Andy – maybe he was *Andrea*. I was entering a whole new world here – a world of other people's futures – and it was exciting.

The first thing I'd done when I'd got home was open up my old address book and write in three new addresses. Anil's. Mikey's. And Simon's. It felt good, doing that. Putting a line through the old ones. Inking in the new ones. It didn't feel like making new friends. It felt like confirming old ones. As if I'd backed them up, somehow. Made them safe. Secured them for the future.

I thought about the boys. It was *great* that Simon was a kind and affable manager. *Brilliant* that Michael had waved the army goodbye and done something else instead. *Incredible* that Anil was designing buildings. And wonderful that, like me, they seemed not entirely at ease with the world of the thirtysomething. I mean, Simon still had a *Back to the Future III* poster on his wall, for God's sake. And Mikey? Mikey tries to cut his hair with an electric shaver.

But what about the others?

When I'd returned from Loughborough – after bringing a tired Lizzie a cup of hot chocolate and kissing her goodnight – I'd excitedly gone back upstairs and reopened the Box, looking for evidence and clues. As far as Peter Gibson went, I found just one letter of note, which I studied with all the tenacity of Columbo. Could this give me any indication about what he might be doing nowadays?

COWABUNGA DUDE!
Yes, turtle mania has hit England and turtle power has been at number 1 for three weeks! Sorry it took me so long to reply to your letter. Boy you live in an exciting area. No tramps on fire here!

'No tramps on fire?' Was this an expression of the time, like 'magic', 'wicked', or, indeed, 'cowabunga'? Or *could* it be a reference to the fact that shortly after moving away from Loughborough I had seen a tramp on fire, and told Peter about it in a letter?

It's been a very hot here lately and on Friday 4th the temperature reached 99 degree fahernheit!! 'Cor what a scorcher!', the hottest in the midlands since 1911!

So. The weather interested him. He was a fan of tabloid-style headlines. And he was a history buff!

In the bank holiday we will be going away in our caravan to where they have tennis courts and a pool on site! Ha-hoo! Hoo-ray!

He enjoyed caravanning. And sports. So much so he would say 'Ha-hoo!'

My paper round is going well, apart from the odd finger getting caught in letterbox's! I have now had 8 pounds from the shop and can't wait for Christmas tips!

An interest in the media. Money-oriented. He had an odd finger.

I have decided one day I want to be an architect in London.
Bye
P. Gibson

Gah. And as quick as that, the trail ran cold.

But still. It raised an interesting question. What *would* everyone be up to nowadays?

When I was about fifteen, my form tutor announced with great excitement that we were all to report at once to the careers adviser, Mr Stott, who had something remarkable to share with us.

'We have a new piece of software in the department,' he announced. 'It is able to accurately predict, based on your skills, abilities, likes and dislikes, your ideal job.'

We all looked, as one, to the rather bruised and scratched beige computer which apparently now held all our futures within its blinking green monitor.

'There is no need for guesswork any more. By simply taking ten minutes to answer all the questions in front of you, the computer will compute the way your life should go.'

I am not sure quite why we trusted Mr Stott so much on this. Many of us had generally stopped taking him particularly seriously as a careers adviser since the day he'd announced his imminent departure as he'd suddenly realised – eight years into the job – that careers advice wasn't the job for him.

But today was different – because today involved *technology*. These were the *nineties* – things were moving on! By the year 2000 *all* jobs would be doled out by robots!

Excited, but nervous, we entered our answers as best we could, and a mere eighteen hours later, the supercomputer had worked it all out.

Justin Betts, a boy who was virtually all muscle and who would later be dubbed a hero by the local paper after single-handedly tackling a burly burglar, was told that his ideal career would be 'midwife'. Chris Jones was told he should be a jewellery designer, Alec Lester an insurance broker, and Daniel Vincent was instructed to pursue a life in medical photography – an odd choice for a boy who once vomited after seeing a picture of a burnt nipple.

And me? Well, with my willingness to work as part of a team or on my own, my ambitions to study German at A Level, and my predicted grade D in maths GCSE, I was uniquely placed to excel as Britain's newest 'quarry manager'.

I am not sure what it is about me that the computer thought would be so useful to the quarry management industry. I had mentioned neither an ambition to manage, nor a particular fondness for quarries. If I'm absolutely honest, I find quarries a little dull. And I wasn't alone in my doubts. No one at school seemed particularly convinced by the results. Chris Jones decided he'd be rubbish at designing jewellery. To this day, I am told Justin Betts is yet to supervise a birth. And just two days later, Daniel Vincent loudly declared that he had seen his last burnt nipple. When we left school, none of us really knew *where* we were heading.

Which is what, I thought, while brushing my teeth and preparing for bed, would make finding out where everyone was so very exciting.

If, that is, I would be allowed.

Don't get me wrong – I was definitely with the right girl. But what's acceptable when you're courting and what's acceptable when you're married are two separate things. Deep down, I knew Lizzie would be happy for me, reconnecting with my past, seeing old names and faces. It might even help her know me even better. But I also knew that this might take time. And there were window frames to paint.

I wondered what Wag and Ian were up to right now.

If only there was someone I could talk to.

'So…' said Hanne, tucking into her bagel. 'What's new?'

It was the next day and we were sitting on a bench in Holland Park. Hanne, my straight-talking Norwegian ex-girlfriend, worked at a radio station not too far away from here. Sometimes we'd meet up for lunch, or a coffee, and talk about the world and our places in it. But today she could only spare half an hour. She'd be meeting her new boyfriend in an hour just down the road.

'Well,' I said. 'Let's see… Ian's moved to Chislehurst, Wag's gone on tour, Lizzie's got a new job. That's about it.'

'And you? How about you?'

'I've been to Loughborough, where I spent the weekend with chefs and architects and gypsy witches and time travellers.'

'Was it a nerds convention?'

Tsk.

'It was *not* a nerds convention, no,' I said. 'They're old friends.'

'You're old friends with a gypsy witch from Loughborough?' she said. 'How come you never mentioned a gypsy witch from Loughborough when we were going out?'

'Well, the gypsy witch isn't specifically my friend. It's her granddaughter. And it's more that she's going out with a friend of mine. Mikey.'

'Who's Mikey?'

'I knew him when I was little.'

'Why were you hanging out with him?' she said, as if it was the oddest thing in the world. 'Someone you knew when you were little?'

'Well... because we were friends,' I said. 'I thought it'd be nice to see him again. I mean, I wasn't sure at first, because it can be a bit weird...'

'It *sounds* weird.'

'It *wasn't* weird. He's just a guy I hadn't seen in about twenty years, and...'

'I've never understood that. I've never understood this obsession with tracking down your past. Why go back? Life is about moving on. That's *why* it moves on. Look – watch!'

She held her finger up in the air and didn't say a word.

'See? That was it moving on!'

'But sometimes you have to look back to look forward.'

Hanne thought about it.

'What does that mean?'

'I'm not sure,' I said. 'But it sounds like something Oprah would say.'

Hanne ignored me.

'People should move on. You know my friend Guro? She still loves Take That. She still believes one day they will reform. It has been ten years, and still on Guro's computer is a Take That screensaver. It's like this Facebook thing. Facebook is ridiculous. People tap-tap-tapping away and tracking people down just to swap trivia... getting little messages saying they're feeling ill or they've just eaten an egg. If I want to tell people I've just eaten an egg, I phone them and I say, "I've just eaten an egg."'

'Why on *earth* would you phone people to tell them you've just eaten an egg?'

'That's beside the point. All I'm saying, Dan, is when you look back, all you ever discover is that most of your old friends now work in IT. It's boring.'

'You do *not* just find that out. I've just told you. One of them's a time lord.'

'Is he really?' said Hanne, not sounding as convinced as I was. 'And what does he do when he's not time travelling?'

'He runs a carvery near a motorway.'

Hanne just nodded and took another bite of her bagel.

'But he's not in IT!' I said, rather offended. 'You said they'd all be in IT!'

'What about the others?'

'I haven't started yet!'

'Ah, so you're *going* to start, then. Because there *will* be others, won't there?'

'I didn't say that,' I said, a little too defensively, but we both knew that there would. That was, after all, why I'd phoned her and asked to meet.

'Can I give you one piece of advice?' said Hanne, with great calm. I nodded.

'Tell Lizzie. I know you and I know how you operate. Tell her now. Get it out of the way and if she says it's okay, do whatever it is you're thinking about doing. You see, that was the thing about you and me. It wasn't the things you did that bothered me. It was the not *telling* me about the things you were *thinking* about doing...'

Hanne had a point. She'd dumped me when I'd started an international cult and not told her about it. Yeah, that's right. That old story.

'So tell me the truth – you're thinking about it, aren't you?'

Sod it. I had nothing to hide.

'Yes, I *am* thinking about it. And yes, I *have* been on Friends Reunited, which I'd previously been *banned* from for being abusive and misleading, and I had a look about. And yes, I *am* a nearly thirty-year-old man who might just be looking to the past to make sense of the future. And *yes*, I've just realised that that's what that Oprah thing meant. And who knows – maybe *you* would call it a third-life crisis, but to be honest who knows how long any of us live these days? This *could* be a midlife crisis, a *bloody great* midlife crisis, for all you know, and...'

Hanne looked mildly shocked at my passionate outburst. I refocused.

'... and actually, *none* of them work in IT, since you ask. One is a famous singer, one does opening ceremonies for major sporting events, and two of them invented the glue on the back of Post-it notes.'

Hanne just looked at me.

'You're thinking of *Romy and Michelle's High School Reunion*, aren't you?'

'Yes, I am.'

'You don't know *what* they do, do you?'

'No, I don't.'

'And you're desperate to find out, aren't you?'

'Yes, I am,' I said.

A pause.

'They're in IT,' she said, and finished her bagel.

Hanne's lack of enthusiasm was frustrating, but what was really frustrating was how right she'd been about telling Lizzie. But who was she to say that all my friends now worked in IT? And what was wrong with working in IT, anyway? These were *my* friends and I was proud of them. A set of people unique to me, just as your set is unique to you.

Discounting Michael Amodio, Anil Tailor and Simon Gibson, there were another nine names in the book in total. And that made twelve names. Twelve names that represented the *best* of my childhood.

I'd immediately sent off a friendly postcard to Peter Gibson's old address, reintroducing myself and asking if he fancied catching up. And then I'd set about finding the other name that Anil had seemed so keen on finding out about. Cameron Dewa. The Fijian kid.

All the Box contained from Cameron was a few pictures, a medal we'd both received after completing the Loughborough Fun

Run in 1988, and a letter he'd sent me after finally leaving town to go back to Fiji. Cameron and I had had so much fun together, riding around on our BMXs in our little green tracksuits. Playing football on the field. Going to the Wimpy and McDonald's and spending our tiny amounts of pocket money on sweets and Garbage Pail Kids stickers, until they'd been banned one day by Mr Williams, the headmaster, for being rude and offensive. Mr Williams had been a kind and generous headmaster, though prone to banning things on a whim. Stickers were banned, MicroMachines frowned upon, the local fair branded a 'rip-off', and then there was the morning assembly when he'd inexplicably decided to ban Wispa bars because they were full of tiny bubbles of air. Mr Williams deemed this 'as good as theft', though he didn't seem to mind eating Aeros. It seemed strange, but Cameron and I, being sticklers for authority, never again bought another Wispa. It can be no coincidence that just ten short years later, Cadbury's stopped production of the Wispa altogether.

The letter Cameron had sent me made no reference to the banning of Wispas, but did, instead, offer a few clues. There was a PO Box address set up by the mail company UPS, for example, which the family were using until they got settled again. There was a reference to his dad's place of work, at the university. And a mention that they were headed for Suva. Cameron also mentioned that he'd just had a strawberry milkshake and it was sunny, but I figured I could probably put those facts to one side for now.

And so I headed for Google.

I typed in 'Cameron Dewa' and pressed 'Search'.

Your search did not match any documents.

Hmm. Okay. Too specific. And so began an hour of wading through website after website associated with the name Dewa. First off, the Division of Early Warning and Assessment. Then the Dubai Electricity and Water Authority. A 1980s Indonesian rock band from Surabaya named Dewa 19. A province of Japan called Dewa. But nothing to do with anyone whose *name* was Dewa.

So I tried another tack. I looked up universities in Fiji. Hadn't he said that was where his dad was going to be working? But there were so many of them…

Central Queensland University
University of the South Pacific
Fiji School of Medicine
Fiji Institute of Technology
Pacific Institute of Management and Development

… and not all their websites had a 'search' function.

I'd never find him this way. I needed another angle… I found the Fijian Yellow Pages, and typed in Cameron Dewa. It came up with 'C. Dewa – Plumber'. *Ha*, I instantly thought. *You see, Hanne? Not all my friends work in IT. Some of them* might *be Fijian plumbers.* But this plumber had a middle initial. I was fairly sure Cameron didn't. I found a link to something called the White Pages, which seemed to be able to give me residential numbers, but how would I know which one was Cameron's? There were no C. Dewas listed – I'd have to find his *parental* home, but there were no Fred Dewas, either… there was a Chetty Dewa, and a Dr Seru Dewa, and a Kumaran Dewa (which made me wonder whether I'd been misspelling 'Cameron' all these years – if I had, my one major talent at school would have been instantly undermined), but no Fred Dewas whatsoever.

I was drawing blanks in every direction, and feeling suddenly a little beaten. I didn't even know for sure that Cameron was still in Fiji.

All I could do was write another postcard. At least I had the UPS address to write to. But as I did it, I slowly realised that surely this would have been shut down years ago. It was a temporary measure. Somewhere to direct their mail while they found a house. It would be nearly twenty years out of date.

I sighed, signed the postcard, shut down my computer and waited for the doorbell to ring.

The Bald Assassin had just jumped out of a third-floor window, reloaded in mid-air, and shot me in the forehead from a distance of about a hundred feet. He landed, giggling, and then ran away, before the sound I'd been waiting well over an hour to hear finally happened.

'Until next time, Bald Assassin,' I muttered, but he was off, annoying someone else and still giggling, so I switched the Xbox off and answered the door.

'Well, the first thing I can tell you is this…' said Paul, pointing at the guttering. 'We're going to need to replace all of that…'

'*All* of it?' I said, but what I was really wondering was why we'd stopped calling it 'her'.

'Yup. And also, see this?'

He patted a part of the wall which looked exactly the same as all the other parts of the wall.

'Ah,' I said, pretending to notice whatever it was he'd noticed.

'You're obviously going to need to protect this…'

'Of course, yes.'

'Have you thought of building a small canopy?'

'Not that much,' I said, which was at least honest.

'Well, you should.'

'Hmm!' I said, tapping my finger on my lips, assessing the problem. 'Okay!'

Paul smiled. This was good. This meant he was now under the impression that, like him, I was a man of action, and that at any given moment I would happily sanction the building of small canopies.

'I could do that for you,' suggested Paul, which was very kind.

'Brilliant!' I said.

Being a boss was *easy*.

Paul left soon after that, having given me a revised quote and asking for a little more money, 'just to secure the right materials'. The work couldn't be started today, because Paul wanted to wait for the optimum weather conditions, and also it was nearly three o'clock and he wanted to miss the traffic. But I'd written him a cheque and he said he'd be back soon to measure up for a 'really beautiful little canopy that'll last for years'. I waved him off and congratulated myself on an excellent day's work. It was a beautiful day. Just the right time of day to start work on the garden! The sun was shining, the birds singing in the trees, and so I went inside and turned the Xbox on. I looked at the socket that needed mending. No. Right now, I had to practise reloading while jumping out of windows.

An hour passed. Maybe two. I was still sitting next to the broken socket with my Xbox controller in my hand. The Bald Assassin was still running amok, and had crept up behind me several times in the past few minutes and bashed me on the back of the head. It was becoming severely vexing. But I'd stopped playing. I was just sitting there, staring at the screen, thinking about what lay ahead. Or *could* lay ahead. And thinking about what Hanne had said. If I was to do this, I had to do it *all*. It would be no good finding just a *few* names from the Book and letting things rest. What would that say about the quality of the other friendships in its smudged and battered pages? No, if I was going to find a *few*, I was going to find them *all*. Cameron. Andy. Ben. Akira. Lauren. All of them. But it would take time. And they could be *anywhere*.

I sighed. Was it a good idea?

This was the question I was pondering as I simply sat there, quiet and still, staring at the screen. Staring *past* the screen. Staring past it so far I almost didn't notice the small, twinkling oval box that had suddenly appeared in the top right-hand corner. I blinked until I could focus on it, and just caught it before it faded out...

theblindsniper_1977 wants to be your friend

Eh? Who was theblindsniper_1977? Why did he want to be my friend? Why was my Xbox getting involved?

But this seemed to be in the spirit of the past few days. Maybe it was a sign. A sign that new friendships can be made. That perhaps new ones are what I should be concentrating on. Not trying to find people who live in Fiji who are also nearing thirty and knew me growing up. But new friendships, with twelve-year-old boys, on the internet.

Whatever. I clicked on 'Accept Friend Request'. Maybe this kid had seen my screen name and liked it so had taken a chance. It happens all the time. I waited a few seconds, but nothing much seemed to happen after that. I was about to switch the Xbox off and do something more useful instead, when suddenly, there it was again... another oval, twinkling message...

theblindsniper_1977 wants to play

I was intrigued now. Whoever theblindsniper_1977 was he certainly seemed keen on me. But it was getting late. The afternoon was slipping away and I'd done precisely nothing. There were still those boxes to unpack, and I should think about varnishing the garden table while it was still sunny, and then I'd also promised to give that banister a lick of paint...

But one more game might not hurt.

I clicked 'Accept Game Invite' and sat back down on the sofa. And then, in my headset, I heard a familiar voice...

'Danny! It's me!'

Eh?

'Who?' I said.

'Who do you reckon?' he said.

I thought about it.

'... God?'

'No. Me! Mikey!'

'Mikey? Michael Amodio?'

'Yeah!'

'But... how did you get inside my computer?'

'You told me your screen name the other night when you saw my Xbox... so I decided to look you up...'

'That's brilliant!' I said. 'Let's play!'

And so Mikey and I ran around a small room, shooting each other, making each other laugh, talking about our lives. And it was just like the old days.

'This is probably the first time I've played you at a computer game in twenty years,' he said, and he was right. We were the videogame generation, raised on Ataris and ZX Spectrums and Space Invaders, Pacman and Kong. In the old days, Mikey had been the first kid I knew to get a Sega Master system – a games console with all the high-tec power of a satsuma – and we'd spent many happy afternoons playing Shinobi, Bubble Bobble and Out Run... those were the days of bulky cartridges and unwieldy joypads... the days when the music CD had only just come out and *Tomorrow's World* declared them 'indestructible', meaning the next day everyone tried to snap and scratch their dad's new CDs and discovered that *Tomorrow's World* was talking out of its arse.

'Things have changed quite a bit since then,' I said, lobbing a grenade his way.

'Yeah,' he said, a hundred miles away but right here in the same room, and blowing up rather dramatically. 'But I was just saying to Nikol, it's *so* cool we're mates again...'

I was touched. I had been incredibly pleased to see Michael again. And it felt good knowing that he felt the same way. Friendship really is a two-way street. You select your mates, single them out. But they have to do the same for you. Otherwise you're a stalker. It's a fine line.

I wanted to say thanks to Mikey – thanks for being so open to the past – but he got his pistol out and shot me four times in the feet so the touching moment was sullied, somewhat.

And then, a message appeared on the screen.

The Bald Assassin wants to play...

'Oh, God,' I said. 'Not *this* nitwit...'

'Who?' asked Mikey, exploding again.

'It's either this eunuch, or this American child who continues to taunt me. He's brilliant at games, just like *we* were when *we* were twelve.'

'What does he want?'

'He wants to beat me again,' I said. 'And to honest, I should really be varnishing the garden furniture.'

'Wow. You *do* sound old. One more game?'

'He'll only come in and beat me...' I said.

'Well... maybe he'll beat you,' said Mikey. 'But you're part of a team now... Team Loughborough... let's *get* him...'

Brilliant!

*

An hour later and I was at my desk, typing an email with furious pace... the thrill of warfare was running high, and it was now time for action. Talking to Michael again had proved to me that meeting with him after twenty years wasn't just about that one night in Loughborough... it was about starting something again. Something that could last for *years*... so long as we wanted it to. We could meet up and hang out whenever we decided. And I wanted more. I wanted to be able to say the same of Cameron, or Chris, or any of the others. But I knew my responsibilities, too. Which is why my email was to Lizzie...

Dear Lizzie
It is I, your husband.
(Dan)

Now, listen, I could have talked to you about this tonight over dinner, but I feel it necessary to put it to you as a formal proposal, so as to keep things above board and businesslike. Also, we are currently within office hours and I thought you might like to maintain an air of professionalism.

As you may be aware, I recently found an old address book containing twelve names. Twelve names that represent the best of my childhood. But twelve names that I've lost touch with.

You will know from recent conversations that over the weekend I undertook a trip to Loughborough, Leicestershire, where I gained an audience with Michael Amodio, Anil Tailor and Simon Gibson. You will find them in my address book under A, T and G. Now, that's three names done. Three addresses updated. I was just wondering if it would be okay if I found the other nine.

I promise I'll do it as quickly as possible. And I'll do whatever you want in return. It's just that, in a weird way, I think I need this. I'm not sure why. I think it's to do with being... you know... 29 and a half.

I await your response with interest. And crossed fingers.
Yours,
D
x

P.S. Michael Amodio helped me beat the Bald Assassin!

P.P.S. You probably do not find that all that impressive.

P.P.P.S. Actually, it was a draw. This is now the least impressive story of all time.

P.P.P.P.S. The Bald Assassin is a child I play at Xbox.

Minutes later, my phone rang. It was Lizzie.

'So you want to do this?' she said, almost straight away.

'Yes. I do. I mean, if it's cool with you, and—'

'You know you don't have to ask me,' she said. 'You're just hitting thirty and you don't like display cushions. Why *wouldn't* you do this?'

'It's really just updating my address book,' I insisted. 'People do that all the time…'

'Not usually in person, though,' and I had to concede, she had a point.

'Listen,' she said. 'I have an idea. One that'll make you feel better about all this and benefit us both.'

'Okay.'

'Meet me at Desperados at eight… bring whatever evidence you need to support your case.'

Eh?

'Desperados? What… that weird little place on Upper Street?'

'That's the one.'

'But you *hate* spicy food…'

'We're not there to eat,' said Lizzie, her voice taking a chilling turn for the ominous. 'We're there to make a deal…'

I was sitting, waiting for Lizzie, next to an upturned wheelbarrow in Desperados. There was a sombrero to my left, an inflatable cactus to my right, a picture of Tony Blair and Gordon Brown on the wall, and a bright yellow mocktail in front of me, so I think you can tell – authenticity was key. Desperados was a Tex-Mex I'd walked past almost every day since moving to north London, and yet this was the first time I'd ever sat in it. There'd just been too many quaint little coffee shops, or *boulangeries*, or places where they look at you like you're mad if you can't tell one olive from another. But this? This was all jalapeño poppers and deep-fried mushrooms stuffed with Mexican cheese. This was good. This was *proper*. This was somewhere I'd have come to if I'd fancied a really posh night out with Ian.

I took a sip of my mocktail and thought about what Lizzie could have meant. A deal? We were making a deal? Perhaps now that we were married, I'd be allowed one small adventure a year. Or none! What if *that* was the deal? She'd wanted evidence to support whatever case I was supposed to make, and so I'd brought some with me. The only postcard I'd ever received from Christopher Guirrean. Pictures of me and Peter Gibson in the school play. The letter from Cameron in Fiji, complete with vague PO Box details. I studied them. And then in she walked.

'Hello, you,' she said, stooping to kiss me.

'Hello!' I said. 'Check out my mocktail!'

'It's very pretty.'

She sat down and ordered one for herself. Apparently, she said, Desperados had once been a place called Granita, and as such was perfect for making deals people could stick to. I have since looked it up, and consider her to be correct.

'So, keeping things businesslike,' said Lizzie. 'Let's cut to the chase. You want to find your old friends. Why?'

'I don't know. Like I said, it feels important. Like I'm getting older. Like things are changing. Like I'm going to be thirty any minute and I want to be like my mate Neil.'

'Neil?'

'Remember I went to that guy's thirtieth birthday? Well, he was surrounded by all the people he used to know. Except he *still* knows them. *I* moved around so much. Mobile phones didn't exist, or if they did, they were the size of dogs and children couldn't even lift them. Text messaging was when you passed a note in class. And Bebo was the scary clown who used to come to assembly...'

I was suddenly getting quite passionate. It was like one of those courtroom scenes in films, where the young lawyer suddenly starts getting all articulate and just.

'And then you found the address book with twelve names...' said Lizzie, for the prosecution.

'Exactly! The Twelve! The Special Twelve! I could call them Danny's Dozen!'

'If you use that phrase even once more it will seriously count against you.'

'I promise I won't! But as we know, I've already met up with Anil, Mikey and Simon. That's three out of Danny's Dozen in just one quick go! And that's already *25 per cent* of the people in the book!'

Statistics. They'll always impress a jury.

'Already, I've written to Peter Gibson. Already, I've written to Andy Clements. And the rest? The rest will be *easy*. I *must* be able to find *Chris*, for example…'

'Which one was Chris again?'

And cue the evidence.

I held up a photo of Chris.

'Chris was my first-ever best friend. He was the first kid I ever met at school. We hit it off straight away. We were these two tiny four-year-olds with Scottish accents and little blazers and ties, and we just *knew* we'd be pals forever and ever and ever…'

'But you weren't?'

I shook my head, a little sadly. This would be a pivotal emotional moment to sway even the hard-faced and fictional judge.

'No. I mean… I moved away from Dundee when I was about seven.'

'Why?'

'Mum and Dad moved and I decided I wanted to be near them.'

'Fair enough.'

'But we had such good times, me and Chris. Proper, carefree times. I can remember learning to ride a bike at the same time as him. Seeing a brand new TV show called *The A-Team* with him. I remember him bringing me a water pistol to make me feel better after Steven Bishop broke my arm. I remember agreeing with him that one day when we were old enough we'd both buy Choppers.'

'Choppers?'

'Those weird red bikes that make kids think they're in *Easy Rider*.'

This was good. This was setting the scene. Even the court reporters and the woman typing it all up would've been on my side at this point. I kept pushing.

'And yet the thing is, from looking through the Box, all I've got to show for my friendship with Chris Guirrean – one of the first and arguably most *important* of my life – is a postcard he sent me when he was seven saying that France was hot and he likes dogs.'

Lizzie considered this vast injustice. But it still wasn't quite enough.

'Who else?'

I was straight on it.

'Tarek Helmy.'

I held up a picture of Tarek, in which he was smiling and waving. Who *wouldn't* want to meet this guy?

'When I moved to Berlin with Mum and Dad for a year, he was this supercool kid. He was a quarterback and one of the in-crowd at this American school I went to, but he was nice and kind, and one day he managed to save me from getting mugged by knife-wielding maniacs.'

They'd actually been knife-wielding *teenagers*, but it's important to heighten the drama when in court.

'And that's *important*, Lizzie. Who knows what effect that could have had on me? And yet I don't even know Tarek any more!'

I now felt I was making Lizzie understand that this wasn't 'just' updating my address book. Making her understand that updating my address book *mattered*. And what's more, I was actually convincing *myself*.

'Who else?'

'Lauren Medcalfe. She was a kind of pen pal. But I was never any good at writing back. Same goes for Andy Clements, although I'm trying to make up for that now. And Cameron Dewa.'

'You've mentioned him, I think,' said Lizzie. Her mocktail arrived. It was almost as yellow as mine.

'He was a Fijian kid. We were best, *best* friends. But then he went home. I thought I was on to him for a while today. Thought I was tracking him down. But the trail went cold. I'm still going to send the postcard, just on the mental off chance that somehow it gets through.'

'To where?'

'To the PO Box they set up about twenty years ago.'

I laid the letter and my postcard down on the table and showed her.

'See? People set up these UPS things all over the world, and get their mail redirected to their temporary home, wherever that might be. But as soon as they've found somewhere more permanent, they shut it down. And I don't have his new address.'

Lizzie was still studying it.

'Sod it,' I said, suddenly realising that was a bad example. 'He's probably moved house sixty times since then...'

I'd made a tactical courtroom error. Highlighted the fact that this wasn't as easy as I'd hoped to make it sound. I was about to say that if I really focused, really put the effort in, I might be able to *find* Cameron, but Lizzie interrupted, with: 'Okay.'

I didn't know what the 'Okay' meant. It sounded like 'Okay – enough of this', and I paused. There was a silence. The case seemed lost. I was about to take a large, sad sip of bright yellow mocktail, when she suddenly said, 'I'm about to tell you something that will both delight and astound you.'

I just looked at her. Maybe there was a chance I could turn this around...

'But first,' she said, 'the Deal.'

I nodded her on.

'The Deal,' I said, importantly. And then, slightly less importantly: 'What's the Deal?'

'The Deal is this. Now as you know, I have no problem whatsoever with you gallivanting around, having fun. It's part of you, and I love it. But I've also seen how, lately, you've been a bit... lonely. I've been busy, and Wag and Ian aren't around, and that's got to be part of why doing this appeals to you so much... but also, I am well aware of how you feel about... display cushions.'

How did she know?

'I *love* display cushions!' I said, defensively. 'I love how they are there just for display and no other reason and how they are not for bottoms.'

'I kind of don't mean display cushions specifically. I kind of mean what they... *represent*.'

I didn't say anything. She was on to me, and she knew it.

'Now maybe this is all to do with looking to the past, and thinking about growing up. Or maybe this is all just fun. Either way, who cares – if you want to do it, you should. But you're going to feel guilty, and I'm going to feel knackered coming back late every night to a house that's even more knackered than I am. So how about this... you can see as many old friends as you like, so long as you put equal effort into sorting out the house. The lights, the sockets, the painting, all that stuff.'

The prosecution had made their case. And I could meet them halfway!

'Today I commissioned the building of a small canopy!'

'And played Xbox?'

'Well... yeah.'

'And googled Cameron?'

'Yup.'

'In equal measure?'

I thought about it. I was being cross-examined. But I could get out of it.

'Define "equal",' I said, cleverly.

'The same.'

Bollocks.

'Then, no.'

Lizzie took a sip of her mocktail and winced. It was a rubbish mocktail.

'Thing is,' she said, 'I know you. And I know you'll put it off. Now I don't mind that. I'm Australian, after all, and we can put off even putting things off. But I am suggesting two things. The first – Man Points.'

Man Points? What were Man Points? It sounded like a headline from the *Loughborough Echo*.

'An odd job earns you a point. Fixing something, cleaning something, painting something – all worth points. The bigger the job, the more Man Points you earn.'

'Where's this come from?' I said, aghast.

'I have four brothers,' she said. 'Accrue enough Man Points' – I knew things were serious when Lizzie would pull a word like 'accrue' out of the air – 'and you can do whatever you like with a clear conscience.'

'Man Points!' I said, but Lizzie hadn't finished.

'The second thing I would like to suggest is a deadline.'

I thought about it. It was a compromise. And she was right. A deadline would be good for all manner of reasons. For her, it would mean a definite end in sight. A chance to indulge me, but not indulge me forever. And for me, it would light a fire behind me… make me *do* this!

'When are you thinking?'

'Your thirtieth.'

My thirtieth. November 16th. It was perfect. It was absolutely *perfect*. The house would be done, and my twenties along with it. I would get to grips with saying goodbye to being a boy with a group of people doing exactly the same – and a group of people with whom I'd *always* been a boy. Plus, the DIY I'd undertaken and completed in the name of Man Points would help me feel like a… well… like a *man*. *Prepare* me. Lizzie had covered all the angles. The case for the prosecution rested. I'd avoided forty years of immediate manhood, and been offered several months of community service instead.

'So…' she said. 'Deal or No Deal?'

I smiled.

'Deal.'

And a high-five in Desperados sealed it.

I wanted to show her how much I appreciated this. I wanted to say something that demonstrated just how cool I was with our new way of life. I suddenly really appreciated all the things that Ian had made me so worried about. I could be ready for them – I *would* be ready for them – especially after this. I wanted to tell her that I was pleased she understood the old me, and that the new me was coming along. That once this was out the way, I'd be so much more able to deal with ciabattas and mohair. But all I could manage was:

'We should go home and look at our cushions!'

'You don't get any Man Points for that,' said Lizzie.

Bollocks.

'But in return,' she said, 'to show you how supportive I am of this new endeavour – because I *am* supportive of it – I am now going to give you a gift.'

I crossed my fingers and hoped it was a kitten.

Lizzie held up the letter from Cameron and pointed to the top right-hand corner.

'What does UPS mean?' she said, knowingly.

'United Parcel Service,' I said.

'Yes. But this... this isn't UPS. This is USP.'

I couldn't believe it.

'Psychic ability?'

'No,' she said, patiently. '*USP*.'

I looked at the letter. I reread the address. She was *right*.

USP PO BOX 978

'But... what's *USP*?' I asked.

'I have absolutely no idea. But I doubt it's the United Service Parcel.'

And then, suddenly, and with no warning whatsoever, I *remembered* something... or *thought* I remembered something... and my eyes must have lit up like fireflies because no sooner had I said...

'Can I just...?'

... than Lizzie had said...

'Let's *go*.'

Lizzie sat on the arm of my chair as I fired up the computer.

'For someone who claims to be an excellent speller, I find it interesting that you struggled to spell USP.'

'I saw the letters and I *assumed*...' I said. 'But I *know* I've seen USP somewhere before. And I *know* that it had something to do with Cameron...'

'Maybe he's psychic,' she said, and I laughed.

I found the internet and jumped in, tapping USP into Google as I did so.

United States Pharmacopeial...

Unique Selling Point...
United Security Products...
Universal Storage Platform...

'There are too many USPs!'
　'But you definitely saw it?' said Lizzie. 'You definitely saw USP?'
　'I'm pretty sure...'
　'Click on History...'
　I did.
　And there I saw it...

usp.ac.fj

At first glance, entirely unremarkable...
　But when you *clicked* it...

University of the South Pacific

That must be it! That must be the university Cameron's dad moved to!
　There was a search bar...
　But *would there be a Dewa*? I typed it in, and pressed Search.
　And up came an article...

Microcomputers in Fiji Education/1984 by Fereti S. Dewa,
Suva, Fiji.

'That's Cameron's dad!' I yelled, and Lizzie clapped her hands
together. 'It *must* be! Fred was what he'd always called himself in
Loughborough to make things easier for people... Fereti must be his
real name!'
　I was now on to something... *we* were now on to something...
　I typed Fereti S. Dewa into Google, and found, to my intense joy
and surprise, a photograph of a man I recognised as Cameron's dad.
A big, bold, silver-haired giant of a man. Distinguished and elegant,
in a suit, making a speech of some kind. And what's more – it had
been a speech made in *London*, just two years before!

I started to read it, but it was a complicated speech, which sounded incredibly important, to do with land rights, and forefathers, and rebellions, and Parliamentary Constitutional Review Committees. I couldn't take much of it in, because I was reading on, scanning through, desperately searching for clues as to where he might live now... where *Cameron* might live now...

And then I noticed this...

The Chairman of the Society, Mr Michael Walsh, introduced Dr Fereti Seru Dewa, who had been one of the two hundred and twelve young Fijian men and women who had joined the British army in 1961. Dr Dewa was elected as an MP to the Fijian Parliament in 1994, a position which he held until the coup in 1999...

It was all amazing to me... I'd had no idea his dad was in the army! I'd had no idea he was a Fijian MP, but had been ousted by military coup! But among all that excitement, and danger, and power, there was just one thing that stood out to me. One thing in particular which made my heart jolt...

Seru.

Dr *Seru* Dewa.

I had seen that name *that very day*. And more importantly, I had seen that name that very day, and it had been *next to a phone number*...

'I think I've got him!' I said.

'Good,' said Lizzie, standing up and smiling. 'In which case, I'll fetch your screwdriver...'

Within ten minutes I had a Man Point score of One.

The Desperados Pact had begun.

Sunday June 19th, 2006

Dear Andy

In the name of friendship past, I am slowly working my way through all your letters, and will now take a moment to answer the issues raised in your correspondence of Sunday February 24th, 1989.

First off, your mum is right – you should not pick at it, as tempting as it may be.

Secondly, I am pleased to hear that your dad has managed to pump sealant into the overflow pipe, but saddened to hear of the damage to the overflow pipe that this has caused. I have no further comment.

Now, to *my* news!

I have found the number of a very old friend of mine – Cameron! I am hoping to talk to him soon and one day maybe even meet up! It is very exciting. Lizzie, my wife (did you ever think we'd get married?! We used to say it would *never* happen! Actually, my apologies if you are not yet married. I hope this has not brought up any issues), has given me permission to see all the people from my old address book... and you're one of them! So what about it? You may well still be annoyed at me for never really replying to all your wonderful letters... if you are, I'm very sorry, but I hope I'm making it up to you now. Although I haven't yet had a reply to any of my recent ones. Maybe your family has moved house, so I'll write on the front of the envelope 'Please forward' and hope that they do.

Get in touch, Andy!

Right. I'm going to try and phone Cameron and then I've got to be up early as I'm varnishing the garden furniture. Life is exciting!

Daniel

P.S. Remember not to pick at it. Actually, it's probably cleared up by now, hasn't it?

Chapter Eight

In which we discover that for every Hitler, there's a Shitler...

It was the next morning and I was up early and already at work, in the garden, with a special brush I'd bought and a tin of teak varnish which I was attempting to open with a small pen.

Paul had promised to come round today, but had phoned and said, 'You'll never guess what – my van's broken down!' I had laughed and said, 'You couldn't make it up!', but a few minutes later, as I thought about it, I realised you could.

Ian hadn't been too happy when I'd told him, over the phone, about the concept of Man Points.

'Man Points?' he said, and I could tell from his voice he was cradling his head in his hands. 'Oh my God, Dan, you've fallen for it. This is how they get you.'

'How do you mean? This means I can find my mates! This is freedom! This is brilliant!'

'No. This is the *opposite* of freedom, and this is the *opposite* of brilliant. This is a *system*. Do you think this system will ever disappear now that it's established?'

'You're talking about it like you know what it is,' I said, churlishly.

'It is one of the oldest systems of human oppression in existence,' said Ian. 'Now you have to *earn* your fun.'

'No, it's not like that – it just stops me feeling guilty about running around...'

'And why do you feel guilty?'

'Because I'm married, and I'm nearly thirty, and I should be...'

'I guarantee you your dad had to earn MPs.'

'MPs?'

'Man Points! 2MP for tidying the garage. 1MP for changing that lightbulb. 4MP for—'

'Shut up, no he didn't, he never had to—'

'YOUR DAD HAD TO EARN MAN POINTS!' shouted Ian, shocking me slightly. 'Think back!'

I thought back, confused.

Dad *had* always been tinkering with things. Painting doors. Varnishing tables. Mending broken sockets. And hadn't I once noticed that he always seemed to be mowing the lawn, or up on the roof... *just before a Carlisle United game?*

Oh my God. My dad had had to earn *Man Points* for his fun!

Oh my God. *I was a subject of human oppression!*

I considered this for a moment.

Was my need to see those twelve friends again – to reconnect with my past – really enough to warrant an entire life of servitude... of earning points to be able to do anything, go anywhere? Was it enough to warrant becoming just another faceless drone heading towards middle age? Wasn't that what Ian had been warning me about all along? Was I destined to become one of the men you saw at IKEA? A Micky Thomas in a Volvo wearing driving gloves and buying Turtle Wax?

I weighed everything up in my head.

I decided that, suddenly, I didn't really mind.

Getting the go-ahead from Lizzie had galvanised me into action. And getting a deadline, too – that helped no end. Now there was a point to all this. Now I knew I had to move fast and think quick. If I was going to meet the old gang again, it had to be by November 16th. For on the 17th, I would become a man, with no time for such childish folly. That would be the day I bought a silver Ford Fusion people carrier like Simon, and stopped cutting my hair with electric razors, like Mikey.

That would also be the day I stopped trying to open tins of varnish with small plastic pens.

I looked at the varnish. I looked at the table. This was *clearly* worth 2MP. And what would that be worth, in real terms? I started to stir the tin, thinking about the night before.

I'd discovered to my dismay that the number I had for Cameron was in fact a fax number... but realised, with no small degree of delight, that I could send faxes on my computer. No one had been this delighted about discovering a fax machine since 1985. Or at least no one outside of Poland. And so I'd sent a fax off into the distant gloom of the London night, through wires and across oceans and towards Fiji... hoping that the words 'Fax Sent' were true, and that the number was still current. I hadn't known what to write, so had kept it brief...

Hello! This is Daniel Wallace! I'm trying to find Cameron Dewa! We were best friends at school! I'm updating my address book! My missus says it's fine! Get in touch? My email address is...

It had felt hopeful but also slightly hopeless. A message in a bottle, cast out towards who-knows-where... but it was better than nothing. And now here I was, making up for it, finally opening the tin and getting only two or three splashes of varnish on my shoes and jeans. Result!

As well as the fax of the night before, I'd also raided the Box again, looking for clues as to where anyone might be. Getting closer to Cameron made me feel everyone *else* was achievable, too. But everything was so out of date, so of its time. Snapshots of the past and, as such, not particularly useful to the present. I'd tried to find Akira Matsui on the internet, but, rather annoyingly, discovered it to be one of Japan's most common names. I found an old address I hadn't tried for Tarek, when I lived in Berlin. I knew that Lauren's grandma lived in Dublin, and that she'd often go there to stay for the summer holidays. I'd printed off a list of all the Christopher Guirreans currently living in the UK, and tried to work out which one might be mine.

And then... as the first few strokes of dark, thick varnish went down on what had been a light and golden table... *then*... I remembered Ben Ives...

*

The reason Ben Ives and myself first became friends was due, in some small way, to Adolf Hitler.

Please don't close the book.

You see, from where you're sitting, 'Hitler' probably has a few negative connotations. And you'd be right – the name Hitler *does* have a bit of a history to it. But in the 1940s and before, there were probably rather a lot of people going by the name of Hitler. There were probably Hilary Hitlers, and Phillipa Hitlers, and Dr Billy Hitlers, and each of them could well have been a lovely individual who was carbon neutral and only bought free-range eggs.

But then along came a frowning dwarf named Adolf, with lots of grumpy speeches and silly ideas, and ruined it for the lot of them. The lovely Hitlers of this world had a tough choice to make: keep hold of their names and be looked at oddly when paying by credit card, or sacrifice years of family history and change their names to something a bit less... y'know... *fascist*.

This is the secret tragedy of the Second World War that you only rarely read about. This, and the fact that tiny moustaches went *right* out of fashion.

And so most of the nice Hitlers had done the sensible thing and chosen new non-Hitler-sounding names, like Lambert, or Butler. Some just adapted the name Hitler, and became Hatlers, or Hotlers, or Hipsters. And once they'd done that, everyone would have nodded and clapped and congratulated each other on having skilfully avoided the very worst name in the world.

All, I would think, apart from one man. One man whose name I first saw scribbled across the top of a copy of the *Bath Chronicle*. One man I had to deliver newspapers to as a teenager. One man who'd managed to choose *the only name* in the *world* which was *actually worse* than Hitler.

Which is why it was my job to deliver newspapers to a man named Mr Shitler.

It was extremely difficult not to be fascinated by Mr Shitler. His house was near the very top of Lyncombe Hill, up a long and winding driveway under fir trees that would do their very best to slap me round the face and neck as I struggled to lug my bag towards the door.

Now, Mr Shitler had obviously never been anything to do with the Nazi party. He'd probably never even *been* to a Nazi party, with their Nazi canapés and Eva prawns. He was a lovely old man with Germanic roots who'd leave me a pound in an envelope at Christmas. Of course, it never fully made up for the war crimes of his former namesake, and I think he *knew* that, but it was at least a step in the right direction.

Mr Shitler's wife, who I think was called *Mrs* Shitler, had passed away some years before, and the Shitler house became slightly grubbier for it, with dusty windows and mud on the porch, and a screw missing from the small brass sign on the door that read, simply, SHITLER.

It was a nice house.

But with the familial decision to go from one name to the other, this kind and gentle old man managed to carry with him all the stigma of the name Hitler, while reaping all the rewards of having a name that began with the word 'Shit'. It just goes to show, I remember thinking, as I popped that morning's paper through the letterbox – no matter how bad you think things can get, there's always someone worse off than you. For every Hitler, there's a Shitler, and I fully expect that phrase to appear on T-shirts very soon.

But it was this discovery of the one name in the world even *Hitler* would have been embarrassed by that first and fully bonded myself and the next name in my address book. Ben Ives.

I'd just given up my paper round in favour of a Saturday job at Argos, where Ben had started the week before. Ben was at a different school to me. Had different friends. Lived on the other side of Bath. The odds were against us from the start. But the very moment I'd casually dropped Mr Shitler into conversation, Ben did what any of us would have done in that situation: he hit me back with three Cockheads who apparently lived in Swindon. He knew they were real, because he'd checked in the phone book, after his mate, Bigfaced Tim, had told him all about them. I told him I thought there were a lot more than three Cockheads in Swindon, and he'd laughed, because that's quite a good joke when you're fifteen.

And so, on our first break together, we got the phone book out to check for weird names. And we found them. And we laughed. And our friendship began to grow. And suddenly – I think it was the moment we found the name Vernon Bodfish – we were mates. Mates bonded by Bodfish, and Shitler, and the drab grey and beige world of gold-plated nine-carat Argos catalogue shopping.

And so that was it for me and Ben. Saturdays became fun, and eventually so did Saturday evenings, as we'd head back to mine and watch *Gladiators* and *Noel's House Party*, and play Mega Bomberman until our legs fell asleep and our thumbs fell off. Pretty soon, it was Sundays as well, when we'd cycle around, or sit in McDonald's, or head down to Quasar for 'serious fun with a laser gun'.

Soon we discovered a love of pranks, and we'd rejoice in each of them, no matter how small. Ben was the first person I called when my mum returned from two hours of shopping still wearing the bright green sign reading I AM A WISE OLD SWISS WOMAN that I'd pinned on her back that morning. Ben rang me to let me know that the local paper had printed the letter he'd written on behalf of his neighbour declaring he was leaving the country to start a hospital in Kenya and was inviting donations. When, using hidden speakers and a microphone, I convinced Mum the cat could talk, I immediately told Ben. When Ben did the same to his, he immediately told me.

Ben was brilliant. Ben was a laugh. And it was with Ben that I'd spend long afternoons looking out of my window with a tiny pair of my parents' opera glasses (never otherwise used) until we saw someone walking past the payphone outside Boots. We had the number of the payphone on speed-dial, and this was the best moment of our Sunday afternoon. I'd signal to Ben to turn the radio up in the background, and, as soon as the unsuspecting stranger answered the ringing payphone, I'd shout, in my very best DJ voice, 'THIS IS DAVE CASEY FROM EXCELLENT FM! FOR TEN THOUSAND POUNDS... *WHAT'S THE PASSWORD?*'

'Oh, Christ...' the person would inevitably say, 'I... oh, my... ten thousand... er...'

'FOR TEN THOUSAND POUNDS... *WHAT'S THE PASS-WORD?*'

'Um...'

Ben would be either doubled over or crying into the binoculars at this point.

'I HAVE TO RUSH YOU – WHAT'S THE PASSWORD?'

'I knew you were doing this,' the person would lie, seeing as no one in their right mind would listen to a station named Excellent FM, 'but, um… I've forgotten the password.'

Now the acting would come in.

I'd give Ben the nod and he'd switch the music off.

'One second please,' I'd say, and then Ben and I would pretend to have a secret conversation.

'Oh, no. Ben the producer, they don't know the answer.'

'Oh dear. That is terrible. Because we have to give this ten thousand pounds away today. The bosses here at Excellent FM have said so.'

'Yes,' I'd say. 'We definitely have to give this ten thousand pounds away today. It is lucky this is not live. Perhaps I could give the person we have randomly called a clue, and then we could call them back and see if they have the answer, after taking that clue into account?'

'Yes,' Ben would say, 'that sounds like a fair idea. Provided the person doesn't mind waiting for a few moments.'

'I'll check,' I'd say. 'Excuse me, but I've been talking to Ben the producer, and as we have to give this ten thousand pounds away today, we wondered if we could give you a clue and then perhaps give you a call in a few moments' time and see if you get the answer right?'

'Yes!' the person would shout. 'Definitely!'

'Okay,' I'd say. 'It is an eight-letter word, and octopuses have these.'

'Right!' the person would shout. 'Okay!'

And then Ben and I would put the phone down, and make a sandwich and drink a glass of Fanta, and Ben would keep his eye on the person next to the phonebox while I had a pee or another glass of Fanta.

And then, ten or fifteen minutes later, we'd call back.

'THIS IS DAVE CASEY FROM EXCELLENT FM! FOR TEN THOUSAND POUNDS – *WHAT'S THE PASSWORD?*'

And then the person on the end of the line would shout something like 'TENTACLES!' And I'd say, 'No! I'm sorry! The answer is "Gullible"!'

And then we'd hang up and collapse on the floor and fight over the opera glasses and who got to watch the person walk away looking confused and counting the number of letters in the word 'gullible'.

Our pranks continued for a long and warm summer. We'd write letters. Invent news stories. Play phone pranks. I once phoned the Halifax head office to tell them I was Dave Casey and I was lost in one of their Bristol branch and could they fax me a map of how to get to the tills. Apparently they sent the manager out to check for me. Ben spent twenty minutes on the phone pretending to be a journalist named Dave Casey and asking a local councillor for their reaction to the breaking news that a local school was to be demolished to make way for Britain's only rubber church.

And it was good. And fun. And *great*. We were mates at the top of our game; a team to be reckoned with. And I was happy.

But then, one day, Ben overstepped the mark.

The unwritten rule in those happy teenage years was that we were a team. And the team never played pranks on each other. The team was as one.

You may find the following rather harrowing.

It was a Saturday morning. I was dressed in my ill-fitting slacks and grey Argos tie. My hair was badly gelled and I cut an awkward, gangly figure as I lolloped down the hill to work, the winter sun bringing every single dented beer can and waterlogged fag end into sharp Saturday focus. Everything was normal as Bath recovered from the night before: the payphone had been bashed and smashed as usual. The subway had been given a fresh lick of mildly offensive graffiti. And, as every week, someone had inexplicably left a single chicken nugget on top of the postbox opposite Millets.

The first of the day's shoppers were milling around Southgate shopping centre ('Bath's largest covered shopping area!' was its only sad boast) waiting for the keycutters to open, and I left the beauty of a bright morning for the flickering striplights that painted the bags under your eyes and yellowed your face.

I'd bought a coronation chicken sandwich and a can of Tizer for me and Ben on the way in, and my first vital mission was to make it to the staffroom to deposit them in the fridge. But there was something not quite right. Something different, as I walked past the wonky pile of catalogues by the door. There were glances, and smirks. A giggle and a nudge.

I nodded a hello to the girl whose till was one down from mine, but she avoided my eye and pretended to be studying the homemade tattoo on her arm. The woman in the jewellery section – whose alarming enthusiasm with make-up has since been made illegal in nine countries – was simply smiling at me.

Nevertheless, being a true and proud Argos professional, I pressed on, through the double doors with the peeling silver windows and up the too-steep steps to the staffroom, where I would make a cup of tea before the doors opened and the horrors began. I was looking forward to seeing Ben that day. I had something funny to tell him, and as well as *Gladiators*, there was going to be a very exciting edition of *Noel's House Party* that night, because I'd seen a trailer and Lionel Blair got a Gotcha. It was going to be a *magical* evening.

But then... then I saw it.

Up on the noticeboard.

Neatly tacked in, a pin in each corner.

A letter.

A letter with *my name* at the end of it.

Which was odd, because I hadn't written any letters. And I certainly hadn't written any letters *here*. Why would I write letters from Argos? I was confused. Concerned.

I stood closer, and began to read...

PRIVATE AND CONFIDENTIAL

Eh?

This was a bad start. A bad start to something that suddenly seemed likely to get a lot worse.

I broke into a sweat.

To: Dr Riversticks
The Reinhardt Private Clinic for Young Men
10–12 Lime Buildings
Chippenham
RE: Your letter of August 18th

Dear Dr Riversticks,
My name is Daniel Wallace, and I wish to point out that your
assessment of the so-called 'outstanding' balance on my account
is plagued with a startling presumptuousness.

What? What *was* this? Who was Dr Riversticks? What was the
Reinhardt Private Clinic for Young Men? And where had I learnt a
word like 'presumptuousness'?

When I originally embarked upon the Genital Exfoliation
treatment ...

On *what*?!

... I was led to believe that the overall outlay of £280.25 would
easily cover the scheduled twelve sessions...

Twelve sessions? I'd had *twelve sessions* of genital exfoliation!? I didn't
even remember having *one*! I think I'd remember having twelve of
anything involving my genitals!

Besides my extreme dissatisfaction with the 'results' of the surgery,
your final balance of £1,326.35 is entirely unacceptable.

Why had I written the word results like that? What had happened
with the surgery? What had happened to my *genitals*? Was it possible
to over-exfoliate them? Who had over-exfoliated my genitals?

I had imagined, when first I embarked upon my journey with
the Reinhardt Private Clinic for Young Men, that the journey

would be short, cheap, painless and successful. I certainly didn't imagine it would make my knackers look like a weeping sparrow.

A WEEPING SPARROW??

Please contact my lawyers at Casey & Bodfish, on all future matters.

No! Casey & Bodfish!? Casey... and *Bodfish*! This... this was the work of...

Sincerely,
D. Wallace

No! *Not* D. Wallace! This was B. Ives! *Ben Ives*! A comrade! A *team*-mate! A... *hang* on...

PS. I am writing this at work so I hope I don't accidentally print it out on all the printers here, because I would be quite embarrassed by that.

... a *bastard*!

Ben Ives had broken the rules! He'd gone against everything that was good and holy in our world! Everything that was right and proper! Everything we'd built up and bonded over! He'd turned me from pranker to prankee! A victim! A mark! A... *loser*! A loser who quibbles over the high price of genital exfoliation!

And to think I'd brought him a can of Tizer.

This was terrible. Terrible! I was humiliated! Humiliated, as I walked out of the staffroom to notice a copy of the letter on the door! Humiliated, as I stumbled past Connie from the stockroom. Humiliated, as I realised that yes – Ben had printed out a copy on every printer in the store, and yes – those copies had been read. And passed around. And photocopied. And, for all I knew, sent to the *Bath Chronicle* and the Associated Press.

This was it! This was war! The army had been split! Torn apart by betrayal and menace! Ripped in two by the actions of a young maverick trying to make a name for himself! A line had been crossed. A line that now separated us. A line too wide to ignore; too wide to reach out and shake hands across. A line that meant *trouble*.

Hours later, at my till, my cheeks still burning, I caught a glimpse of Ben Ives as he came down from the stockroom. He looked slightly apologetic; slightly shamefaced. But I knew what was happening inside of him. I knew because I had been like him once. I knew the feeling of elation, the bubble of joy in the base of the gut that comes from a prank that hit the target. And he knew I knew. And I knew he knew I knew. But now... now I was a different person. I had learnt my lesson well. The lesson of the victim.

I turned around. I had work to do. Good, honourable, Argos work. Those fancy, gold-plated BEST MUM IN THE WORLD sovereign rings weren't going to sell themselves.

But soon... soon I would come up with something to get him back. Soon I would conquer the master. I would use what he had taught me to exploit his weaknesses; I would find the chink in his armour and, when the moment was right, I would strike. Strike like the panther! But it had to be good. It had to be right. It had to be better than his; he'd really nailed me with that genital exfoliation. Which is a sentence I never thought I'd write.

But guess what? As the weeks passed, as one month slopped into another... I never got Ben Ives back. Yeah, so I tried, once or twice. But he was on to me. He found the *Jackie* annuals I'd hidden in his backpack. He knew, when I phoned up in a funny voice to tell him he'd won a competition and he was to make his way to Germany immediately, that it was me. He was always one step ahead. And annoyingly, he knew it. Gradually, he became more arrogant about it.

'Give up,' he'd said one day, as we left Argos. 'You're never going to pull it off. Admit you're in second place and maybe we can start doing stuff again...'

But I was too proud. I didn't want to be in second place. All I wanted was for us both to be in first place. The old team. Back together. But the only way for that to happen was to get even; to prove my worth; to regain equality.

I was quite down about it. I knew, deep inside, that Ben was the better prankster. I knew that perhaps I needed him to bounce off; to make my own pranks that little bit better. The split had caught me unawares. Now I knew that somehow he would always catch me out; that my prank would never live up to expectation; that he'd know it was me in an instant. My confidence was rocked.

Maybe all we needed was a bit of distance.

And that's kind of what we got. A week or two later I was moved to the stockroom. I didn't see Ben as much. I began to watch *Gladiators* on my own. Later, Ben got a job at Superdrug, and he started hanging out with a kid named Gary, who had his own video in his room. They could watch *Gladiators* whenever they liked.

Soon, my days at Argos were over, and thus, my last link to Ben Ives.

It was a shame.

Suddenly now, in London, halfway through varnishing a garden table on a bright and sunny summer morning, I was consumed by an overwhelming urge to see him. To tell him that upon further reflection and after more than a decade of thought, his accusations of genital exfoliation had been excellent; that he'd got me and that I didn't mind; that I would happily take second place if only we could be friends again...

Within moments, I was at my computer. I thought back to what Anil had implied. That these were opportunities to be grabbed. That the past is as important as the present. That I shouldn't pass up the chance to right a wrong. That wrongs were there to be righted. That sometimes that's how you make peace with the past.

I retraced my steps of the night before, and then... I found him. I knew where he was, and what he was doing. I knew some of what he'd done, and some of what he hoped to do. I even knew what he looked like.

It was all rather impressive. Ben Ives was now a journalist. On a paper somewhere outside of LA. Writing features, and opinion pieces... a review of a touring production of *Pirates of Penzance*... a lengthy diatribe on the links between oil and war... a feature about a strange group of people called 'Furries' who enjoy dressing up in big furry pig costumes, or bear costumes, or Snoopy costumes, and then having intimate relations, which he'd titled *FUR THE LOVE OF DOG*... and next to them all, under his byline... a picture.

It was him! It was *definitely* him!

But as I looked into those eyes – and this is something I am deeply ashamed of – I couldn't help but feel a twinge of annoyance. A twinge of regret that I never quite managed to get him back. It sounds silly, and childish, and stupid, but looking into those dark Ives eyes brought something else out in me...

What had Anil said again? That I shouldn't pass up a chance to right a wrong? Well, here was a wrong to be righted. The letter on the Argos staffroom noticeboard! That was the real wrong! Not the falling out of touch with Ben Ives – but the catalyst. The kick-off. The *reason*. This... this was a wrong worth righting!

But no. Wait.

That is not what Anil meant.

No. He meant I correct the past nicely. Make *positive* moves.

Yes. I'll forgive and forget. Email him nicely. Ask him how he's doing. Lay the past to rest. Ignore the fact that he'd informed half of Bath I'd been undergoing an intensive course of genital exfoliation which had left my knackers looking like a weeping sparrow. Ignore the fact that he'd gotten away with it. Gotten away with it because we'd never got *even*. And we'd never got even because he was *expecting* it. *Waiting* for it. *Wanting* and *willing* it to happen. And how do you get even with someone who *wants* you to? Who's *waiting* for it? None of my plans had ever been quite good enough, quite *right* enough to carry out... because now I see he was *expecting* retribution. *Expecting* a comeback. *Expecting* my revenge!

And now, as I sat in London, a million miles away from such immature and childish things, a million miles away from having to *prove* myself... a strange and satisfying thought occurred...

Would he still be expecting it after fifteen years?

To: Ben Ives
From: ManGriff the Beast Warrior
Subject: YOUR 'ARTICLE'

Dear Ben Ives,

I got your email from a friend of mine, Domino Bullets, at the recent FurCon in Miami.

My name is ManGriff the Beast Warrior and I am a Furry.

I would like to speak with you about being a Furry.

You appear to have a problem with us Furries. Your article FUR THE LOVE OF DOG describes us thus:

'A bizarro world of animal love and human failings... they dress up as animals, but why these people think they can hide behind their costumes is beyond even the most eccentric mind...'

This is outrageous. We enjoy dressing as furry animals, talking and, yes, sometimes making love. You do not. So what?

You may well know you have become known as Ben Lie-ves by some of the higher powers at FurCon – Ujagi Mokanda and Panda Al in particular. Your duplicity at once united and split many at the DeathStar BBS in Washington and the MidWest FurFest and you have been the subject of many debates (you have come to represent the media as a whole for many thousands of Furries in the US of Americans).

I am coming to LA in the next month or so and I will be calling by your offices where you work to see you. I would welcome the chance to tell you how it really is. I think that you should write another article about Furries – one that shows things how they REALLY are.

Can you let me know your availability for the next month please.

ManGriff

(Tom)

Chapter Nine

In which we learn that when you look back, most of your mates do work in IT...

My email to Ben Ives had filled me with childish glee. I had tried to *hook* him. Reel him in. ManGriff the Beast Warrior was on his way, and there was nothing Ben could do it about it. I'd been slightly worried, though. Ben was a smart cookie. Hard to fool. But that had been when we were in Bath. He was in LA, now. This kind of thing must happen to him all the time.

The next morning, however, and I was concerned. I hadn't heard back from him. Maybe I'd pushed it too far.

By mid-afternoon, I knew I hadn't.

To: ManGriff the Beast Warrior
From: Ben Ives
Subject: RE: YOUR 'ARTICLE'

Er, hi ManGriff/Tom

Just picked up your message – I'm just about to go into a meeting for the rest of the day but I'm more than happy to meet with you – in fact I would welcome the opportunity.

I realise that I upset a number of Furries thru my piece – I got some nasty emails about it – but certainly I didn't realise it had become such a hot potato in the US Furry community. And in fact I think I have been well and truly misrepresented. I don't know who Domino Bullets is, nor what DeathStar BBS is, perhaps you could fill me in? It would be interesting to consider a follow-up piece, depending on my editor's feelings.

Do you have any particular date in mind? I could do the afternoon of the 21st. Are you in LA?

All the best,
Ben Ives

Ha. This was *great*! Ives was *mine*! Now all I had to do was keep this going for a while – at least until he'd booked a meeting room or shown some sign that I'd tricked him, and then I would reveal all. Revenge! Revenge was on its way! After fifteen years! Well done, Wallace!

I bounced around my room for a moment or two, thinking about what to write next. Ben Ives would rue the day he'd made a target out of me. But the best thing was, he was currently rueing the day he'd made an enemy out of the Furries – those poor, misunderstood people who innocently enjoy the simple pleasure of dressing up as animals and having sex. This was for *them*.

I decided to up the ante. Which, if you add the word 'lope' to the end of that sentence, sounds like something a Furry might do.

To: Ben Ives
From: ManGriff the Beast Warrior
Subject: RE: YOUR 'ARTICLE'

ROOOOOOOAAARRRR

Ben,

This is EGGSELLENT news. My girlfriend, the Stormy Leopard, has asked me to ask you this: in her 'human' form, she is developing a performance piece based on being a Furry, which she has developed over the years. She wanted me to ask you whether you and your staff would be interested in a small performance of this piece when we meet. For my part, I believe it is amongst the only things that will truly help you understand the way that we Furries have to live. Here's to the follow-up story!

With thanks,
ManGriff

There. I was introducing a new layer: a new player. A new Furry for Ben to deal with. The Stormy Leopard. Who was she? I had no idea. I would find out when Ben did.

I also admired my own use of the word 'Eggsellent' instead of 'Excellent', and hoped Ben would assume this was some kind of special Furry speak, even though eggs very rarely turn out furry.

I was having fun. I realised I'd have to pay for it. I had MPs to earn.

I went outside and got the varnishing brush out of the shed.

'So, what've you been up to?' said Ian, putting his pint down on the table. He'd called, out of the blue, and said he was heading into London for the day. He sounded quite down about it, as if leaving Chislehurst was the worst thing a man could ever go through. We'd decided to watch the Costa Rica versus Poland match, in a pub just off Tottenham Court Road.

'I've been doing a lot of DIY,' I told him, importantly.

'Ah,' said Ian. 'Of course. How many Man Points are you on?'

'DIY is *important*, Ian. It is a vital stage in my evolution towards adulthood. Already, I have had several meetings about my guttering, there's a ladder in my hallway, I've decided to get a canopy and I've varnished half a table.'

'You must be exhausted,' said Ian, and I made an exhausted face and nodded. Poland scored a goal.

'Well, how about you? How's Chislehurst?'

At this, the heavens above Ian's head opened – angels sang, and he was bathed in a glorious and golden light.

'It is wonderful,' said Ian, his eyes shining. On his shoulder, a small fairy was playing a harp. 'It is just *wonderful*. There are the caves, of course – miles of history and mystery...'

I was sure he'd got that off a pamphlet.

'... and the local culture. The high street has several restaurants and pubs. And did you know that Malcolm Campbell, former Land and Water Speed Record Holder, was born in Chislehurst and indeed is buried in St Nicholas Parish Church?'

I shook my head.

'I did not know that.'

'Yep. It's not all about London, you know.'

I looked at him.

'You miss it here, don't you?'

The golden light disappeared and the fairy on his shoulder popped.

'Yeah, a bit, yeah. There's only so many times you can visit an internet café. Particularly when you already have the internet. But how about Wag? Have you heard from Wag?'

'I got a postcard,' I said. 'He's in Belgium.'

Ian looked at the TV while Costa Rica had a near miss.

'Who'd have thought the three of us would have such an amazing summer,' he said. 'Me in Chislehurst, Wag in Belgium, and you varnishing a table.'

I suddenly got a little defensive.

'I've told you – I haven't *just* varnished a table. And I'm only halfway *through* varnishing it, anyway. I've been updating my address book, as well.'

Ian wrinkled up his nose.

'How long does *that* take?'

'Quite some time, actually. I'm going some way back.'

'How far back?'

'Right the way back.'

'To when?'

'To when I lived in Dundee. That conversation we had – the one about being in touch with my roots. The one about only being able to go forward once you've looked back. It struck a chord with me. And then I found this old address book and met up with some old friends, and it hit me – that's what I should do. See what the old gang is up to. See how they're coping with being nearly thirty. Reconnect with my past. Like you said I should.'

'*I* said that?'

'*Yes*, you said that.'

'It must've been that Taiwanese lager. Won't you just find out that all your old mates work in IT?'

'Why does everyone *say* that?' I said, outraged. 'Probably 0.001 per cent of the population work in IT.'

'Well, it seems a bit odd to me. All this reconnecting.'

'What? You said I should do it!'

'I meant you should do things like stay in bed watching reruns of *Murder She Wrote* and *Magnum*.'

'But it's been *great* – one of my mates has solved time travel. And at the moment I'm pretending to be someone called ManGriff the Beast Warrior in order to entice another!'

'Well, when you put it that way, I'm a lot happier about the situation.'

Poland scored again, and Ian went to get the pints in.

'*I've* done it, you know,' he said, setting them down on the table.

'Done what?'

'The schoolfriends thing. I've looked them up on the internet. Facebook, and stuff.'

'Hanne says Facebook is stupid.'

'*Does* she?'

'Why do you look so surprised?'

'She asked to be my Facebook friend last night.'

What?

'Anyway,' said Ian. 'I even met one of them for a drink one day.'

'Who was he?'

'Steven Macintosh.'

I love the way whenever anyone tells you about someone they went to school with, they give you their full name. It is at once unnecessary and vital, conjuring up images and contexts and a feeling of childhood. And everyone does it. Somehow just saying, 'a kid at my school' doesn't work anywhere near as well as saying 'Gareth Sawbridge', or 'Michael Kirkland', or 'Sally Watkins'. It is my contention that if Jesus had gone to a British school in the 1970s or 1980s, the Bible wouldn't simply make reference to Mark, Luke or

John. It'd be Mark Witherenshaw, Luke Fielding and John Pepperwhite from Bethlehem Junior School for the Holy. Still, Jesus was a right one for nicknames. Just ask John the Baptist – *he'll* tell you.

'And what was it like meeting Steven Macintosh?' I asked.

'I was quite surprised I went,' said Ian. 'But I suppose I was intrigued. I'd tried once before to get in touch with someone, but they didn't reply. And in actual fact, I'm not sure *I* would've normally. It's a bit weird, isn't it, hearing from someone you've not heard from in so long? You just kind of think, I'll leave that friendship there.'

I thought back to Cameron Dewa. Had he got my fax? Would he *ever* reply? Was he doing what Ian was suggesting? I had his address – I could always surprise him. *Force* him to meet with me. But he lives in Fiji. Doing who knows what. It would be a hell of a trip just to knock on someone's door and ask if they're coming out to play.

And then there was Ben Ives. Would he have replied if he'd thought those emails were from me, and not ManGriff the Beast Warrior?

Meeting Simon and Mikey had been easy – because Anil had been there. He'd given things a sense of normality. A sense of happy coincidence. We could all just pretend that I'd happened to be in Loughborough and kind of bumped into everyone.

Maybe Ian was right. Maybe this *was* weird.

'But did you at least have fun with Steven Macintosh?' I asked, hopefully.

'Put it this way,' he said, taking a sip of his pint. 'He now works in IT.'

On the way out of the pub, I texted Hanne.

'Have you eaten any eggs today?' I wrote.

'What?' was the reply.

'Oh, never mind, I'll just check your Facebook.'

'It is a BUSINESS UTILITY!' she shouted.

'I suppose you'd say the same about your Take That screensaver too.'

Ha.

My journey back from the West End was on a tube train packed with men with Polish flags painted on their faces and one lone Costa

Rican. The World Cup was in full swing and London was a happy place because of it. At each stop on the way to King's Cross, more fans would join straight from the pubs. Or, at least, more Polish fans. I sat next to the Costa Rican most of the way home, for vital moral support. I even tried to look a bit Costa Rican.

At King's Cross I left the station happy and lager-relaxed, though thinking about Ian's experience with Steven Macintosh. Was that really was it was like for everybody? Did it *have* to be like that? My BlackBerry buzzed in my pocket, alerting me to new messages.

I got it out and looked at it.

New emails.

The first made my heart leap slightly.

It was from Ben Ives.

To: ManGriff the Beast Warrior
From: Ben Ives
Subject: RE: YOUR 'ARTICLE'

ManGriff, hi. Thanks for your mail. But I am not sure a physical performance piece by your girlfriend would be appropriate! LOL, sorry.
B.

Gah! Oh well – I would have to try a different tack. Ives still wasn't on to me. That was good. That was something. I'd been slightly dispirited by my meeting with Ian, but at least ManGriff lived on. I started to think of what I could do next, but all thoughts of mischief left me instantly as I looked at the next name on the list...

Because it was a name I just hadn't been expecting.

The name was Cameron Dewa.

I immediately clicked it open.

Daniel! Hello!
    Our housegirl in Suva forwarded me your fax! How funny to hear from you! Where in the world are you? What are you doing nowadays?

I couldn't believe it! It was Cameron! And he sounded pleased to hear from me! I wrote back immediately.

Cameron! I'm in London! Where are you?

The wait was excruciating. I began to walk up the street, towards home. By the time I'd reached the kebab someone had left on the corner, my BlackBerry buzzed with Cameron's reply...

Wow! I'm in London too!

I stopped in my tracks. What?! Cameron was in *London*? *Fijian* Cameron? Cameron I'd last seen in *Loughborough*? He was *here*? I looked around, just in case he was somewhere to be seen. That sounds stupid now I tell you, but how many times could I have walked past him in the street and not known? How many people might we know in common? Where does he live? What does he do? Why had we never met up? There were too many questions – too many exciting things going through my head! I hit Reply...

You're in London!? How come? Where?? Doing what?

But I needn't have asked. I scrolled down and saw his email had been sent from Dutch Rabobank, London...

I dialled 118 and gave them the name...

'*I've got the number for Dutch Rabobank on Thames Hithe in London...*' said the lady, and I hung up, because I had what I needed...

Thames Hithe! That was... that was *close*.

My BlackBerry buzzed. A reply. I was hungry for more news. Cameron! Cameron the banker! He could be doing *anything* there! A high-rolling financier! A dealmaker and a dealbreaker! A suited and booted head of international and legal affairs! I clicked it open.

I work in IT.

Right. Don't tell Ian or Hanne.

I read on...

Hey – if you're in London too, we should meet up sometime!

I smiled, and laughed, but I didn't reply. Because I was already looking at my watch and checking how long it would take to get to the river.

I could be there in fifteen minutes.

Chapter Ten

In which we learn that every day,
a million coincidences nearly happen...

I jumped out of the shuddering black cab and there it was: Dutch Rabobank.

A large, glass-fronted building inches from one of the busiest roads in London. There were people everywhere. Important-looking people, wearing important-looking shoes, striding about, importantly. Through the windows I could see men hurriedly walking into rooms with sheets of paper in their hands. Women throwing their hands up in the air and talking loudly on their headsets, probably to other banks, in Tokyo and New York and Rome. They all looked quite angry. And I'd thought the Dutch were laid-back.

I stood back and studied the building. So this was where Cameron undertook his IT work – fixing computers and solving problems and generally keeping the banking world from meltdown, after which I imagined dams would rattle and burst, buildings would topple and meteorites radically change course and aim for London.

I'd moved with great speed and stealth upon hearing Cameron's news. A quick trip home to raid the Box for a few items of Cameron-specific paraphernalia and then into a cab. If a meeting happened, and it was awkward, I'd decided, I could always literally pull something out of the bag, as a kind of Show & Tell element to the proceedings. But deep down I also knew that I was bringing with me proof. Proof of our friendship. Proof that we'd liked each other. Proof that we had a history. Just in case the new, grown-up Cameron wasn't as keen on meeting the new, grown-up Daniel as I was on meeting him. Because I was, as you may have worked out by now, keen to meet him; so keen that I didn't want to wait until we'd fixed a date. I'd decided that *now* was the time. Now was the moment to strike. But I didn't want to just hang around outside his work and then surprise him. That would be too stalkerish. No. I had a *far* less stalkerish plan: an anonymous note.

Yes. That was *much* better.

'Excuse me,' I asked a man standing outside. 'What's the closest pub to here?'

'That,' said the man, proudly, 'would be the Peepy Cheeks!'

'The *Peepy Cheeks*?' I said, slightly alarmed. It didn't really have much of a pub ring to it.

'The, er… the Samuel Pepys,' said the man, with a little laugh. 'Calling it the Peepy Cheeks is a… kind of joke. We *all* say it round here.'

Cameron must have the time of his life with this lot. But I didn't want the man to feel bad. So I said, 'It is a very good joke, and one which I will use myself.'

He seemed to feel a bit better after that.

'Hi,' I said to the lady behind reception. 'Does Cameron Dewa work here?'

She tapped his name into her computer.

'Yes. He's in IT. Would you like me to phone him?'

'No… but… could I leave him a note to collect?'

She frowned slightly, but said, 'Okay.' I took my backpack off, got out a piece of paper and a pen, and started to write.

HELLO
CAN YOU COME OUT TO PLAY?
I'LL BE IN THE PEEPY CHEEKS…

I figured that was mysterious enough to catch his attention, but familiar enough for him to know that this was not an elaborate mugging. And I figured that by not saying, 'Hi! It's Daniel! I knew you twenty years ago!', there was less chance of him getting weirded out and deciding against showing up.

I handed it over to the lady, who had an envelope ready, and I noticed her glance at it. And then at me. I thought about what I'd written, and realised that, yes, it did indeed sound like some kind of homo-erotic invitation. Perhaps this lady thought I had a thing for IT consultants, and spent the vast majority of my days traipsing around the banks of London tempting men out to play, based solely on the promise of seeing me in my peepy cheeks. I wondered whether I should tell her the real reason I was leaving an anonymous note for one of her IT guys, but she'd already popped the note in an envelope and started dialling.

Christ! She was dialling Cameron!

'Hello... Cameron? There's some kind of... *message* for you down here.'

And I don't know what she said next, because I was out the door.

But at least I knew he was *in*! I knew that Cameron Dewa was somewhere inside the building in front of me! It was exciting.

But I didn't want to see Cameron yet. Not right this second. It didn't feel right invading his territory like this after so long. What if he got embarrassed? What if he didn't actually want to see me after all these years? What if he thought I was someone else? I wanted meeting up to be *his* choice, as well as mine. We should meet on neutral ground, and the Peepy Cheeks represented just that.

I started to walk away... but then couldn't quite do it. Cameron was *on his way*. On his way, to collect my dubious message! What would he look like after so long? What would he be wearing? How tall would he be? Would I recognise him?

I glanced back inside the building. He'd probably be there any second. I hid behind a lamp-post and started to stare at the people milling around the reception area. Maybe I'd stay just long enough to catch a glimpse. Long enough to make sure he'd been given the right envelope.

Thirty seconds passed. No one had come down yet.

Another thirty.

Hmm.

And that was when I started to drift off...

*

In 1988, when Cameron and me were enjoying the heights of our friendship, the world was a very different place. There were no winters in the late 1980s... just long and hazy summers followed by Christmas day and then the summer again. The Berlin Wall was yet to fall. Iraq was a country only four people had ever heard of, all of them living in Iraq. And Phillip Schofield was the most famous man on the planet.

Schofield was everywhere. This was his world, run by him, featuring him, celebrating him. He was on TV every day. He was on posters on bedroom walls up and down the country. A typical edition of *Fast Forward* magazine, which I found in the Box and to which both Cameron and I both subscribed as children, has no fewer than four thousand mentions and eight hundred pictures of Phillip Schofield within its 32 small pages.

Fast Forward was ahead of its time; a publication I couldn't wait for each week. With its insightful interviews ('If you were a biscuit, what biscuit would you be?') and its understanding of the important things in any twelve-year-old's life (Andy Crane, Timmy Mallet and the crazy new phenomenon of 'mountain' bikes), this was a magazine it was impossible to do without. It was *vital*.

It could do hard-hitting facts:

10 Completely Amazing Facts About Nathan Moore From Brother Beyond!!
Number 4: He once came second in a dance competition when he was 14.

It could do heartwarming, celebrity interviews:

'I see old pictures of myself and I've got green smudges around my eyes and a flick hairdo and I just scream.'

Kylie Minogue, next to a photograph of herself with *blue* smudges around her eyes and a perm so tight she could survive a fall from another planet.

And it could do exclusive, you-heard-it-here-first gossip:

'An exclusive bit of goss has reached our ears here at FF. Tony Robinson – Baldrick in the Blackadder *series – has been involved in mega secret talks with film chiefs who have been so impressed with his role as Private Baldrick in* Blackadder *that they definitely want him to take over from Michael Keaton as the next Caped Crusader in the Batman movies!'*

It seems incredible now that that never happened.

But mostly, like I say, *Fast Forward* was about Phillip Schofield. What makes him tick. His thoughts and philosophies. Whether he watches *Neighbours* or not ('Yes.'). It seemed that *Fast Forward* magazine was certain that, like the Bible before it, it was vital to the state of the nation that these facts were passed on down the genera-tions; that Phillip Schofield's every whim and wistful glance down a lens was communicated to the children of the world, so that we may prosper and grow in a safer, better, cosier world. These facts... these were the things we all needed to know to survive junior school in the 1980s. Phillip Schofield trivia was like knives are now.

Of course, every now and again Cameron and I would realise that *Fast Forward* was trying to give us a *new* hero. You'd get a page dedicated entirely to Nigel Mansell facts ('Number 2: Nigel goes to church quite often when he is at home'; 'Number 9: The Mansells once had to sell their family home because they had run out of money'), but no one cared. No one gave a *shit* about Mansell. Mansell was no *Schofield*. Schofield was our *leader*. He was the only person in Britain who was even *remotely* interesting, and *I* knew *everything* about him. His favourite colour (red). His favourite drink (orange juice). What kind of biscuit he'd be if he were a biscuit (a wafer). *All* the important stuff.

But then, one day, a new man came into my life, in a way I just wasn't expecting. A man who would become so important to me over the next year or two that everything would change absolutely. I was to become obsessed. Utterly and totally *obsessed*. Within a year, every inch of my bedroom wall – and I employ no exaggeration here – would be covered in pictures, articles, posters and artwork of him. I would have a number of T-shirts with his face on. I would come to the conclusion that this man was the coolest, kindest, most talented and wonderful man the world had ever produced. Cooler, kinder, and more talented and wonderful than even Phillip Schofield. And even now, I do not use those words lightly.

The man's name?

Michael Joseph Jackson.

Within a matter of days, 90 per cent of the Phillip Schofield trivia stored in my tiny brain would disappear – some of it, unbelievably, *forever* – in favour of MJ facts. Height! 5'10". Shoe Size! 10 (European size 42). Favourite colour! Red (same as... oh, God, you know the fella... the one who thinks he's a wafer).

My signed Phillip Schofield photograph was relegated to the bit of my wall hidden by my desk, just above a picture of a Smurf and a photo of my nan.

I could not believe I had never heard of Michael Jackson before.

And I had Cameron Dewa to thank for it.

I had been staring at the window of the Dutch Rabobank with wide, vacant eyes for nearly five minutes. I'd been lost in thought and realised I was simply staring at a reflection of myself. I snapped out of it and focused my eyes on what was behind it... to notice, with some degree of horror, that it was the receptionist's face. She was looking back at me with what looked like real concern in her eyes. She'd been joined by a man in a suit who was also looking at me, now. He'd just made a phone call of some description and started to talk to the receptionist without taking his eyes off me. I smiled at them and nodded, as innocently as I could manage, but then caught sight of myself again. I was a man with a backpack hiding behind a lamp-post outside an international bank staring intently at the receptionist just minutes after handing over what I'd imagined she'd *thought* looked like a homo-erotic invitation but which *now*, in this new and sinister light, looked far more like a *coded warning*.

I tried to look nonchalant, and put my hands in my pockets, before realising that if an armed response unit had been dispatched this was *exactly* the kind of thing they'd be waiting for. I whipped them out of my pockets again, possibly too quickly to look entirely normal, then started to whistle, before breaking into a jog.

Behind me, all I could hear was the whirr of CCTV cameras as they rotated to catch me.

Inside, a small internal voice was shouting, 'PEG IT!'

I'm ready to admit something to you now. Something I wasn't sure I'd be able to do. But telling you about the Cameron days makes me think it's all right...

There was one extra name in that address book, which I didn't mention before. One extra name I'd included on this unofficial list of great mates. One extra name I'd put down there, along with a picture and an address. An address I had written to on more than one occasion.

The World of Michael Jackson
PO BOX 92873
Encino, CA
USA

I had written to Michael Jackson to invite him to Loughborough. It would be the school play soon, and I'd thought perhaps he might like a free ticket (I know people). As it turned out, the closest I would ever get to Michael Jackson was walking through the town centre one evening and experiencing the heart-stopping delight of spotting him in the bargain bookshop on the corner. 'There he is!' I thought. 'He's in Thompson's Bargain Books! He must have read my letter and decided he needed to see *The Princess and the Pea*!' And as I walked closer, and took in the cruel and devastating truth – that this was just a waxy cardboard cut-out to promote his new book *Moonwalker* – my heart hit the floor, and I felt more disappointed than I thought it possible to feel. I boycotted Thompson's soon after. Mainly because they told me I couldn't have the cut-out.

The obsession had started after Cameron had been round my house and suddenly pulled a battered C-60 tape from the trousers of his turquoise cotton tracksuit.

'This is my brother's,' he said. 'Have you heard of *Thriller*?'

I shook my head. I wasn't all that interested. My main interest was recording the theme tunes to my favourite shows by placing a tape recorder next to the telly and hitting Record and Play at precisely the right moment to avoid the announcer's voice. I had *The A-Team*, *The Littlest Hobo*, *Grange Hill*, *Streethawk*, *Wac-a-day*, *Airwolf*, everything. I had no time for this other, childish stuff.

But then Cameron flipped open the cassette player and pressed Play. And in that moment everything changed. This was the most incredible music I had ever heard! It told a story! There were sound effects! What the hell was it?

'There's a video,' said Cameron.

'A *video*?' I'd said, wide-eyed.

'My brother has it. All these dead people come alive and they start dancing. Like this.'

He did a little zombie dance.

This sounded too incredible to be true.

'And Michael Jackson turns into a wolf and he starts dancing like this.'

He did another little dance.

I wanted to do that! *I* wanted to dance like a little wolf!

'And there's this other album,' he said. 'Called *Bad*.'

'Why's he called it *Bad*?' I asked.

'Because Bad means Good,' said Cameron, wisely.

'Oh!' I said. That was clever.

Within a matter of weeks, I had become unhealthily obsessed with Michael Jackson. The letters I wrote him talked openly of my admiration for his charity work. I dissected his lyrics and explained what they meant to me – the twelve-year-old boy in late 1980s Leicestershire. I asked after his chimp, Bubbles, and told him I hoped his hair had stopped hurting after he got burnt doing that Pepsi ad. And I loved the fact that Michael Jackson loved children. I mean, he *really* seemed to love them. There they were in his videos. In his films. Round his house. He was a grown man who seemed to prefer hanging out with boys my age! That was brilliant!

My mum and dad didn't seem to share that view, but what did

they know? They didn't even know his favourite colour, or all the words to 'Liberian Girl'! How was I supposed to take *them* seriously? Losers!

But me and Cameron knew *all* that stuff. We were Loughborough's number one Michael Jackson obsessives. And we'd always said that one day, when we were old enough and able to, we'd go and see the man, for real. It seemed an impossible dream. And, like most impossible dreams, it never, ever stood a chance of happening.

I sipped nervously at my pint. The Peepy Cheeks was filling up with the post-office crowd. By which I mean a crowd that had just been in the office, not a room full of postmen.

Around me were men with shiny hair and tailored suits, talking loudly and laughing at the slightest thing. One of them banged the table every time he spoke, apparently on a one-man mission to turn the word 'Banker' into rhyming slang.

I had a seat near the entrance, so I could look out for Cameron and prepare myself for his arrival. I honestly didn't know how he'd react to me just turning up and asking if he could come out to play. Maybe he had things to do tonight. Maybe he had a family, or had to pick someone up from school. Maybe he was allergic to pubs, or had a history of violently assaulting people who surprised him. I just didn't know what Cameron would be like now. I only knew what he *used* to be like.

Twenty minutes passed, and there was still no sign of him.

Then thirty.

Hope seemed to be fading. But then, maybe Cameron was still running on Fiji Time. Cameron had *always* said he ran on that. This meant that he could be as late as he wanted for anything he chose and simply blame it on the people of Fiji. I had a feeling this only worked if you were actually Fijian yourself. It would be difficult for me to be late to a job interview and then blame it on the Swedes. But Cameron embraced his excuse on a near-daily basis. When I'd made him promise and swear to meet me at two o'clock outside the Curzon to watch *Who Framed Roger Rabbit*, he'd finally wandered in at around four, and caught the last five minutes.

'At least I got to see who framed him,' he'd said. 'That's the important thing.'

And I suppose he was right.

And then, with no warning whatsoever, in he walked.

He saw me and pointed.

'*You!*' he said.

Cameron was unmistakably Cameron.

He was taller, and broader, and wider... but he was Cameron.

'I had no idea you were trying to track me down!' he said, settling into his seat. 'I only found out from that fax! They forwarded it to me in London, and I said, oh my gosh, I *remember* this guy!, and I told my wife, I said, I was at this guy's house practically every day when I was a kid! So I thought I'd give it a shot and reply.'

'Did you ever try and look *me* up as the years went by?' I said, with a little hope in my eyes.

'No,' said Cameron.

Oh.

'But every so often I wondered where you were in the world, if that counts. I think we all wonder where our friends are now. It did cross my mind that perhaps these days you were a psychopath, leaving dodgy notes for me around the world. But life's about risks. I figured it was worth the risk.'

I took that as a compliment. It was official: meeting me was worth risking murder. It's not something I get a lot.

'So where do you live now?' I asked.

'In Essex,' he said. 'I get the train here every day, quite early, and then—'

Hang on...

'That goes through Bow! I think that goes past my old flat!'

So Cameron had been closer than we'd ever thought. The trains which run past my old flat run within two metres of it. That meant that for the past few years, Cameron and I had been within spitting distance, every day, twice a day. Yeah, so only for a split second each time – but that's a *lot* of split seconds. And that's a *lot* of spit, over not much distance. The tracks must've been *soaked*.

A strange thought occurred... I wished I had a map. I wished I could somehow trace the lines of people's movements through the years... not just the movements of their daily routine, but the times they ventured out of it. The times we might just have bumped into each other. The times that coincidences are made of. Cameron's daily routine had brought him closer to me than I'd ever thought could be likely – but who knew how many times I'd walked past him as he sat in a café, or a pub? What if that was true of the others? What if I'd walked past Akira Matsui, or Peter Gibson, or Lauren Medcalfe on my way to meet another, newer friend? What if I'd been on holiday at the same time and in the same place as Ben Ives? Or at a gig? Or in the same cinema? What if tonight I would walk past Christopher Guirrean without even realising it – without even looking up to check? It suddenly struck me that every day a million coincidences *nearly* happen.

'It's a small world,' said Cameron. 'But it feels pretty big when you're a kid. Hey – are you still into MJ?'

'Michael Jackson?' I said. 'No. That sort of faded away. You?'

'No. Michael Jordan took over. When we went back to Fiji I got kind of obsessed with basketball. I had to go to a Chinese school at first, and they didn't really have a natural talent for rugby, so all we did was play basketball, and I loved it. I ended up playing for Fiji.'

'You played *basketball* for *Fiji*?' I said, amazed. 'Seriously?'

It made my North Leicestershire Under-Tens Boys Swimming Championship seem almost like some kind of regional sporting award for children.

'Yeah... we played against America, against Australia, against New Zealand... I wound up scoring nine three-pointers in the game before the world final, but then sprained my ankle so couldn't go through... I was pretty annoyed.'

'But still! You played for a national team! You played for your *country*!'

Cameron looked proud.

'I suppose.'

And then he looked even prouder.

'I was also in a Coke ad.'

'You what?'

He nodded.

'I was in an advert for Coca-Cola.'

This seemed to me to be the whole point of something like Friends Reunited. Why write 'I enjoy peanuts and am unmarried' when you can write 'I played basketball for Fiji and advertised Coca-Cola'?

'It was when they had their new plastic bottles out, and they didn't want to frighten everyone with them by just putting them in the shops.'

'That would have been *very* frightening.'

'So they did this advertising campaign. I happened to be walking by the studio, when someone I knew ran out and said, "Hey – what are you doing for the next hour or so? How would you like fifty bucks and some free Coke?"'

That seemed to pretty much sum up the advertising industry.

'I had to run along a beach with a girl and then stop and drink some Coke. They expected you to hold the bottle in the air miles away from your mouth and then pour it in for thirty seconds, non-stop. I kept getting it down my top, or my mouth would fill up and it would go down my chin. I got it in my eyes at one point and then coughed and sprayed the girl with Coke. It wasn't the look they were going for.'

'Did you manage it?'

'I went through nine bottles. I was getting shaky from all the caffeine and my tummy was full of liquid. In the end they made the girl do it instead. She did it first time.'

'Oh.'

'When I saw the ad I noticed that all the foundation they'd made me wear had mixed with the Coke and made me look all lumpy. I looked like one of the zombies from "Thriller".'

'Still. Another ambition realised.'

'It was as close to being Michael Jackson as I ever came. I remember we always said that one day we'd get to see him.'

'Yeah. But then you grow up.'

'Yeah. But then you grow up.'

Cameron was now married, to a Fijian girl called Nadine, who he'd met at school. Nothing had happened at first – she was concentrating on her band, 4Jams, he was playing basketball with a load of Chinese blokes. And then, while working in a factory, they'd finally fallen in love. Cameron found work as a piano tuner, Nadine found part-time work here and there, and one day they'd upped and moved to London. It was a happy story. But then Cameron said...

'You know my mum passed away?'

I was shocked, and hit by a wave of sadness. When you leave people for so many years – when there's no contact, no updates – you somehow assume that everything is okay. That no tragedy can possibly happen because *you're* not there to see it. That because your world revolves around you, surely nothing happens without you. But that's not how life works.

'God... Cameron, I'm so sorry.'

'Yeah,' he said. 'But Dad's doing good. He's remarried now. Living in a small village in Yorkshire. There's not really much of a Fijian community up there, so he's a bit of a celebrity...'

Which reminded me of something. Something incredible. Something about Cameron.

Because when we were growing up, Cameron Dewa was hiding a *secret*...

I hadn't known about Cameron Dewa's secret until a month or two after our final, tearful goodbye. It had been a horrible goodbye. In our minds we were going to be friends forever, and probably live side by side in a caravan park until we were 80. It was a goodbye so traumatic that in the end the only way I could find to cope with it was through the medium of poetry. I had written a poem entitled 'Cameron Is My Best Friend', through which I was able to exorcise the pain and trauma.

But now that I think about it, all the clues to the secret were there. Clues pointing towards something I really should have known, given the hushed whispers and quiet mutters as we'd cycled around Loughborough, or kicked footballs, or swapped fascinating Michael Jackson trivia.

There was the fact that I knew that his dad, Fred, was someone important back in Fiji. But then, *everyone's* dad was someone important back then. Then there was the fact that it seemed like returning to Fiji was almost some kind of *duty* for the Dewas, rather than a choice. But ultimately, and most importantly, there was the Friday after school, just before Cameron left Loughborough for good.

That Friday was the Friday of the school play. I wasn't in this one – despite the fact that my accent now met with all accepted East Midlands guidelines. Cameron, however, *was* – playing a key, tree-based role in a forest scene. School was over and the sun was shining. Cameron and I cycled away on our BMXs, through the playground, past the magic tree and on, towards home. At the newsagent's near Anil's house, we stopped for some aniseed balls and a drink. We knew our time was running out, but neither wanted to say anything, in case somehow that made the end come faster. And so we rode wordlessly up the hill towards Spinney Hill Drive, turning the corner into the cul-de-sac until we saw something astonishing. Well – something that astonished *me*.

A long, black limousine parked right outside my little house.

With a smart, suited driver in it.

A small Fijian flag above the grille.

And a licence plate with FIJI 1 written on it.

I skidded to a halt. Cameron stopped beside me.

'I think that must be my dad's friend,' he said, as simply as that.

We edged our way past the limo, pushing our bikes and keeping our heads low as a sign of deference to the man within. I couldn't quite believe it. A limousine in Loughborough. You don't get limousines in Loughborough. Even when Barbara Windsor, the most famous person Loughborough had ever seen, had arrived to open that Kwik Save on the market, it had been in a metallic green Austin Princess. That meant whoever was in my house was even more important than that woman who'd been in *Carry On Camping*.

We opened the front door, took our shoes off and walked into the front room. And there they were… Cameron's dad. My dad. The Fijian Minister of Defence. The Ambassador to Fiji. And my mum serving finger sandwiches.

What were these people doing in my living room? Who *was* Cameron's dad? What was that man doing in the limo outside?

'Yes,' said my mum. 'The driver. Apparently he has to stay outside and keep a lookout.'

A lookout? For what? What was going on?

'I tried to offer him a cheese sandwich,' she said. 'But he said he couldn't take one on the grounds that I might be trying to assassinate him.'

She said this as if people were constantly turning her sandwiches down for fear of political assassination.

It turned out that the Minister of Defence and the Ambassador had come all the way to Loughborough to congratulate Cameron's dad on finishing his doctorate at the university. The completed doctorate which meant he would now return to Fiji as soon as possible. Cameron's dad had wound up stuck for things to show them in Loughborough – I believe they'd already had a Wimpy *and* seen the Woolworths pick 'n' mix – and so decided to bring them round to our house for a cup of tea.

Cameron and I had a sandwich and discussed it.

'How come these guys are in Loughborough?' I asked.

'Oh... you know,' he said. 'They're friends of the family. Hey – did you say you got a new He-Man?'

And we went and played with Ram-Man.

Later that evening, the limousine gave me and Cameron a lift down to the school play – where Cameron was preparing for his role as a magical tree in an enchanted forest (a role that consisted mainly of him standing very still and every now and then squeezing a small bottle of talcum powder which represented fairy dust) and we got out, like Hollywood stars.

As it would turn out, all this had been a small moment in world history.

'I remember that!' said Cameron, putting his pint down. 'The guy with the main guy was supposed to make sure that he didn't give away any secrets about Fiji. But your mum got it all out of him within ten minutes. She got Fijian military secrets from him. And while he was away, Rambuka held a coup in Fiji. He made himself President. All while your mum was making them little sandwiches.'

'My mum got secret information out of the Minister of Defence?' I said, shocked, as Cameron nodded. 'Using little sandwiches?'

I bet Mata Hari would be pissed off she didn't think of that one. Which reminded me of something... something to do with Berlin...

'It was quite a coup!' said Cameron, and we both fell about laughing. Cameron looked delighted with his pun. This was brilliant.

'I think that the limousine outside our house was the first time I actually knew about... your secret.'

'My secret?' said Cameron.

'Yeah... your secret...'

Because it *had* been a secret. At least from me. Only after Cameron had gone did I find out the truth. Only after he had gone did I find out my best friend Cameron Dewa – the smiley Fijian kid going to the standard state school in the middle of Loughborough – was essentially...

'You're third in line to the throne of Fiji.'

Yes. Third in line. To the throne. Of Fiji!

'Oh, that,' said Cameron, dismissing it. 'That wasn't a secret. I just didn't think it was very relevant. And it's not exactly third in line. It's more like part of an extended royal family. I really didn't think you'd be all that interested.'

'Not all that interested? Cameron! You've just said the words "Royal Family"! Do you have any idea how many people I told about winning the swimming gala? How many people I told about the conker championship?'

'Hey, I come from Fiji. *Everyone's* in-line to the throne...'

'That's not true... wasn't your granddad, or your great-granddad... oh, *what* was he, again?'

'Well... kind of the King.'

'*That* was it!'

'But *I'm* only a chief.'

'*Only* a chief?'

'There are a few chiefs in Fiji.'

'It must be *great* being a chief in Fiji!'

Alcohol brings out the truth, doesn't it? Because it *must* be great being a chief in Fiji! This was great. It was me and Cameron! Together at last! We were on our third pint and I slapped his arm in a look-at-you-you-big-Fijian-chief kind of a way.

But he turned and looked at me with fury in his eyes.

'NEVER TOUCH MY ARM!' he yelled. 'IN MY COUNTRY IT IS A SIGN OF GREAT DISRESPECT TO TOUCH THE ARM OF A CHIEF!'

My arm shot back so fast it left a vapour trail. If I could've tucked it inside my body I would've.

Cameron looked furious.

And then, suddenly, he didn't.

'But seeing as it's you,' he said, 'another pint?'

An hour later and we had reminisced about the Great Loughborough Fun Run, about school playtimes spent on nothing but running around, about our families, our friends and our pets. We talked about school, and about old teachers who'd gone unmentioned for *years*.

'Do you remember that frightening one? Mrs Adams?'

'Yes. I used to feel a little bullied by her.'

'Me too,' said Cameron. 'I wanted to join the orchestra but she wouldn't let me because I wanted to play the trombone and she said that was unbecoming.'

'I used to get my own back,' I said. 'Once, during the summer holidays when I knew she went back to Wales, I used to phone her house and leave messages on her answering machine, when answering machines were incredibly rare.'

'What *kind* of messages?' asked Cameron.

'I used to get high on bottles of Panda Pops, and then ring up and just say, "Potato" down the phone.'

'Potato?'

'Yeah, but I'd put the effort in. I'd shout "Potaaaaatooooo!"'

Cameron's eyes widened.

'You shouted "Potatooo" at Mrs Adams? Why "Potatooo"?'

'I have absolutely no idea.'

'How often?'

'Every day or two for three or four weeks. When she got back she had about forty messages, all just saying, "Potaaaatooooo!"'

'Potaaaaatooooo!' said Cameron.

'Potaaaaatoooooooo!' I said, which I believe made the point.

'And she never found out it was you?'

'She recognised my voice immediately and told my parents I was abnormal.'

'Ah. Well. You used to like doing stuff like that,' said Cameron, and immediately I thought about telling him about ManGriff the Beast Warrior and Ben Ives and Argos. But Cameron had a glint in his eye, and he held up his mobile and said, 'Do you still have Mrs Adams's number?'

It was so tempting.

As the pints went down and the glasses piled up, hunger set in. We found a Burger King round the corner. I asked the lady behind the counter if she had one of those golden paper crowns, and if she did, could we borrow it because my friend was a Fijian chief, but she looked at me like I'd been drinking.

'Hey, I brought something with me!' I said, slurring ever so slightly.

'What is it?' said Cameron, sitting down.

'A poem!'

Cameron made the kind of face all nearly-thirty men say when you declare you've brought a poem with you.

'A good one, though!' I said.

I scrabbled about in my bag trying to find the small, colourful notebook I'd last used in the 1980s. The one with NO GIRLS ALLOWED written in it and various doodles of classmates along with brief character assassinations.

Cameron started to munch down on his Whopper while I found the right page.

'Aha! Here it is!' I said, and then cleared my throat to read.

I began. Loudly. Solemnly. With deep and meaningful resonance.

Cameron Is My Best Friend
By Daniel Wallace

Cameron shifted about in his seat a bit. He looked mildly uncomfortable. But I took this to be humility – after all, it's quite a thing to have your name in the title of a poem. Especially a poem as important as this one – one that told the story of an entire friendship. I continued.

> Cameron, Cameron!
> With your face like a plum!
> Skin soft as a baby's bum!
> You are my best friend! My best friend!
> A rum pum pum pum.

I think that rhyme still stands up today. I continued.

> You have come to my school!
> Where we both played the fool!
> And now you must go!
> To Fiji!
> Wherever that is.

We didn't take geography until high school. I pressed on.

> I will never forget you!
> We will be friends for all time!
> Our friendship can't be summed up!
> At least not while making it rhyme.
> Goodbye old buddy!

And, with a flourish of the hand, I brought the piece to an end.

Cameron sat, in awed, stunned silence.

I allowed him a moment to take it all in. Sometimes to truly appreciate a piece of work like this, you have to give someone their space. There had been a lot of important imagery to appreciate.

And then I looked to one side. There was a man staring at us. He was wearing a blue cagoule and half an onion ring was hanging from his mouth. He'd been listening to my poem, and watching carefully as one grown man sat in Burger King and read out a poem he'd written about the other grown man. I suddenly realised there was no way of explaining the situation – no way of telling him I'd written that poem when I was eleven and this was the first time we'd seen in each other in nearly twenty years and so to mark the occasion I'd decided that Burger King was the place to read it out. Because, as unbelievable as this may seem, that would sound even *weirder*. He clearly thought I'd written it this afternoon, and then summoned Cameron to Burger King to let him know just how I felt about him. I managed to communicate all this to Cameron using just my eyes. He managed to communicate a panicked 'I *know*!' using just his. Quietly, we finished our burgers, and silently made our way to the door.

We stood by a bus stop outside and looked at each other for a second. This had been fun. Good, honest, childlike fun. We both knew this would be the moment we would say goodbye. And we both wanted to delay it a bit.

'So… we'll have to do this again,' I said.

'Definitely,' said Cameron. 'We'll have to email each other or something.'

'Sounds good, yeah.'

But had we done enough to be pals again? Had tonight been enough to warrant a definite beginning to our friendship again – or had it just been a fun night out?

'So… do you still have royal connections?' I asked him, just for something to say.

'Nah,' he said. 'I mean, back in Fiji I get more privileges. I can stay in my village and people have to give me free food and lodgings, and be very quiet around me.'

'You have your own *village*?'

'Nabuso. My village is the area regarded as the people from the bush. The tough and violent people. No one messes with us. My people recently wrote to a church in England to apologise for eating a reverend 136 years ago. He'd taken the comb out of a chief's hair, which is frowned upon, so they cooked him and ate everything except his boots.'

'Your people *ate a vicar*?'

'A reverend. But yeah. Hey, you'll have to come out to Fiji one day! I'll show you round the village!'

I nodded. But, like our grand plan to see Michael Jackson, it seemed like just one of those things people say. Especially if they're minor Fijian royalty.

There was a slight lull in the conversation, signalling, I thought, the end of the evening.

'Well...' I said, extending my hand.

'Listen,' said Cameron. 'What are you doing now?'

I shrugged.

'I was going to go home.'

'What? The night is young!'

It wasn't. It was already applying for a bus pass.

'What do you suggest?'

'The American Embassy.'

'The American *Embassy*? Why the American Embassy?'

Cameron smiled.

'There's a karaoke party on.'

'A karaoke party? At the American Embassy?'

Yeah. Cameron still had connections.

And so the chief and I caught the bus.

What followed that night is, I imagine, bound by some kind of official secrets act, but let me tell you one thing: ambassadors can't dance for toffee.

We sang, and we laughed, and we said our goodbyes and exchanged numbers, and I was certain that *this* time, I'd got Cameron back for *good*.

I went home, buoyed by the happy randomness of the evening, and made myself a cup of tea.

I stood there, and thought about how, actually, that poem wasn't all that bad. Maybe I should write *more* poetry. Yes. I should definitely write *more* poetry.

And then I turned my computer on, and, though my eyes were blurry and my typing slightly drunken, I had a go...

To: Ben Ives
From: THE STORMY LEOPARD
Cc: ManGriff the Beast Warrior
Subject: RE: My performance

Meeeeeoooooowwwrrrrr.

Hi Ben

It's Alison here – the Stormy Leopard!!
    I believe you and your colleagues have agreed to listen to some of my poetry and thoughts on the 21st at 1pm in your offices in Llllllos Angeles. I will need a suitable space and also a changing area so if you have any ideas thank you
    Here's one for you, would appreciate you're comment's. It is called, simply, DANGERFACE.
    Night time!
    Danger!
    There's a noise over there!
    I strive, stealthy, stalking my prey, because I am a leopard
    What a day
    Night time!
    Night time!
    Move like a panther, clouded like a skyline
    At night
    I am a woman, I move like a leopard, which is what I am
    I am Alison – are you? No. For we are as one...
    In the dark.

Thanks Ben, see you all soon, with bells on (literally!!!)
The Stormy Leopard

P.S. I will need volunteers for some of the dances.

Chapter Eleven

In which we learn that often,
the future takes ages...

I woke up, the next morning, with a smile on my face as wide as a cat.

I'd had a great night. With a great old friend. Yeah, so I knew that, thanks to the Desperados Pact, I now owed Lizzie for my night out at the ambassadors' disco. But that was fine. I knew precisely what to do. Finish varnishing that table. That was roughly equal to a night out, surely? Well, getting the bus there, anyway. And, when I rolled over to check the time, I found a note...

> Hey baby... didn't want to wake you. All going crazy at work. Could you do me a favour? Could you get some shopping in? I'm going to be back too late to do anything... L x

Excellent. Easy MPs. Duly noted.

I turned my phone on and thought about the night before. That had been my first 'cold' meeting with an old friend. And it had gone well. Me and Cameron were reunited. There was definitely something in this. In reconnecting. Rewiring friendships. Buffing them up. Giving them a polish. Returning them to their former glory. Cameron had proved that. I only hoped he felt the same way.

Bzzzz.

I looked at the screen. I had a voicemail.

I dialled it up.

'*You... have... nine... new messages.*'

Eh? *Nine?* It was only quarter to ten!

I listened to the first one.

Silence.

A crackle.

And then...

'POTAAAATOOOOOOOO!'

I laughed, and flicked to the next one.

'POTAAAATOOOOOOO!'

And then...

'POTAATOOOO!'

Plus six more 'Potaatooo!'s, each of them delivered with enthusiasm, gusto and power. Either Cameron was amusing himself on his way to work, or Mrs Adams had really been biding her time before wreaking her revenge.

Which suddenly made me think of Ben Ives and giggle again. If my plan was working, he would now be starting to worry that ManGriff the Beast Warrior and his oddball girlfriend really would be turning up to his offices near LA in order to perform a selection of poetry and wisdom for him and his colleagues. He'd said no, of course, and that it wouldn't be appropriate, but I'd ignored him... or, rather, the *Stormy Leopard* had...

But had he replied to my slightly drunken email?

I checked.

He *had*.

To: The Stormy Leopard

From: Ben Ives

Subject: RE: My performance

Hello 'Stormy Leopard'

Um... I'm slightly dubious about this now... I think there has been a misunderstanding. I told ManGriff that a performance would not be appropriate. I had a very quick look at your poem and it seems very personal and heartfelt. It is also clear and succinct, which always appeals to me. But to be honest, I am more of a prose man – I very rarely read poetry. Anyway, I have to get on.

B.

Oh, joy!

This was *working*! Okay, so Ben was dubious, but he was saying he didn't want it to get out of hand, which just proved all the more that he thought it *was* going to happen. The old Ben would have been on to me in an instant... he'd have *encouraged* the poetry, made it bigger, odder, shown he was in on the joke... but that was the suspicious Ben. *This* was *grown-up* Ben. And I was getting him right where I wanted him.

Life was... *fun*!

I got up, whistled a bit, thought about watching Iran versus Angola, put some music on, jumped online, did the weekly shopping, and went and found my varnishing brush. I wanted to finish that table off quick-smart. Because I was happy, and I was charged, and also... I'd sneaked a look at the Book and I knew *exactly* who I wanted to meet up with next... someone I'd been reminded of when talking about little sandwiches and spies with Cameron...

Me and my mum and dad moved to Berlin in 1990, just a few months after the Wall had been pushed over and a new sense of excitement had rushed through Europe. I'm sure if I had properly understood all the political goings-on, *I* would have been very excited, too. But for me, the mere fact that we were in 1990 was enough to have me almost giddy with delight. It was a new decade! And we were only ten years off the year 2000! And in the year 2000, *everything* would be different. I knew this, because of all the comics I was reading. There was the *Beano*, sure, and the *Dandy*, as well, but there were also the dozens of ancient comics my cousin had thrown my way – comics with names like *Eagle*, *Boy's World* and *Fury*. These were the comics that painted the way I thought the future would be going. A future of robot servants, and silver home pods, and personal aluminium jetpacks. I'd lose myself in copies of *Action*, *Tiger* and *Millennium*, but remember feeling particularly dispirited in 1989, when I picked up a comic from the late 1960s to see a group of glamorous travellers from a sexless future, wearing one-piece body suits and carrying rayguns, startling a group of Earthlings by jumping from a silver disc and shouting 'WE ARE FROM THE YEAR 1989!'

I'd looked out of my window at that point. Dad was mowing the lawn. Suddenly it looked like the future would be a long time coming. But for the Germans, the future they never thought they'd see was happening right now. For the East Germans, especially. They didn't need personal aluminium jetpacks. The idea of a well-stocked supermarket was as alien as any alien.

For Dad, whose academic work centred almost entirely on East and West Germany, being where the future and the history were happening was vital. So it was decided. We were off. But then – the *really* good news: I would be going to an American school. An *American* one!

Like every boy who'd grown up in the 1980s, I knew that America was the most exciting and incredible place known to man. It was a giant McDonald's-sponsored adventure playground, where the kids divided their time between summer camp and Disneyland. It was huge and vast and neon, and, for all I knew, people really *did* live in silver home pods, and have personal jetpacks, and travel through time scaring Earthlings. What was *absolutely* for sure was that they wore wicked jackets, and played American football, and had names like TJ and JT, and ate hamburgers and caught bad guys and played basketball and baseball and looked coooool. They'd tell people to 'hold the rye' and they were always talking about their 'ass'! They'd say 'you ass!', or 'look at my ass!', or if they were *really* angry, 'Ass you!' They had the best flag and the proudest people and they were never afraid of having a war or doing explosions and *everyone* had a gun. People were *always* getting shot, or shooting people. Plus, all the *best* and most *trusted* and *nicest* people were Americans – Michael Jackson! OJ Simpson! Peewee Herman! – and I, Danny Wallace, would be going to the John F. Kennedy International School for Cool Kids Who Rock Out! I would play baseball and hold someone's rye and talk constantly about my ass! I literally could not believe my luck. I immediately packed the tape I'd made of all the American TV theme tunes I'd recorded, knowing that this would be a brilliant ice-breaker when it came to making friends. Or 'buddies', as I'd now have to call them. Brilliant! I'd have *buddies*!

Four months later, we'd sold our Honda Civic and bought a VW Camper van in British racing green. This would be the shonky, backfiring van that would take us out of Britain, through France and into Germany, piled high with suitcases, boxes and backpacks and never more than a minute away from the threat of a breakdown. It would stutter and splutter, and every hour or so a new and foreign symbol would light up on the dashboard and Dad would get the manual out and say, 'Now what does *that* mean?' We'd spend light, summer nights in ill-equipped camping grounds on the way, driving up mountains and through valleys, with our rickety, farting van put-put-putting a trail of oil all the way from Spinney Hill Drive to – at long last – Berlin.

Over the course of the next year in Berlin I would make some incredible friends. Amy. Brian. Josh. And, of course, Tarek...

The first thing I'd learnt about Tarek was that he was a former child star in one of Germany's biggest sitcoms. He hadn't told me this himself – this was before I'd even met him. It was a boy called Jan who'd told me, in hushed, reverent tones, while pointing Tarek out on the playing field during PE.

PE was the only lesson I had that was taught in German. Even German was taught in English – although I suppose that makes sense, now that I think about it. Basketball, baseball, football – all of it was accompanied by a grumpy man with a beard shouting instructions at you in German. For the first few months I had no idea what was being shouted at me, and so would panic and simply give the ball to someone else as quickly as I could. As it turned out, that was actually all I was ever being told to do. Sport wasn't really my thing. But it *was* Tarek's. He was a big lad, muscular and powerful, and 'in' with the bigger boys in our year. Tarek would play American football as the star quarterback, and he'd knock baseballs for miles, and, despite being German, he looked like the all-American kid. He kept his child-star past quiet, but it was something that everyone knew, and rumour had it he still got asked for autographs when travelling on the U-Bahn or walking through Berlin. I didn't know how people recognised him. He'd been small when he was on telly, with huge round glasses, playing Tom – the cute, smart-talking son – in the top-rated comedy hit, *I Married My Family!*.

Here is the synopsis that will greet you, if ever you decided to look it up on the German side of the internet...

I Married My Family!
The divorced Angi lives with their three children Tanja, Markus and Tom in Berlin and possesses a small fashion shop. Over its, friends Bille and Alfons Vonhoff become acquainted with it in a party, the advertising commercial artist Werner Schumann originating organized by Bille specially for it from Vienna and conceal to it also after several appointments first the existence of their children. When it experiences from them, it decides nevertheless to marry and draw with it and the lady housekeeper Mrs. Rabe into a large house the whole family! In the course of the series Angi and Werner get still another baby, Franziska.

A stark slap in the face for anyone who has ever dared to doubt German humour.

But not only that – now for the *really* cool bit. Tarek had also been in *The Goonies* – one of the defining films of my childhood! Well, not 'in' it, exactly. But his *voice* was. Well, not in the English version. But his voice played a huge part in the translated *German* version. Audiences ever since have heard him bring to life one of the finest comedy roles in American cinema of all time... that of Chunk.

Chunk!

Tarek was *Chunk*! The funny fat kid off of *The Goonies*!

How impossibly glamorous was my new life? No one in Loughborough had *ever* been in a translated version of *The Goonies*!

Bearing all this in mind, I think it's fair to say that Tarek had me at the Truffle Shuffle.

My first day at the John F. Kennedy International School had been nerve-wracking. Dad was already hard at work in Berlin, and Mum had landed a job as a translator with the American Military Police, working alongside tough-talking New Yorkers with guns. But I was a thirteen-year-old boy at a new school, in a new country, where, thanks to the differences in the two education systems, I was in a class where everybody was an entire year older than me. And these were mainly Americans; these were *big* kids. One of them had a moustache. I would not have been surprised if several of them had wives.

But I found the whole thing unutterably brilliant. It was like landing a part in *Degrassi Junior High*. People talked about 'recess', and said 'math' instead of 'maths'. Intercoms went 'bong' and loud American accents talked about band practice and psychology class. The only American thing we were missing was a spelling bee, which I'd have loved, being *excellent* at spelling, and *especially* excellent at spelling the word 'bee'. All the kids wore Nike Airs and Reebok Pumps and drank sodas, and everyone had their own locker. And best of all were the jackets. The coolest jackets in the world. JFK jackets. Dark blue, with leather arms, and your own name sewn into the front in silver thread; $115 dollars and worth every penny. There was a large 'B' on the front to indicate you were from Berlin, and on the side you proudly proclaimed you were destined to graduate in the Class of '94.

Plus, Berlin was at the centre of world events. The Wall had fallen. Germany had held its first free elections. America, Britain, France and Russia were preparing to pull out all military presence. Germany would be a fully independent, unified state. On October 3rd of that year, I'd be swept along in a crowd of West Germans at midnight, through the Brandenburg Gate and towards the hugs and embraces of East Germans. In my mind it is as romanticised as any historical moment. Although I do remember there was a bloke peeing on the side of a police van, and another bloke having a fistfight with a bicycle, so perhaps it wasn't quite as romantic as I'd have liked.

Every morning as I walked to catch the 7.37 bus to school – which I was always careful to point out was *continental* time – I'd pass fifty or so American soldiers running past me singing their army songs. Tanks would regularly roll by our flat. One morning, during a history lesson with Herr Camp, we were told we'd suddenly become a terrorist target. Iraq had invaded Kuwait and kicked off the first Gulf War, and our American school bus was now to be constantly flanked by two jeeps full of armed soldiers. Bags were checked as you boarded by two mountainous black guards with assault weaponry. You had to get up extra early to tune in to the Armed Forces Network to see if school was on a 'Charlie' or a 'Delta' alert. I think 'Delta' was the best one because it meant two days off school, and jeeps with roof-mounted machine guns would patrol the streets outside. Every week we'd practise a bomb evacuation, which means I am now better at avoiding bombs than I am fire. I suppose that makes me about average at avoiding firebombs.

Here is how I managed to sum up the entire Iraq conflict in my school diary.

> I hope Saddam sees sense and pulls out. I do not want war.
> On a lighter note, it is not raining much at the moment.

I was now rifling through the Box and finding more and more evidence of my time in Berlin. Tarek's entry in the Book listed him as living in the former West Germany, and even had a phone number. I'd tried it, but to no avail. But there were clues elsewhere. A copy of the JFK Student Directory. An address of a mutual friend. And dozens of photos of the old gang in Berlin... photos of us on lunch breaks, when we'd walk down to Zehlendorf and buy currywursts and chips. Photos of us on a school trip to Brussels. A class photo, signed by everyone, on the last day of school – a sad day for me, because it indicated a return to Britain and an end to JFK. A sad day for my friends, too, because, with America pulling out of Germany, whole military families would now be saying goodbye to Berlin too. My friend Amy, whose dad was a diplomat, was heading back to Washington, DC. My friend Josh, whose dad had flown for Pan Am, was heading back to Boulder, Colorado, and had made me memorise his address as a sort of bizarre rhyme. Brian, whose dad was in the army, had his ticket for Buffalo, New York, and was packing up already. We'd all shared that time in Berlin... but for all of us, it had come to an end. But how about Tarek? Had he stayed on at JFK and graduated in the class of '94? Would he still be in Berlin?

The doorbell rang. I answered it.

*

'So… been busy?' asked Paul the builder. He was halfway up his own ladder inspecting the location of the new canopy. I stood at the bottom with a mug of coffee. This made me look more like a boss.

'Oh, you know…' I said. 'Yes. Sort of. I've ordered some shopping online and varnished a table.'

Paul looked over to the end of the garden and spotted my handiwork.

'Christ – *you* did that?'

I was mildly offended.

'Yes,' I said. 'With varnish and a brush.'

I was *sure* that's how you did it.

'Bloody hell.'

I looked over at the table, proudly. And then the pride sort of disappeared. It suddenly didn't really look all that varnished. It just looked like a table someone had liberally dripped varnish over. I'd been in quite a rush to get it done – to prove to Lizzie that I would live up to the Desperados Pact – but really, I'd just wanted to get on and track down more of the names in the Book, and this streaky, patchy mess of a table was the result.

'Well. It's not quite finished,' I said, defensively. 'I've been a bit distracted. With important work.'

'You must've been,' said Paul. 'You've not even done her legs.'

I checked. He was right.

'It's an ongoing project,' I said. 'I am taking my time with it. With her. With it.'

'Well, I'd start again, if I were you… I could do that for you, if you like, for a bit extra…'

Paul was undermining my confidence in the job. Plus, it was apparent that I still didn't know when to correctly identify something as a lady. I resolved to do the legs myself before Lizzie got home, and left Paul to get on with building the canopy. But twenty minutes later, after receiving a phone call asking for a quote, he told me he'd brought the wrong screws and would have to return in a few days, when he'd ordered the right ones. I told him there was a DIY shop just down the road, but he frowned and shook his head and assured me they would not have the right screws, so I said okay, and told him to keep me updated. I was secretly pleased he was off. Being in charge of Paul was tiring. And besides, I had *real* work to do, and a can of varnish remover to buy a little later on...

I sat down at my desk just as a text arrived. It was from Hanne.

> *I think I should reiterate that I only use Facebook as a business utility and not as some kind of social networking site and the pointless Take That obsession is Guro's, not mine. Understood?*

I suggested she go and cook an egg.

I hit the internet and tried to find the website of the John F. Kennedy International School... and it got me thinking...

One of the strangest things about our move to Berlin was the day I'd had to fight off a renegade KGB agent who'd broken into our flat.

Now, you might wonder why I've never mentioned this before. It is, after all, quite a nice sentence to say. It's the kind of thing I have to stop myself from telling complete strangers at bus stops or in Post Office queues, as it has the effect of making me seem a little bit mental, like saying 'My friend Simon has solved time travel', or 'I know the German Chunk' would. It is, however, fact: I once fought off a renegade KGB agent who'd broken into our flat.

Actually, 'fought off' is probably a little strong. And I've no proof that he was 'renegade' – he might've been a real stickler for the rules. But he *was* KGB. And he *did* break into our flat.

I'll explain.

My dad is a very good friend of Britain. He pays his taxes, he picks up after himself, he never litters and he always observes the countryside code. The East Germans, on the other hand, thought of him slightly differently. According to official secret police files released as the Wall took its tumble, they'd decided my dad was an Enemy of the State. His official file brands him as *feindlich negativ* and a menace to East Germany, thanks to his work studying various exiled writers and vocal critics of the socialist government.

It is something I had never realised about my dad, but it suddenly made him something just short of James Bond. And from the evening I stared the KGB in the eye, small events in my child-hood slowly started to make sense. The fact that sometimes, in Dundee, when you picked up the phone and hadn't even dialled a number yet, there'd be someone on the other end already waiting for you. I'd assumed that was just how phones worked. But no. It turned out this was MI5, possibly trying to see if my dad was a double agent. Which would have been weird, seeing as how he wasn't even a single one. But sometimes, Dad would finish a conver-sation, put the phone down, then remember with a tut and a click of his fingers that he'd forgotten to mention the one vital thing he'd phoned up about. So he'd pick up the phone again, only to hear his own conversation being played back in a room with a couple of men commenting on it.

'Hello!' he'd shout. 'Can I use my phone again?'

Whereupon you'd hear two men shouting 'shit!' and spilling their coffee while pressing various buttons.

I remembered the day Special Branch turned up at our house in Loughborough. And the day we found out that a woman I'd always thought of as a mere busybody who was always turning up to our house and asking what we were up to was in fact a part-time spy for the East Germans. I wouldn't have minded so much if she'd come up with a decent codename, like Hawkwind or Raven-tits. But the letters she sent the East German secret police were just signed 'Anne'... which lent a potentially exciting situation a sort of beige tinge.

But then there was Frederick. Frederick was *brilliant*. Frederick was the world's most rubbish spy, sent over to Loughborough to infiltrate our small family and keep tabs on my dad. His brief was apparently simple: pretend to be a student, win my dad's confidence and report back.

Sadly for Frederick, his cover story involved pretending to be twenty-two, when he was a man quite clearly in his early forties. This was also in the days before Google, so when Frederick came to the business of his clever disguise, he couldn't actually look up what students in the late 1980s in England were wearing. He had to *guess*. Which is why he turned up in the student bar looking like Doctor Who, with a huge Oxbridge scarf, hat, tweed jacket and leather briefcase, in a futile attempt to blend in with people holding lagers, wearing stonewashed jeans and talking about whether the Smiths would ever get back together.

His plan, however, was *genius*. He would use *my* middle name in order to strike up a rapport with my dad, and then claim to be Swiss, not East German, in order to fox us. The flaw in the plan was that he didn't seem to have read the family file all the way through. He seemed to have stopped at my middle name. I believe the initial conversation with my dad went something like this.

Frederick: Hello Professor Wallace! I am twenty-two but perhaps look older! Look at my clothes – I am undoubtedly a student! My name is Frederick!

Dad: Frederick? Goodness! That's my son's middle name! You must join us for dinner and we can talk about this further!

Frederick: Well, that would be wonderful! I am not from East Germany, by the way, so do not be suspicious of me. I am from Switzerland instead of that.

Dad: Really? My *wife* is from Switzerland!

[pause]

Frederick: Oh.

Dad: You must talk to her about being from Switzerland!

Frederick: Yes.

Dad: Where are you from in Switzerland?

Frederick: I am not 100 per cent sure...

Dad: You're a spy, aren't you?

Frederick: ... Yes.

And Frederick disappeared the next day.

Dad kept much of this quiet from me. Not on purpose; it just didn't really seem to bother him very much. It was just a part of everyday life, becoming normal very quickly, in the way that filling up your car for the first time is exciting but soon becomes a trivial annoyance. But it was the night of the KGB invasion that made me think of it further.

It happened like this. A month or so after we'd moved to Berlin, we had a new neighbour. His name was Bogomolov and he'd been a former adviser to Gorbachev, but had been sent away, as advisers sometimes are. He'd got talking to my dad in the hallway one day, and soon enough they agreed to play ping-pong together. The fact that my dad was playing ping-pong with the former adviser to Gorbachev (and that's another sentence I can never say in queues) was enough to raise suspicions, and within a week a new set of Russians were living down the hall. But these were *different* Russians. They were brooding, and odd, and they wore all black, and despite their cover story of being experts in German, they didn't really seem to speak it very well. I couldn't help but wonder whether somewhere in the world Frederick had been promoted. We'd been tipped off by two or three people that the new Russians were KGB, but simply shrugged it off... until the night they'd waited for my parents to leave the house and get on a train. Thinking I wasn't in the flat, they'd lain their hands on the skeleton key to the flats, and I'd heard a rattle of the door as a burly man tried to make it fit. Finally it clicked into place, he turned it and in he stormed... and there I was. Standing, like Macaulay Culkin in *Home Alone*, holding the Louisville Slugger baseball bat I'd started taking to school every day, and probably wearing the most frightened face in Germany.

The man looked at me. I looked at the man. My grip on the bat tightened. An hour seemed to pass, but just a moment later he growled something in Russian that soundly faintly terrifying, turned and ran out of the door. I slammed it shut and looked through the peephole, but he'd gone. A second later I heard the main door of the flats slam shut too. He'd legged it. I had successfully repelled the KBG.

Dad thought the man had been there to plant a bug, which I remember thinking was vastly unimaginative of the spy. Frederick would have probably pretended to be a Chinese ping-pong pro in order to glean *his* information. Now *that's* a spy.

I still have the Louisville Slugger, by the way. Because it was a present. A present from Tarek...

The JFK website was packed with more blasts from the past. Names I hadn't seen or thought of in years, like its own private Friends Reunited. An alumni page gave me brief snapshots into people's lives, through email addresses or small photos. But nothing seemed to have been updated since about 2002. It seemed Rob Busch was now a dentist in Miami. JC had joined something called the Ministries of God Theological Church in Atlanta. Jan Zimmerman now seemed to be some kind of professional hacky sack player in Zurich. And Tarek? Just the words… *left JFK in 1992…*

Where would he have gone?

A brief Google search under his name showed various possibilities. Was he the Tarek Helmy who was now Associate Professor of Clinical Medicine Division of Cardiovascular Diseases in Cincinatti? No.

Was he the Tarek Helmy who was teaching at the King Fahd University of Petroleum and Minerals in Dhahran? Not likely.

But there… at the bottom of one particularly long entry, was the name Tarek Helmy and four letters which seemed to strike a chord… BAHS.

What was BAHS?

I clicked the link.

Berlin American High School.

Of course! Our rival school! The one we'd always been pitted against in unsuccessful basketball games! The kids who used to wear the burgundy Happy Days jackets to our blue ones! Had Tarek defected? Gone to the other side?

Yes!

I found a sentence, entered onto a messageboard, almost exactly a year before…

If you went to BAHS class of 94 we should have a reunion.
Would be cool to see you again. Tarek.

I couldn't believe it.

Tarek was doing what *I* was doing! Exactly the same kind of thing! Just one year earlier! Maybe *he* had an address book to update! Plus – there was an email address! Had I found him?

I quickly started up my email. I would write to him straight away.

But, as it opened up before me, something stopped me.

The bing-bong of a new email.

Peter *Gibson*! The day just got better and better.

Someone had found *me*! And it was Peter Gibson! Peter Gibson who liked caravans! And said 'Cowabunga!' And had an odd finger!

I checked the message…

Hello. I don't know if you remember me, or even if you're the same Daniel Wallace, but it's Peter Gibson here. I was bored and looking at Friends Reunited, so I thought I would say hello… if it's you, Hello.

I laughed and shook my head. He'd happened to be looking at Friends Reunited, and happened to see my near-brand-new entry. He had no idea that just a week or so before I'd sent a postcard to his old house in the hope that somehow it would get to him…

Were we *all* doing this? Were we *all* looking for each other now that we were approaching thirty? Were we *all* going through the *same thing*?

I now felt like I was firing on all cylinders. Maybe today was the day I should try and find the others, too… Chris! Akira! Lauren! And then I realised that if I was going to tell Lizzie about my day, about the unrivalled successes of the afternoon, I'd better get on and do something useful. A deal's a deal, after all. Hey – I could unvarnish that table (2MPs). How long could *that* take?

I was about to switch the computer off, but paused for a moment, and then, for the sake of completion, checked one more thing.

I made my way to hotmail…

Oh…

Uh-oh…

To: ManGriff the Beast Warrior
From: Ben Ives
Subject: RE: YOUR 'ARTICLE'

ManGriff,
Sorry about this but the more I think about this the more I
think it's a piss-take. Can you please send me a photo of you
as 'proof'? Apologies but this is a bit bizarre.
Ben.

Oh, *bollocks.*

Ben Ives was losing his nerve. Or... was he *on to* me?

I had a decision to make. Come clean and admit it was me before
he worked it out or stopped all communication. Or push forward,
and try my luck. Push forward, and go for the big one...

But how?

Chapter Eleven-and-a-half

In which we learn the power of persuasion...

'I'm not doing it,' said Ian.

'Please,' I said.

'No.'

'Please,' I said.

'No.'

'But... *please*.'

'Absolutely not.'

'One photo. Just *one* photo.'

'Not even one photo.'

'Come on!'

'*You* do it!'

'If *I* do it, he'll know it's me!'

'What if someone *sees* it?' he said.

'*No one* will *see* it,' I said. 'I promise you, no one will *ever* see it!'

'I feel very uncomfortable about this.'

'I swear to you – it will be *very* dignified,' I said.

To: Ben Ives
From: ManGriff the Beast Warrior
Subject: Photo

Hello Ben

This is not a joke – please do not insult us any further than you have already.

Please find attached my picture so you recognise me during our meeting.

Grateful thanks

ManGriff the BW

Tuesday 22nd November.

One day I saw a pcice of Vandliesame. Ir is bad

vandalism

Chapter Twelve

In which we learn that a friend is worth a flight...

I'll be honest: the day hadn't started off brilliantly.

It was Lizzie's first day off in weeks and she was inspecting the work that I had completed on the house in order to make up for the work I had completed on my address book. I had realised this day was coming after my successful recent exchanges with Ben Ives and had set to work. I had painted the small toilet near the stairs, and done so with great speed and enthusiasm. However, today, in the cold blue light of the afternoon, I realised I had *literally* painted the small toilet near the stairs.

'I can just scrape those blotches off,' I said, trying and failing to scrape them off. 'It is a standard decorative technique.'

Lizzie had smiled and nodded and said nothing, and I silently hoped she wouldn't notice the paint on the carpet.

'And the paint on the carpet?' she said.

'Yes,' I said, 'I was just about to say. And the paint on the carpet.'

There was a pause.

'Well, what about it?'

'I was trying something. I don't like it,' I said. 'It's going.'

'I also noticed that the table outside looks... *unusual.*'

I peered out of the window and saw a half-varnished, half-unvarnished mess. There were streaks down the legs and a small strip of wood was missing where I'd been a little aggressive with the scraper.

'Do you like that look?' I asked, hopefully. 'It gives it quite an aged appearance. Almost... *like an antique*!'

I raised my eyebrows to show she should be impressed. Women *love* antiques! This, however, didn't look like an antique. It looked like shit.

'Well... I suppose I'm a traditionalist,' she said, kindly. 'Either varnished or unvarnished would be fine. You decide.'

'Right. I will give it some thought.'

'Also, the shopping you ordered arrived.'

'Good!' I said, relieved that there was a success story in there somewhere. 'That is excellent news!'

'Yeah... it's just... well... did you *mean* to order what you ordered?'

'Of course! I thought it through thoroughly.'

'It's just,' she said, ignoring me, 'you seem to have ordered everything in *catering* size. We have a box of cornflakes the size of a telly and the ketchup won't fit in any of the cupboards. It's a bottle nearly two feet tall. The delivery man actually asked me if we were starting a business. It took three of them to bring the bags in.'

I was never very good when it came to understanding quantities. The internet had just offered me choices and I'd simply ordered the biggest. See? I'd have been a *rubbish* quarry manager.

I needed to distract her.

'The guttering is coming along fine, as is the canopy.'

I pointed at the guttering and then at the place where the canopy would go in an extremely confident and able manner.

'Well, when I say that, I mean it's all still in the planning stages, really. Paul was here yesterday but the screws he'd ordered didn't fit so he's having to order some from a man he knows, but he's away in Poland and they're specialist screws so I had to give him some extra money for them.'

'Right. And I see the ladder is still in the hallway.'

'Yes. That's true.'

'Why...?'

I thought about it.

'I thought I could use it for mending that broken socket.'

We both looked at the socket. It was three inches off the floor.

'Or I could just kneel down.'

Lizzie said 'hmmm' and walked away, quietly.

I decided not to mention the good news about Peter and Tarek.

*

It turned out that Peter Gibson was now living and working in London as an architect. In London! And as an *architect*! Just like Anil. I thought back to what Ian and Hanne had said about all my mates working in IT. Well, so far, only *one in five* was working in IT, and *he* had his own village in *Fiji*. Plus, *two* in five of my friends were *architects*: a statistic that only I – and architects – could probably lay claim to. I wondered again what everyone else was up to. Would Tarek have continued with the acting? What other voices would he have provided to the German cinema scene? As with Hamlet, where else is there to go once you've played Chunk from *The Goonies*?

Peter was living with his girlfriend in Tooting, was enjoying the World Cup and couldn't wait for tonight's England game, and was as keen as I was to meet up. His email suggested a date a week or two away, and I'd decided that gave me more than enough time to either revarnish or unvarnish half a table, mend a broken socket and scrape some paint off a toilet. If only I could drink half a gallon of ketchup, I'd be straight back on track, Lizzie-wise. And so Peter and I had agreed to meet up.

Right. To work. I found my way to a DIY site and tried to look up the best method of removing paint from a carpet.

And then my phone rang.

'For someone who lives in Chislehurst, you're spending a lot of time in London,' I said.

'Well, I can't help it, can I?' said Ian. 'Where else can I go to get dressed up like a bloody bear? And anyway, it's the World Cup! You've *got* to watch that in the pub with your mates. *Your* words, not mine.'

England were playing Portugal and the place was *rammed*.

'I thought you said they had pubs in Chislehurst.'

'Yeah, but not like the Royal Inn. They've got pistachio nuts here. And olives.'

'*Olives?*' I said.

Was this it? Was Ian joining me? Had *his* earthquake begun?

'Yeah, olives. They're like fancy grapes.'

No, it hadn't.

We looked at the telly in the corner. Portugal had a near-miss and the pub screamed its relief. The game was already in extra time. We'd been late into the pub because Ian had wanted to stop for a Chinese that he claimed I said I'd buy him for dressing up as a beast warrior. And we'd only made it this soon because Ian had seen some distressing vandalism in the toilets of the restaurant that had raised some controversial issues.

'How do you get paint out of a carpet?' I asked, distracted.

'We nearly went out of the World Cup there, and you're asking about painting carpets?'

'I was just wondering.'

'I dunno. Use a hammer or something. So I don't need to ask what you've been up to. More DIY?'

'Kind of. I met up with my old mate Cameron, too. The one I was telling you about?'

'Oh yeah. *Does* he work in IT, then?'

'He's a Fijian chief. But yes, he works in IT.'

'Who else?'

'I'm in touch with various others.'

'No one, then.'

'It's all coming together, Ian. Peter Gibson is close. We've got a date in the diary. And Tarek Helmy from when I lived in Berlin – I'm on the trail!'

'Berlin? That's where the final's happening.'

'The final what?'

'The final countdown. What do you reckon? The final of the World Cup!'

England had the ball and looked dangerous. The crowd reacted. But a brilliant tackle from Portugal and the moment disappeared.

'And what about this Ben bloke?' said Ian. 'The one I dressed up for?'

'Ben Ives. I worked at Argos with him. My first-ever Saturday job. He spread a rumour that I'd undergone genital exfoliation and that my knackers looked like a weeping sparrow.'

Ian spluttered into his pint. I thought it was in disbelief but it's actually just something he does.

'A weeping sparrow?' he said. 'I'm not sure that even makes sense...'

'I know! But it didn't seem to matter! Connie from the stock-room couldn't stop watching me walk about in case it was true.'

The referee called time. Nil-nil. Extra time was over.

'So when are you meeting him?' said Ian, turning away from the screen.

'I'm not. I'm just pretending to be ManGriff the Beast Warrior who initially wanted to have a quiet word with him about an article he'd written for the newspaper but who is now organising some kind of animal poetry event in his office.'

'Eh? So you're not actually meeting him?'

'Once I'm sure he's totally gone for it and booked a conference room or something I'll reveal it was me all along and the justice will be sweet. That's all I need. I'll give him a bell and we'll chat and I'll update my address book there and then.'

Ian was thinking.

'Doesn't sound... quite in the *spirit* of what you're doing, though...' he said.

I thought about what he meant. He had a point. All I wanted to do with eleven out of the twelve people in the book was celebrate. Celebrate our friendship and our childhood in the hope that we could celebrate our impending adulthood too.

'I know what you mean,' I said. 'But a bit of revenge is called for in this case. Once I reveal it's me, it'll all be fine again.'

'No, no, not the revenge thing. I think the revenge thing is *good*. *Called* for. You *have* to get him back. I just mean...'

The pub crowd started to applaud. Initially I thought someone had scored. But they hadn't. Penalties were starting.

'You just mean *what*, Ian?'

'Well, you're trying to *meet* everyone else, it seems. The Loughborough people. The IT guy. All you're doing with this Ben fella is *phoning* him.'

'He's in LA, mate. LA's a bit further than Loughborough. Cameron I met up in London. And I'm going to meet Peter here too. No – this is new media revenge. Something he'd never have dreamt of fifteen years ago. This is the right and proper way to pay Ben Ives back... and I'm enjoying it. It's the best way.'

But inside, a little pocket of sadness had opened up. I knew Ian had a point. The spirit of the activity demanded a meeting. But what else was there to do?

'Do you *want* to meet him?'

'Course I want to meet him.'

'Then you should meet him.'

Ian had had an idea. There was a sparkle in his eye.

'If England win this game,' he said, pointing at the screen, 'then *you* have to go to LA.'

'What're you on about?'

'It's a bet! You *love* bets!'

'Ian, I *don't* love bets.'

'You *used* to.'

'Once. And it was only *one* bet! *One* bet and I'm tarred for a lifetime!'

'Quick, get drunk,' he said, trying to hold my pint up to my lips.

'*One drunken bet* in the *last century* and that's all people think I do all day!'

'If England win on penalties, you have to go to LA to reveal your-self to Ben Ives in person! You have to stroll up to him and say, "It was me all along! *Now* who looks like a weeping bloody sparrow!?"'

'I'm not doing it, Ian.'

'It'd be such sweet revenge! Do it!'

'I'm *not doing it*!'

The pub started to make the noise it usually makes when some-one's about to kick their penalty. A low, rising 'oooh', stopping the split second the ball's kicked... the ball kicked by...

'Lampard's missed!' shouted Ian, but he was all but drowned out by the other shouts of anger and sadness. England were one-nil down.

'I'm *still* not doing it.'

'The odds are in your favour, Dan! Do it!'

Portugal's turn. Simao bashed his in. One-nil to Portugal.

'I'm still not doing it,' I said, and I'd curse myself for this moment of weakness later on, but I was actually considering it, now.

'Come on! Quick! Decide now!'

Hargreaves equalised for England. The pub exploded. One-one.

'Ian, this isn't one of those times. This is a more grown-up me.'

'That's what you're supposed to be *fighting*.'

'No – this is what I'm supposed to be *accepting*! In my own way.'

'Do it!'

Viana for Portugal. The pub went quiet. He jogged up, struck the ball…

And missed his penalty.

The pub exploded again, louder, harder, more fiercely.

'I *won't* do it!' I said, but Ian couldn't hear me. It didn't matter.

'Go to LA! Put your fate in the hands of the football gods! You used to say yes all the time, for God's sake!'

'I do say yes! I say yes *more*! And it's led me towards growing up. I live in north London. I get paint out of carpets and nearly varnish tables. We've *established* this.'

'You're supposed to be reconnecting with the past.'

Gerrard stepped up to take his penalty and the pub fell silent. He kicked the ball hard and fast, but – unbelievably and to the cries of the people around me – *missed*. Somewhere, a woman nearly fainted. A fat man swore loudly and a Portuguese bloke in the corner kept very still.

'Your chances are better than ever,' said Ian. 'England's losing! Agree to it!'

'No…'

'Agree!'

'No…'

Petit ran at the ball and struck it. Portugal had missed again too. The windows shook in time with the cheers. This was shredding my nerves. England were still *in* it. But time was running out. Who was taking it? What would I say to Ian? I just had to stay strong…

Jamie Carragher stepped up.

'This,' said Ian, 'is your *chance* to hang on to your youth.'

'It's not about hanging on. It's about *moving* on…'

'This is your chance to do something big and stupid and *just like the old days*. The days when you'd jump on a plane and head to Inverness at the drop of a hat! The days when you'd text me to say you'd be late for the pub because you'd decided to go to Belgium!'

'But I'm *married*, Ian. I'm nearly *thirty*.'

'Fight it! *Do* something! Take action!'

'I *am* doing something! I'm reconnecting! I'm updating my address book!'

'And you're not even willing to leave the country? For an *old friend*? A friend's worth more than a flight. And this is your chance,' said Ian. '*This is your chance*!' And I looked into his eyes. And I looked up at the TV screen. And I saw Carragher preparing himself. This was his moment to take the lead. To win it for England. To send me to LA to come to face to face with an old enemy; to make that old enemy *a new friend*.

Fuck. How would I explain this to Lizzie? How much DIY would equal a *trip to LA*?

'Okay,' I said. 'Let's do it.'

The whistle blew. Carragher bounced on his heels and began his short run. Ian and I involuntarily stood up. The crowd's shouts grew. The world slowed down by a third. Carragher struck the ball with power and grace and elegance...

... and...

Carragher had missed, and two minutes later both Postiga and Ronaldo had scored for Portugal. And that was that. England was out of the World Cup.

And I was walking back to the tube, utterly relieved that I would never have to go to LA. Never have to meet Ben Ives in the flesh. That I was *moving* on, not *hanging* on...

So why was I so annoyed?

Ian's words were ringing in my ears.

A friend's worth more than a flight.

And when I got home, and I turned on my computer, I still found myself annoyed, and I still found those words bouncing around my ears.

So much so that when I saw the words 'New Mail', and read the contents within, I had booked myself a flight just twenty minutes later.

Sod it.

I was taking *action*.

To: Ben Ives
From: ManGriff
Ben
Did you get my photo? Is the 21st still on?

To: ManGriff
From: Ben Ives
Hi
Okay! Yes. I did. Sorry I needed 'evidence'.
I guess stranger things have happened. 21st okay.

To: Ben Ives
From: ManGriff
Great. I will let everyone know.

To: ManGriff
From: Ben Ives
Everyone? Thought it was just the three of us.
That is still best for me. A coffee and a chat only okay?

To: Ben Ives
From: ManGriff
Well, I'll do what I can.

To: ManGriff
From: Ben Ives
?

To: Ben Ives
From: Gamron the Viking Dog
Hi Ben!
Gamron here (Simon)!
I hear we are all meeting up on the 21st to run through some of
the Stormy Leopard's poetry.
We're all really excited to see what she's come up with this time!
We'll see you soon,
Gamron the Viking Dog
P.S. Would you be up for an interview for our website?

To: Gamron the Viking Dog
From: Ben Ives
Er, Hi Gamron/Simon,
Can I ask: how did you get my email? ManGriff did not mention
you were coming. Think it would be best if it's just me and
ManGriff and his girlfriend right now.
Ben

To: Ben Ives
From: Katherine Jameson [bettythefrog@hotmail.com]
Hello Ben
What time on the 21st?
Betty

To: Betty the Frog
From: Ben Ives
Hello Betty
Did you get my details from ManGriff? I'm just having a
quick coffee and a chat with him on the 21st –
sorry you were misinformed.
Ben

To: Ben Ives
From: Betty the Frog
Ben
I actually heard about the event thanks to dark fox, who forwarded me an email that JaJa Bah at DKB (!) received. But ManGriff Lord of All Enemies is a friend of mine too.
See you on the 21st for the big event!
Betty

To: Betty the Frog
From: Ben Ives
Betty
It is not an 'event'.
Ben

To: Ben Ives
From: Jon Bonnaud
Subject: Yes
Yes I would like to attend the brainstorming on the 21st.
Jon Bonnaud

To: Jon Bonnaud
From: Ben Ives
Jon,
Who are you? It is not a brainstorming.
Ben

To: ManGriff the Beast Warrior
From: Ben Ives
ManGriff,
Slightly concerned. Am happy to meet up briefly to talk
about the article, but have started to get mails from strangers.
Not appropriate, really, I'm very busy all afternoon. If that's
a joke, stop please. If not, then the same.
Ben

To: Ben Ives
From: ManGriff the Beast Warrior
I'll take your details off the mailout.
But we *are* definitely on for the 21st?

To: ManGriff the Beast Warrior
From: Ben Ives
Yes, so long as there's not hundreds of you.

From: ManGriff the Beast Warrior
To: Ben Ives
Cc: iamthestormyleopard@hotmail.com;
bettythefrog@hotmail.com; jonbonnaud@hotmail.com;
spaceroach@furrytongue.com; darkfoxhiding@aol.com;
thementalistsalmon@juju.tk;
whos_afraid_of_the_pickle@jamjam.net;
tickles_the_spider@furry.co.uk;
gamronthevikingdog@hotmail.com;
stickleback_stan@theone.me.uk; fish_bod@casey.com;
biffothebigbluebear@rampart.com; Jennyt@lexfoliation.com;
JaJaBah@horatio.net
Subject: Poetry and Fun in LA!

Dear all,

Okay, we have to sort this out. I know that there has been some excitement about the poetry event on the 21st. But we need to put a limit on numbers as I believe Ben is getting nervous about lunch orders etc.

Just myself and the Stormy Leopard will now be attending. Stickleback Stan and Tickles the Spider – sorry, guys... next time!

Betty – we need to take this out of the newsletter and off the website ASAP! Also, remove Ben's cell number from the mailout.

I will let you know how it all goes.
ManGriff

                                        To: ManGriff the Beast Warrior
                                              From: Ben Ives
                                                        ta.

Chapter Thirteen

In which we learn you can often catch Danny
rubbadubbin' in a club with some bubbly...

I had spent the several days before the flight wondering whether
perhaps I should cancel. Whether perhaps I should stay in London
and work on the house. Whether perhaps I should make do with a
phone call and a catch-up.

Well, I'd been wondering all that, *and* emailing Ben Ives ever
more obsessively.

But Ian had been right, in some senses. To reconnect fully and
properly required a face-to-face meet-up. And hey – it's not like this
was in danger of going on forever. I had until November 16th. The
day after, I would buy Lizzie all the cushions and potplants she could
eat. Literally.

Plus... this felt... *fun*.

That's not to say I didn't feel slightly guilty. I did. I wasn't working at the moment and I'd asked Lisa, my agent, to turn down any
meetings for the time being. When she'd asked why, I'd cited
'personal' reasons, which is an excuse you can use on any occasion
without fearing any follow-up questions. But really, it was because I
was *excited*. Plus, a deal's a deal – Lizzie had set out the rules and I
was obeying them. To make up for the fact that I would be gone this
weekend, I'd mown the lawn, replaced a doorknob and bought a
new doorbell. I'd begun to enjoy myself somehow, so bought a tin
of paint from the man at the DIY shop who had inexplicably started
calling me Rhodri, and I'd painted the window frames. They looked
amazing. So I tried to find other things I could paint. I painted the

handrail next to the stairs. Immediately, it looked brand new and I patted myself on the back for being such an expert. I went outside and painted the little garden wall that surrounded the flowers and bushes. I was proud. It lent the garden a Mediterranean feel, and so I moved a terracotta pot that the previous owners had left behind and suddenly it all looked like something out of a magazine. But terracotta is such an *orangey* colour, and so, in an amazing moment of creativity, I painted it white. And then I'd noticed I still had more than half a tin left, so I started to paint the shed. This was going *well*.

I was now a man of some responsibility, unable to simply board a plane and leave the country, and I understood that. I was, for one thing, a *boss*. I'd called Paul and instructed him I would be away this weekend and therefore would not be around to let him in to begin the canopy and the guttering. He'd listened attentively, but then I'd had to spend a couple of minutes reminding him who I was and what he was supposed to be doing for me. He said he could maybe sort things out this week, only his assistant was ill and he wasn't feeling too good either.

All of this had, though, meant I could board my flight with the beginnings of a clear conscience. I sat quietly and read my complimentary copy of *High Life* magazine, and there, over three or four pages, was a huge and colourful feature on… Los Angeles.

I wolfed it down. LA looked exciting. Dangerous. *Exotic*. A place of fun and shenanigans. Ben Ives must *love* it there. There were muscly men rollerskating near the beach. Girls in bikinis eating ice cream and dancing. Yellow cabs, and bright sunshine, and neon lights, and billboards and cops and film stars.

But, as I looked around me, and at the stewardess starting to point out the emergency exits, I remembered that I wasn't going to LA.

My plane would land in Berlin in an hour and forty minutes.

Tarek's email had made me remember exactly why we'd been friends. It was warm, and inviting, and immediately made me feel like we hadn't been apart for sixteen years. It was like nothing was missing… and it was full of promise, too. He'd told me to look him up the next time I was in Berlin, that we had so much to catch up on, that there were so many things he wanted to remember with me, that I should absolutely, *definitely* come back over…

And so I'd decided I would. There and then. *A friend's worth a flight*. Yes. A friend *is* worth a flight. And so I'd started the booking process – a booking process that reminded me that a friend would have to be worth a hotel, too. But yes. A friend is worth a flight *and* a hotel, I assured myself. And a taxi from the airport. Yes. A friend is worth a flight and a hotel and a taxi to *and* from the airport.

Yes.

But I'd begun to feel slightly nervous. Finding a hotel had proved difficult. Two separate websites which individually checked availability throughout the whole of Berlin had both come up with just one option… a hotel next to the Ku'Damm, right in the heart of the city, at a nightly rate of £290.

£290! A *night*! I struggled to see where the money could possibly be going. There was no talk of king-size beds, or duck-down duvets, or complimentary champagne, or any of the things you'd expect and demand as you handed over your 290 quid. There was just a picture of a room. A very normal, German room.

The lack of accommodation, and the high price, were both, I knew, down to one thing. I was heading for Berlin on the day of the World Cup final. The day all eyes would be on the city. It was Tarek who'd suggested it. He'd said we should meet up, have a chat and a beer, and then go and watch the final on one of the big screens near the Brandenburg Gate. It just seemed too perfect not to do. Me and Tarek, hanging out again, in the most exciting place of the moment. And so I'd bitten the bullet, bought an overpriced ticket and booked an overpriced room. Ah well. Hang the expense. I'd live in luxury for a weekend in the name of friendship. To make it work, though, I'd had to cancel my meeting with Peter Gibson. But that was fine, I reasoned, as I stepped off the plane and walked into the arrivals lounge. Peter would be okay about it. He was in London, after all, and now that contact had been made, I could see him *any time*. Who'd begrudge me a trip to see an old friend on a night like this?

I turned my phone on and immediately received a message.

Why have you painted everything white?? Why did you only paint half the shed??

Well, Lizzie maybe, but that was fair enough.

Now that you and I are best friends, I'd like to present you with a new rule of travel. One which I hope you will treat with all the gravitas and seriousness you have come to treat *all* my important advice.

Never get a hotel room based on a picture you see on the internet. Because, sometimes, those pictures are *actual size*.

If I'm honest, I was mildly suspicious from the very second I caught sight of my plush, £290-a-night, luxury Berlin hotel.

For a start, there was the fact that, as per the website, nothing so far was really screaming 'plush'. Or 'luxury'. In fact, there wasn't really much even screaming 'hotel'. For the price of a night in the Dorchester, its location was undoubtedly excellent – ten seconds from one of central Berlin's most exciting streets. But location isn't everything. Sometimes a hotel needs a little more. Like locks. Treat this as piece of advice number two.

The lack of a proper lock was my first clue, as I stood outside, fruitlessly pushing a doorbell from which wires spilled out liberally, and noticing the scratched and scruffy door secured by nothing more than an open brass padlock. Not one of those big ones, either. A tiny one. The kind you'd give to a child so that he can lock his pencil case. Then there was the broken lawnmower on the stairs. The peeling wallpaper and cracked, blackened windows. I found myself tutting as I passed these, noting what a lick of paint could do for those frames. And then there was the fact that, as I found the lady sitting behind the plastic desk in what the sign above her peroxide head insisted was the reception area – but which also appeared to be someone's bedroom – she seemed incredibly surprised to see me there at all. I knew this because her eyebrows were somewhere around her hairline. But then, these were eyebrows she'd drawn on herself, so who knows *what* she was thinking.

'You booked on internet?' she said, perplexed. She was young, and Polish, and I may well have been the first guest she'd ever seen.

'Yes,' I said.

'But... you have read description of the room?' she said.

Another clue for me, there.

'Um... yes,' I said.

'Well... we need you pay now, before I can give key.'

This was suspicious. If I'd been buying a car or adopting an orphan I might have thought twice. But I handed over my credit card and shrugged. I'd seen a *picture*, after all – surely I didn't need to see anything else. The lady ran the card through the system, never once taking her eyes off me, and then handed me a massive key, attached to a large block of orange plastic the length and width of a brick, but heavier.

'Are you here to see football?' she said.

I nodded.

'Kind of,' I said.

'You must be very big fan,' she said. 'You must *love* football game.'

'Well, I'm here to see a friend as well,' I said. 'An old friend.'

'He must be *very* old friend,' she said.

'Yes,' I said. 'He's 102.'

I laughed lots and lots. She didn't laugh at all. Her eyebrows remained perfectly still and blue.

'You go down this,' she said instead, pointing to a corridor somewhere off to the left. As I wandered off, I turned round to see her still looking at me with a mixture of confusion and fear on her face. I walked on.

There was a strange smell in the air. It was manly, and musky, and reminded me of cheap nightclubs and angry, fighting men. As I found my room, I also found the source of the smell. The cleaner – and it's hard to call someone that when they actually look dirtier than you do – was doing a spot of air freshening by walking down the hallway with her finger jammed down on a can of Lynx. This is how I used to make my room smell nice when I was a student, and it did not work. I scrabbled to get the key in the lock and managed to force the door open just in time to avoid total saturation by the smell of a thousand teenage boys. And then I saw my room. Well, I couldn't help it. One step in and I was already halfway through.

It was tiny. Absolutely *tiny*.

Every piece of furniture had been shoved into one small corner. The TV – one of those wood-panelled push-button ones that one day no one will believe ever existed – was rammed with the sink, the bin, everything, all into one corner. There was a dirty bar of soap face down on a damp table. The window couldn't be opened because it was jammed shut by the communal bins outside. There were wires where lights should have been. The cold tap spat water around the bowl, unpredictably and perilously close to the telly. There was no toilet or shower. There was a three-inch gap between the floor and the door. I stood there and blinked at it all a few times. And then I blinked a few more times, because the cleaner must have been in here with the Lynx a few minutes ago and the fumes were prickling my eyes. I looked around me and tried to convince myself that this was £290 well spent. And then I realised that looking around me wasn't helping my case.

I went out. I'd be making friends again with Tarek at six. For now, I'd make friends once more with Berlin.

When I'd first arrived in Berlin, in 1990, I had never been anywhere like it before. The closest I'd been was probably Leicester, and it's very hard to get excited about seeing Leicester. It had been the height of summer and the city was bright and vast. From my little seat at the back of the van I'd looked up as we drove down Unter den Linden to see the Brandenburg Gate in the distance. The entire street was lined on both sides with precisely the same model of pale blue Trabant – the car which millions of East Germans would save for millions of years to buy. The same car which, in thirty years of production, was never once updated or changed. The same car which was originally supposed to have been a three-wheeled motor-bike, but which the designers decided to change at the last minute and sell as a car. It was an incredibly odd sight. There must have been hundreds of them... and now, as I walked down the same street, I couldn't spot even one. Just beemers. And Mercs. And slick, silver Audis. Things had changed. So I went to try and find the Berlin *I* knew.

Almost immediately, I found myself riding the U-Bahn to Oskar-Helene-Heim, the tube station I'd used every day in Berlin. At the stand outside, I bought a currywurst and a beer, with chips and mayonnaise piled on top, just as I'd done when I was thirteen. Apart from the beer, I mean. I walked past my old flat on Gary Strasse, the scene of the KGB invasion, with its parquet floors and tall white walls. I wandered through the park that I'd first eaten Oreos and drunk Mountain Dew and played baseball in... past the duck pond which froze solid in the winter and which I once fell into trying to rescue a frozen fish which turned out to be a large brown stick. Down the streets around Dahlem, where I'd cycled with the small Russian kid who'd lived downstairs. Grisha. *Grisha Kozlov.* I wonder what *he's* up to these days?

I got the bus down to Zehlendorf, towards JFK. I walked through the park next to it, and remembered the shaving-foam fight on the last day of school, when the entire park had turned white, and the entire park smelled just as my hotel room smelled now. I found the tree that Tarek and Josh and I would sometimes sit under when we couldn't face geography and would decide to skip class and eat apples. And then I hopped back on the U-Bahn and made my way into town again, doing my best to take in exactly the landmarks I remembered best as a kid. The Gedächtniskirche, the church in the centre of Berlin, with the spire damaged in the air raids of the Second World War still as it was... the KaDeWe shopping centre and the bright blue Mercedes sign that shines over a darkened Berlin like a second moon... the TV Tower, built as a symbol of communism – but which annoys all communists on sunny days as a giant cross appears on its huge, curved windows... then, further into town, a stop at Checkpoint Charlie, where somehow, sixteen years on, men are still making a living from selling pieces of the Berlin Wall which must surely have run out a day or a week after it actually fell... where tourists snap up symbols of the past, tottering home in oversized Russian military gear, or having their passports stamped with the words CHECKPOINT CHARLIE.

Seeing Loughborough again after so many years had been one thing. I'd found it interesting that the Wimpy was still there, for example. But seeing Berlin, a city which had been through so much, been given a second chance, been made into the *capital* of Germany while I'd been *living* there, was quite another. It was such a confident city. Confident of its place, of its cool, of its future.

Perhaps, of course, it had something to do with the World Cup. All around me, all day, had been football fans in various states of dress and sobriety. I'd seen desperation in the face of a wild-eyed Italian, tapping strangers on the shoulders and holding up a sign saying ICH BRAUCHE A TICKET. I'd seen love gently blossom between a girl in a France top and a boy in an Italy top. I'd seen tension, as a drunken Italian in a central square kicked a ball as high as he could in the air, only to watch with simple-faced horror as it came smashing down on a table full of Germans and beers. I'd seen a man inexplicably wearing a North Korea shirt, a girl bringing a pizza to a cheering group of rival fans, and a poodle that someone had sprayed red, white and blue. The atmosphere was incredible. Berlin was a party town at the best of times. Berlin was a party town, in fact, at the *worst* of times. But now Berlin had a *reason*.

I wandered down a side street, away from the Ku'Damm, and found the pub that Tarek and I had agreed would be our meeting point. From here, we could easily make our way to the Brandenburg Gate to watch the final on the big screens. I found a seat on a bench outside and sat in the late afternoon sun. A group of very drunk Germans were at the next table. One of them, sporting a look I genuinely thought had died out as the Wall came down (moustache, spiky-topped mullet, tight black jeans and large white trainers), was leading the group in a rendition, bizarrely, of 'Rule Britannia'. There appeared to be no reason for this whatsoever, and no reason for the group to segue seamlessly into 'The Final Countdown'. It was a bold move, combining two such distinct genres with such reckless abandon, but it worked out for them, and I had to applaud their progressive attitudes. Internally, I mean. I didn't stand there and applaud a load of blokes with mullets singing 'Europe'. But I smiled my appreciation, and they looked at me and raised their glasses and cheered. Berlin was a lovely place to be.

The men, though, quietened down as they saw two guys

approach. They were tall, and broad, and they looked like trouble. One was wearing a hoodie with his cap pulled down low. The other was wearing a basketball top over a T-shirt and a similar cap. I could see a small spark of bling – nothing too flashy, just hints – but I looked away the second I thought I'd caught the eye of one of them, choosing instead to find my Coke suddenly and profoundly fascinating.

A bad thing involving strangers has only ever happened to me once, on the night of my eighteenth birthday, when I'd been walking happily through Bath, and a group of lads had caught my eye and strode confidently up to me.

'You called my name,' said the first and biggest of the three.

'Um… no, I didn't,' I said, which was true. I didn't even *know* his name.

'Well, you called me a twat, then,' he said.

There were so many things I *nearly* said at that point, but eventually settled on, 'Nope,' which turned out, oddly, to be the *wrong* answer, as they started trying to hit me with their chubby fists, all at once. (Although a terrible experience, I did at least manage to accidentally steal the biggest lad's watch as, ten years too late, I finally did as Karate George had advised and attempted to work on my block. Having worked at Argos, I knew this watch – a Seiko – was worth at least sixty-five quid, so it wasn't such a bad night, all told. Although I later destroyed the watch with a hammer and threw it off a bridge.)

The thing is, I'm a firm believer in the kindness of strangers – in the fact that strangers really can be friends you haven't met yet – and other things you might sometimes find on a bumper sticker. I relish the chance to meet new people, and I have found that wherever you go on this strange little earth of ours, you will generally find that they are good. But rightly or wrongly, sometimes you feel awkward. Sometimes you feel strange. Sometimes you feel nervous. You shouldn't – there's generally no reason to. But as the two big lads in their hoods and their caps sat down next to me, I suddenly felt all three.

I shouldn't have. Because one of these strangers *was* a friend.

'Danny?'

*

As soon as I'd realised it was him, Tarek and I had hugged, and shaken hands, and then slapped each other on the shoulders, like men.

'So *cool* you came over here!' he said.

'A friend's worth a flight!' I said. 'I've *always* said that!'

We started to gabble incoherently about the old days and all the memories we shared, like two old women with too much to say. It must have been slightly off-putting for his friend, a tall and handsome man known as Chris. Well, Chris to his pals – 'BRD' to everyone else.

'What does BRD mean?' I asked.

'*Beste Rapper Deutschlands*,' said Tarek. 'The Best Rapper in Germany.'

This was quite a confident name. How had his mother known that her baby would *be* the best rapper in Germany? It'd be terrible if he'd turned out to be *rubbish*.

'It's my artist name,' explained Chris.

'How do you mean?' I asked, and Tarek told me.

BRD!
BRD, in short the best rapper Germany's, celebrates his new entry with a song that leaves no question unanswered. Those, who do not know him will tremble and can go home. Those who listen to him will be part of a new era. He works knowledgeably with the German language without appearing cheap. Battle? Yes of course, but finely chiselled, of high karate, he lets the whole German scene splinter, like Glass. BRD is proud but does not glorify anything. The more one hears him, the more facets will be opened. Statement meets announcement and become a powerful word tornado of images which are exploding in one's brain. It is difficult to explain BRD and his songs in words. What remains is complete bewilderment... "it is true. Life make me hard and almost spiteful, I am like somebody working on an Oil-rig. Day and night occupied..."

Tarek, as you may have worked out by now, does not work in IT. Nor is he an architect, a Fijian chief, or a bloke who's solved one of the great human mysteries of all time. He is, instead, it turns out... one of Germany's premiere hip-hop artistes.

Yes.

I couldn't believe it, either. It was *brilliant*.

He certainly looked the part. He'd gone from respectable and bespectacled to the kind of bloke you see in music videos holding Uzis and shouting that life is terribly unfair, but it's so *lovely* to have bitches and dough.

And the more he told me about his new career, the better it got. Tarek was one of the brains behind Hitmen Music, a collective of German hip-hop figures with their own label, studios and a growing and glowing reputation... and BRD was one of its first artists. I was rather impressed and deeply happy at the turn of events. I'd only been in Germany a matter of hours and already I was sitting next to the country's best rapper.

And here was Tarek. A little older, a little bigger, a little wiser. And very proud of *der Beste Rapper Deutschlands*.

'We're pressing the new single, right now. And we got a new distribution deal, so things are going well. Life's good, man. Company's doing well, I've got a baby girl... I got married, to Anna-Re. I met her through hip-hop, she does it too. How about you?'

'Married as well. Not to a rapper though. And no kids.'

'Do it – it's the best thing in the world.'

'But the rapping,' I said, keen to know more. 'How did that start?'

I was struggling to remember music class and whether rapping had been an option.

'You remember Marcus from school?' he asked.

'Yeah – Marcus the rapper?' suddenly realising all the clues were there in his name. 'Used to hang out with that big ginger lad who called himself MC Quite White?'

'Marcus, yeah. Well, him and me, we were just rapping all the time, trying to get a deal, and eventually we signed to Warners, signed to Universal, brought out lots of records...'

'Seriously?' I said, genuinely amazed. 'You brought out *records*?'

This was incredible. My friend had brought out records. I shook my head, and swelled with pride. This made the whole Chunk from *The Goonies* thing fade *right* into the background.

'But when the last group we had split in 2000, we thought, hey, maybe we should do our own thing. Try and start a label, try and bring stuff out, so we hooked up with this guy we know called Axl, and we figured we could just make our own music and use the money to make even *more* music...'

'But is there a big rap scene in Germany?'

'Yeah – and for ten years we were the number one English-speaking group in the country, and...'

'*Ten years?*'

'Yeah. We were bilingual – a lot of people would try rapping in English but it would sound ridiculous because they couldn't even speak it. We could do both. It's just telling stories about how kids in Germany live, the only way we know how.'

It made complete sense. Tarek's accent was a subtle blend of American and German – perfect for his job, and the kind of accent I'd heard every day at JFK. So much so that by the time my year was over, *my* accent was mildly distorted too. We hadn't gone back to Loughborough at the end of the year. We'd moved to Bath instead, where I'd had to start making friends all over again, this time with a strange English-American accent. It had brought about its own set of problems. Once, at a dinner party my parents had dragged me to, I'd spent three or four hours talking to the same elderly woman, when, halfway through a story in which I was talking to her as I'm talking to you now, she'd put her hand on my arm and said, very loudly, 'YOU SPEAK VERY GOOD ENGLISH.' I hadn't known what to say, so just thanked her, and continued with the story. Only at the end of the evening did it turn out she'd thought I was Belgian.

Tarek and the Bester Rapper Deutschlands seemed to be very nice men indeed. They'd met on the scene, in dark and dingy hip-hop clubs, when Tarek used to rap too.

'But then I stopped, and started producing instead.'

'Did *you* used to be the BRD?' I asked. 'When you were an... R... D?'

Tarek looked at me blankly.

'Or were you called something else?'

'I go by Potna Pot.'

For a horrible moment there, I'd assumed Tarek had said he was off to buy some pot, but he was actually just telling me his name.

'"P.O.T." stands for Phat Overloadian Tarikh,' he said, and I'd closed my eyes and nodded, like I'd been about to jump in and guess exactly that.

'I mean, I still MC. I'm a team with a DJ. He does the music, I do the mic. We have a couple of gigs every month. DJ Reaf and Potna... we're called Hit 'Em Up Sound...'

HIT 'EM UP SOUND!

At the beginning of 2002 Reaf and Potna got into contact via a common acquaintance and felt immediately that they got on with each other! The two decided to tackle a new project. And as the two do not like to pay for entry tickets and like to drink free of charge – they thought: 'Why don't we form a Soundsystem?'

Competition and battle is the butter on their bread, and Reaf and Potna did not wait to be asked and went to many clubs across the whole republic, making many clubs unsafe! To the deepest north or the sunny south, Mr Reaf and Mr Potna bring their monstrous sets to your clubs!

'But what would you rap about?' I asked.

I'd never really been into rap. Many at JFK had tried to get me into it, playing me dainty little ditties such as 'A Bitch Iz A Bitch' and 'Fuck Tha Police', but it was never something I felt I could really relate to, particularly as I'd thought the police did an admirable job under sometimes very difficult circumstances.

Tarek thought about how to answer the question, and I tried to think what stories *I* would tell if *I* could rap about *my* inner-city struggles, but stalled when I couldn't think of a rhyme for 'canopy'.

'You know, we're just trying to portray stuff for the people that live here. BRD is trying to make music for people like him. Normal kids, raised normal. Trying to live your life, trying to get by, getting into trouble – though nothing that bad...'

BRD nodded silently and then joined in.

'And then on the other side,' he said, 'you've got the Turkish, Arab and African kids rapping about not being treated fair… and knife stuff is big right now.'

'*Knife* stuff?'

'Yeah,' said Germany's best rapper. 'It's dangerous 'cos the lyrics are nasty. On the one hand I don't want no censorship, but on the other a lot of kids pack knives now to look cool.'

Tarek agreed.

'Just like when I used to listen to NWA they used to say 80 per cent of the people who listened were white suburban kids, it's the same here. Kids sitting in a mountain village somewhere listening and thinking, "That's what Berlin is like." That's the way we used to think of Compton. But, yeah, Berlin's at the centre of it now… but a lot of it is wannabe gangsters, which we're totally not into…'

While he'd been talking, I'd noticed a middle-aged couple on another table glancing at Tarek and muttering something. They didn't really look like hip-hop fans. And then I realised – maybe the kids at school had been right. Maybe even after all these years Tarek still got recognised from that sitcom. I asked him and he blushed slightly.

'Yeah, a couple of times a week I get recognised. The sitcom was pretty big. It can be frustrating because they want signed photos, but all I've got is my rap pictures, and they don't look so keen when they see them.'

I could see what he meant.

'I suppose,' I said, 'it'd be like asking for a photo of the kid from Jerry Maguire and being given a picture of a big man pointing a gun at you instead.'

And then a memory shot back to me. An autumn evening. On a bus.

'I remember once we were on the school bus, and you reached into your bag, and you… you showed me your *gun*.'

It sounded ridiculous, now I said it. Like it couldn't possibly have happened. But things like this did. I refer you to my KGB adventure.

'Can that be *possible*?' I said. 'Did you have a *gun* at school?'

Tarek looked slightly awkward, but BRD laughed.

'Yeah. That was the same thing. I thought it was cool. No reason to have a gun in Berlin at all. It was the videos and the music. I'm not proud of it.'

I had been. I'd written about forty letters the next day to all my mates in Loughborough, basically just saying, 'My mate Tarek showed me his gun!'

'We were scared about our jackets being taken,' explained Tarek. 'I did protect myself with that gun, too. Someone tried to take my money and my shoes and I wasn't gonna let that happen. I pulled the gun out and shot him twice.'

There was a silent moment as I took the information in, processed it, and then decided I'd better process it again, because somewhere along the way I'd apparently gotten the impression that Tarek had just said he'd shot a man.

'Sorry, you did what?'

'I shot this guy.'

What?

'You shot someone?' I said, my eyes suddenly cartoon balls of terror. 'You *shot* a guy?'

'Yeah. Twice.'

What?

'In the face, I think.'

WHAT?

'You shot someone *twice* IN THE FACE?' I said. Maybe if I just kept repeating what Tarek was telling me he'd realise he'd made a mistake and meant 'hugged', not shot, but then, how often does someone hug you twice in the face?

'Yeah. And then I ran away.'

This was all too much.

'You shot someone TWICE and then RAN AWAY?'

Tarek just nodded.

I couldn't quite believe it. My old friend, sitting in front of me like a gentle and respectable man, a pillar of the German hip-hop community, this German Chunk... was *admitting a murder to me*! Just twenty-five minutes after having met him for the first time in sixteen years! Christ... maybe he'd just been waiting all this time to tell me. Maybe that's why he'd been so keen to meet up. I started to panic... what if I was now, by some weird German law, somehow *in* on it? What if I'd broken the law just *listening*? Was I to blame now? Those forty letters might now be considered evidence!

'Well... what happened?' I asked, desperate for a happy ending, but aware that the reason that stories that involve men shooting other men in the face never appear on *Jackanory* is that they very rarely *feature* a happy ending.

'Oh, nothing probably. It was just a gas gun. It just burns your eyes for a bit. I've been shot with one. It's not too bad. Why? You thought that was a *real* gun?'

I thought back to when I was a kid.

Yes! Of *course* I'd thought it was a real gun!

'No! Of *course* I didn't think it was a real gun!'

'You did, didn't you?'

'Well, a bit, yes.'

And then, as I have done so many times in my life, I found myself very grateful indeed that my friend was not a murderer.

I bought Tarek and the best rapper in Germany a drink to celebrate.

BRD had to go off and meet someone for a bit, and Tarek and I were wandering through Berlin, swapping stories and catching up. I told him about my address book, and who I'd already met, and about my letters to Andy Clements, and he seemed to love the idea. He'd done something similar himself, he said, but hadn't managed to follow up on it too much.

'I'd love to see more of the old gang again,' he said. 'People from the old days. I think it's a natural thing. Like Josh.'

'Josh, yeah...' I said. *What was that rhyme he made me learn again? The one with his address in it?*

'Those days were really special,' said Tarek. 'They *meant* something. Everyone accepted each other – usually in schools there are dividing lines. But with us, everyone liked each other – rock, hip-hop, grunge, sports, skaters – whoever you were, if you were cool, you were cool. It's a pity that sometimes people let the special days go.'

The streets were packed with football fans, all making their way to the Brandenburg Gate, not one of their faces showing anything other than happiness, or excitement. It felt like we were at the very centre of the world.

'Now, we could go and stand and watch the game with everyone else,' said Tarek. 'But a group of friends are meeting up in a bar round the corner. We could get food, and beer, and maybe even a seat…'

I thought about it. We were in Berlin. On the night of the final. With a chance to feel like a part of history.

'I think,' I said, remembering Ian, 'that the World Cup was *made* for being in a pub with your mates…'

'It's all about friends, man,' said Tarek, and I smiled.

And so we turned around and went to the pub.

'So you went to school with Tarek?' asked a man in a baseball cap, tucking into his pizza.

It was a minute before kick-off and everyone had ordered a Meaty Maxi Meat pizza – an enormous, towering thing packed with a variety of indistinguishable meats. You might as well have popped a slice of cheese on a farm and been done with it.

'I did!' I said, losing myself in the memories for a second. 'Our school was a *special* school.'

'You went to a *special* school?' said the man, wide-eyed, and I had to correct myself.

'Well, no, hang on, the *school* wasn't a *special* school. It was a school that was *special*. It was just after the Wall came down. I hadn't seen him until tonight, so I had no idea he was a rapper and had once shot a man.'

'These things happen,' said another man, just one of six people associated with Hitmen Music to have arrived in the past few minutes. BRD was laughing in the corner and Tarek had just given someone a complicated handshake. I felt a little out of place – mainly because I was wearing glasses and didn't know how to shake hands like that.

The whistle blew and the noise in the pub increased with it. This was it! The *final*!

And then, like something out of a film, a slick, new, blacked-out Mercedes with blue neon involved screeched up outside the pub and two men got out, slamming the doors behind them. One of them was quite large. The other was almost exactly the opposite.

'Axl and Papo are here…' said Chris.

Axl looked like a bit like a Hispanic gangster. Papo did not. He was what you might call a rapper of restricted height, and had kind eyes, a shaved head and a broad smile.

'Danny, this is Papo,' said Tarek, and we shook hands in the only way I knew how.

PAPO!
Small man very big! Papo is not new in the business – he does not rap only since yesterday, he touches with each line! With the powerful voice of a hurricane he demolishes whole concert halls! The contents of the songs mirror his past, present and future and he gives us an insight into his own thoughts, blasting our ears with the naked sounds of life! Papo is real and this is how we experience him!

I was quite surprised that Papo was involved in the destruction of whole concert halls. He seemed a remarkably polite and quiet man, content to sup on his beer and chat.

'So you've been finding people you used to know?' he said.

'Yup. It's been great. In fact, I was supposed to meet a guy called Peter Gibson today but couldn't because I was coming here. He's an architect. But I've also so far found a Fijian chief whose villagers ate a vicar, a bloke who runs a carvery and who's solved time travel, and, of course, a rapper.'

'That's pretty good,' said Papo. 'You'd think they'd all work in computers or some shit.'

He meant 'something' there, he wasn't implying all my friends would *actually* work in some shit, like IT farmhands.

'Yeah, it's been great.'

'But you're just meeting people from your address book?'

'Well, they all earned their places in it, in one way or another, I guess. I mean, I'd like to meet loads of others, too, but where do you start? At least like this there's a system.'

'But what about other people? Seems a pity you can't see them just 'cos they're not in your book…'

Papo was right. It seemed wrong to deny the millions of other people I have met in my lifetime the pleasure of a reintroduction. Instantly I thought of Grisha, the Russian kid who'd lived downstairs from me. And Josh! Even Tarek had mentioned Josh. But what could I do?

There was a rising cheer as Italy took the ball and attacked the French goal mouth. I wondered whether Ian was part of the same cheer back home, or Chris, or Pete, or Cameron. I thought about what else over the years we'd been a part of without thinking about it. Those moments in time or history when all focus is on one thing. Where had they been when the Wall came down? When Diana died? Where were they on 9/11? The world seems a lot smaller on days like that. No matter *where* someone is, you feel united somehow.

I looked around and saw another complicated handshake getting under way, and wondered whether there was something I could do to feel more like I belonged. I had an idea.

'Papo,' I said. 'I was wondering. What could my hip-hop name be?'

'What do you mean?' asked Papo.

'Well, you're called Papo. Tarek is called Potna Pot. Chris is BRD. *He's* called Axl.'

Papo had a think.

'Danny... Dan... D...' he said.

'Danny Dandy?' I said, in disbelief.

'No, no, I'm just thinking...'

'Because Danny Dandy would be a *rubbish* hip-hop name,' I said. 'I mean, I don't want to tell you your own business...'

'No, you can't be called Danny Dandy,' said Papo. 'But how about...'

He looked at his beer.

'D-man?' he said. 'Like Demon.'

'Demon!' I said, delighted.

'Yeah! Demon!' said Papo, and we slapped our hands together like they do in films, and then shook on it.

'Hey, Danny, you want another beer?' asked Tarek, sitting back down again.

'Yes, I do, and it's "Demon",' I said, before, inexplicably, 'bitch.'

Papo laughed, and I attempted a complicated handshake.

I had definitely found my place in life, and it was among the German hip-hop community.

Tarek looked at me like I was odd.

Two hours later and Berlin had exploded into a celebration of the green, white and orange of Italy. Suddenly there were people on mopeds everywhere. Fireworks. Hugs in the street. Taxis screeched by with happy faces pressed up against the windows, Italian flags trailing behind them. Tarek and I watched with a satisfied detachment.

'Okay!' he said. 'So I guess that's the World Cup done. You wanna see our studios?'

'The crib!' I said, trying desperately to remember other phrases I'd heard on MTV. 'Let's mosey on over to your crib!'

'Mosey on over?' asked Tarek.

It must have been country night on MTV.

Axl, Tarek, Papo, BRD and I squeezed into the Merc. I sat in the middle of the back seat, between Papo and BRD, who shifted about uncomfortably. Axl cranked up the stereo and rolled down the windows, and there we were, looking like a proper hip-hop crew, cruising through the streets of Berlin, waving at girls, nodding in time with the beats, looking supercool. Well, *they* did. To be absolutely honest, I looked like the studio accountant. Or one of those nerdy lawyers you see in films getting mixed up in Mafia capers. But I was enjoying myself.

'Hey, put something of *yours* on the stereo,' I said. 'Something from Hitmen Music!'

Axl laughed, found something, and hit Play.

Immediately, the bass in the car started earning its money...

Boof... boof boof...

And then a familiar voice...

Potna Pot!
Who's Potna Pot?
Potna Pot!
Bitch! Who's Potna Pot?

It was Chunk from *The Goonies*!

'Potna Pot?' I said, delighted. 'That's *you*!'

Tarek nodded, happily. I was excited!

'Bitch, that's *you*!' I said.

'Yeah… you should maybe not say "bitch" so much,' said Tarek, quite calmly.

Maybe I was *over*-excited.

But this was *brilliant*. It was like sitting in a car with someone while listening to their theme tune. And *everybody* should have a theme tune.

Catch me in the club, rubbadubbin' in some bubbly!
Potna Pot!

'It's very powerful,' I said. 'And it's not often you hear the word "rubbadubbin'".'

The boys considered this, and all agreed I was correct.

We pulled up and stopped on a typical German street, maybe ten minutes away from where we'd been. I could just make out bakeries and a small supermarket on the corner, as we made our way through the darkness and into a courtyard, towards an arched doorway. I suddenly felt inexplicably tough. This was the lure of the gang. Now, Tarek and his pals were in no way a gang. They were a group of genuinely warm, polite and happy young men. But they *were* a crew. They were pals, together, in a tough city, working away at making their dream come true. And it *was* working.

'Every cent we make,' Tarek said, 'goes straight back into the business. We work fifteen-hour days. We're not interested in becoming famous. We do this just because we love it and it feels important. It's documenting lives.'

I loved Tarek's attitude. And I believed what he was telling me. Too many people are driven by fame. Tarek had tasted it as a kid, thought it was okay, but knew it wasn't important. What was important, it seemed, was who was around you. What you were doing. How you were. Tarek loves his family, loves his mates, loves his work. Tarek had it all worked out.

Axl found the key and let us in to the world of Hitmen Music. Up ahead were studios, a lounge, a kind of green room and various offices for various office duties. There were huge speakers everywhere, plenty of soundproofing and, of course, the Hitmen Music logo – an Uzi in front of a treble clef. On the table in front I noticed two half-full bottles of Jack Daniel's, various ashtrays, dozens of beer cans and no less than six packets of Rizlas. Hip-hop, ironically, is very rock and roll.

'Check this,' said Papo, flicking a switch.

The lights were low, and immediately the room was filled with the voice of BRD, who looked on, proudly. It was his new single. 'WER???'…

WER???

'WER???' is full of clean punch lines, of which one does not have the feeling to have heard them for 1000th time!

Authentic text which do not need to show – with a raised finger – that one is a Berliner! BRD is proud but does not glorify anything. The more one hears him, the more facets will be opened!

BRD with his impressive career as a Hip-Hop-Artist and his versatility as a musician, producer and songwriter, proves with each song again his creative potential. One can wait with great anticipation for further hits from his pen!

We all stood about and nodded our heads.

I looked around and I felt like I'd made a bunch of new friends. BRD, Papo, Axl and, of course, Tarek. They'd welcomed me in, treated me so nicely, named me 'Demon', made me one of the gang. I was touched.

I listened to a few more tracks, and Papo played me a short video of BRD in a dark and dingy Berlin basement club. The crowd were loving it as he rapped, loudly, confidently, fully in control, all of it in German.

My pocket suddenly buzzed. A text.

Hey baby. Haven't heard from you. All okay?

Aw. Lizzie. In all the excitement of arriving in Berlin, rediscovering old haunts and finding Tarek, I'd forgotten to tell her I'd landed safely. I wrote back.

It's great! I'm with Tarek! He's a hardcore German rapper!

Moments later, Lizzie's reply arrived.

What?? Are you okay?? Jesus, come home safely!

I'd thought that was a bit of an overreaction and shook my head at the prejudice that the hip-hop community must have to deal with on a daily basis, but then I looked at my 'Sent messages' and realised I'd written 'Rapper' with one 'p'.

Tarek had disappeared for a second – which was probably just as well given my libellous text – but returned with a gift.

'Take this,' he said. 'It's one of our CDs. I hope you'll listen to it.'

'I definitely will!'

'Right – the bar!'

The night was coming to an end and Tarek and I knew it. We were sitting outside at the Strandbar, yards from the River Spree, with sand underfoot and tropical plants all around. It was a hot night, with a happy atmosphere, and the distant, irregular toot of car horns the only reminder that the World Cup had even happened.

'Maybe we should get some bubbly,' I said, 'so people could catch you rubbadubbin' in it.'

Tarek laughed and I looked over at his pals.

'You've got a nice bunch of mates,' I said.

'They're cool. And Papo even said he felt a bit inspired to try and find an old friend of his. I said he's not old enough yet.'

I laughed, but I didn't know what Tarek meant.

'Can I ask you something?' I said, and Tarek nodded. 'You mentioned you've been doing this too? Trying to track people down, I mean?'

Tarek nodded.

'It was all to do with turning thirty,' he said, and I kept quiet, even though all I wanted to do was shout 'Me too!' But it slowly dawned on me what he'd meant about Papo.

'I don't know why, but every time I looked for someone, or found the old school website, I would think about turning thirty. When I found someone, or I talked to them, I'd always ask them if they'd turned thirty yet. I don't know why. I don't know why it was so important. But it started because I found this old website for my first school. There were about forty people looking for friends they'd known in the seventies. About twenty people trying to find people they knew in the eighties. But from the nineties there were only two or three. And that made me think, maybe people gradually want to reconnect with the past. It's a cycle. It happens to nearly everyone. And I thought, well, maybe it's my time. And it seems like you're the same. Have you turned thirty yet?'

'I'm a few months off,' I said.

'I was too. It was coming. I turned thirty-one last week. Seems like you're exactly one year behind me.'

It did. And it seemed strange. I'd found a kindred spirit here.

'It was a strange thing, turning thirty,' said Tarek. 'I wasn't scared of it. It's just that "thirty" sounds so much older than "twenty-nine". Your twenties are gone. That exciting period, that whole decade, when you're becoming your own person. And now you realise you're supposed to *be* your own person, and if you don't feel ready, or you're not sure you're ready, it can be scary, somehow. In a way I miss being young. When you see a kid who's seventeen, eighteen, on the streets, you can see what it feels like. Not worrying, being cool, being indestructible, and suddenly when you're about to hit thirty you worry that all that is gone. And for me, that's why I looked for my friends. It's why I looked for *you*.'

'You'd looked for *me*?'

'Sure. I'd even sent an email to one I thought was yours.'

This was incredible to me. Sometimes, in years gone by, I'd wondered where people were. Wondered if they'd ever wondered where I was. Maybe right now someone is wondering where *you* are, how *you* are, what *you're* up to.

'Who else?' I asked.

'Josh. The three of us had so much fun together. It seems a pity all that's gone, man.'

How cool would it have been if the three of us could have gotten back together? Just for one night. One night in Berlin. That would've been amazing. And then I realised... maybe there *was* a way...

'When Josh moved back to Colorado, he made me learn his address, like a little rhyme... the number of the house rhymed with the street name...'

The only other time in my life I'd been forced to learn an address was when I was five years old and living in Dundee. A Malaysian kid named Zairul told me I had to go and visit him when he moved back to Malaysia. I promised I would and asked him where his house was. He told me it was number 3. To this day, a part of me still wants to try and find number 3, Malaysia. But how about *Josh*?

'It was... *something* Drive. 635 *something* Drive. Or 195 *something* Drive. It ended in a five and it was a drive, and it scanned perfectly... and it was in Boulder, Colorado... and his dad had a weird name, didn't he?'

'Yeah,' said Tarek. 'His dad's name was Chuck.'

'Chuck! That's it! But what was the address?'

Tarek shrugged, and said, 'Why?'

'Give me a second,' I said. 'What's the number for German international enquiries?'

Tarek told me and I dialled it up.

'*What country, please?*'

'America, please...'

'*City and State?*'

'Boulder, Colorado...'

'*Name?*'

'Miller.'

'*Address?*'

'Ah...'

'*Address, please?*'

'Well, it ends in a five, and it's a Drive.'

'*Sir ...*'

'Please! This is really important! It's C. Miller, in Boulder, with those details!'

'*There are* a great deal *of Millers in*…'

'Please! I'm in Berlin with a very old friend of Mr Miller and we're trying to get through to him with some vital news, and all we're missing is the…'

'*I have a C. Miller at Lindauer Drive*…'

'That's it! Lindauer! That's *it*!'

I high-fived Tarek, took down the number and high-fived him again.

'Shall we call him?' I said. 'Shall we call Josh?'

'Yes – but last I heard he'd moved to Missoula…'

'Well his parents might have a number for him if they still live there… what time's it over there?'

'Morning! Do it! Call Josh!'

I dialled the number and Tarek and I held our breath. The dull monotone of the American ring crackled slightly down the phone, as if to remind us just how far away we were pinning our hopes… but no one was answering… *if only his dad would pick up*, I thought… and then…

'Hello?'

Hang on. That wasn't Josh's dad. That was a *very familiar voice*. That was…

'Josh?'

A pause.

'Speaking.'

I couldn't quite believe it.

'Hey, this is… this is *Berlin* calling…'

There was a split second where Josh may have blinked a few times before working it out.

'… Danny?'

'Yes! And not only me! Tarek's here too!'

'What? You *serious*? How *are* you guys?'

'We're great! How about you?'

'Life just kind of goes on, man… how did you know I was here?'

'We didn't!'

'But I just happen to be in the house for a coupla days, visiting my dad. I just walked in and picked up the phone. I live in Anchorage, now. Alaska, man...'

What were the chances of this? Of me and Tarek being together after all these years, of remembering even part of an address, of phoning the number, and of a man who doesn't live there any more and usually lives in *Alaska* being there and picking up? It felt like it was *meant to be...*

'What are you doing in *Alaska*?'

'Just doing my thing, dude, you know me. I'm into cross-country skiing at the moment so it seemed like a good place to be.'

'Where did you used to be?' I said, secretly relishing the word 'dude'.

'I was in New Mexico. The skiing is pretty bad there.'

Same old Josh. Dry as a bone. I smiled. It was good to hear his voice.

And then it was like he suddenly realised the odds that had been against us all ever speaking again.

'This is... well, this is *cool*,' he said.

'Here's Tarek! He's a rapper now!' I said, taking care to accentuate the double 'p'.

I passed the phone over and then watched as Tarek had a delighted conversation with a friend he hadn't seen in sixteen years, and I felt proud that I'd been able to make that happen for him, just as he'd made it happen for me by agreeing to meet up.

When the conversation finished, Tarek looked at me with joy in his face.

'He told me he'd looked for us both over the years on the internet but never managed to get in touch!'

'Seriously? I guess we're *all* doing it.'

I was starting to think there was something fundamental to all this. A human rite of passage we all go through. Maybe it's just easier for us than it was for our parents. The world is smaller these days. A man from London *can* go to Berlin and phone America, all in the same matter of hours, and along the way reignite two separate friendships. Tarek agreed.

'Maybe,' he said, 'this looking-back thing... maybe it's to do with responsibility. It can be scary. I mean, not getting married, because getting married was really cool. My wife being pregnant – that was really cool too. But the day your child is born is really scary. The day I picked my wife and my kid up from the hospital – *that* was scary. The fact that you now have a kid which is yours to look after for eighteen years... that's terrifying. Plus our apartment was very small and we had no money whatsoever. But soon the kid becomes the only thing you care about. My wife, she had a better job than I did so she went back to work after three weeks, so I raised our daughter for the first two years. And it was hard, a lot of times. But now when I look at the relationship she has with me... that's great. She's a daddy's girl. And I wouldn't change a thing.'

Suddenly I realised my own crisis of confidence had been the most trivial thing in the world. Why had display cushions and lattes and Latvian brunches worried me? Tarek had had a child to raise under difficult circumstances. *That's* responsibility. And he was only one year ahead of me. Our desires to reconnect with the past had crossovers... but his reasons were more pure than my own shamefully trivial ones.

'So what I mean is, it's cool to hang on to your past,' he said, thoughtfully. 'If you don't remember your friends, you don't remember your life. If you compare the things you remember with your friends, you can get the whole picture – who you were, what you were like, maybe even why you are like you are. Sometimes, someone else will remember something that was huge in their life, but which was tiny in yours...'

I was suddenly reminded of something. Something I really wanted to tell Tarek. Something I wanted to thank him for. I looked around. Papo and BRD were deep in conversation. Axl was chatting to someone else. I felt I could do this without embarrassing him.

'Do you remember,' I said, 'one day after school, we were on the bus. I was heading home, you were going off to play basketball or something. And there were these kids on the bus, these older kids?'

Tarek screwed up his face, trying to remember where I might be going with this...

'... and I'd just got one of those JFK jackets. The cool ones with your name sewn on in silver, and the leather arms...'

'Okay...' said Tarek, struggling to place the day.

'And one of these kids was staring at me, and his friends were making jokes, and then when he caught my eye he pointed at my jacket, looked me straight in the eye and gestured that he had a knife.'

'Ah,' said Tarek. 'Yeah, that was always happening. They stole my Redskins jacket, too. A group of kids with knives. You don't hear it so much these days. So did they take your jacket?'

'No!' I said. 'That's just it! I told you what was going on, and you stared back at them, and they kind of backed off, and then you stayed on the bus with me for a few extra stops until they'd gone. You had to walk back for ages and you nearly missed your basketball game!'

'It... sounds familiar,' he said. 'I *kind of* remember it.'

'But that was such a big thing for me!' I said. 'I'd been looked after by my mate, in a foreign city, when I'd been scared.'

'Maybe that's what I mean when I say that for you, it was a big event in your life. And for me, I played a small role. But I'm pleased I could.'

'Thank you, Tarek,' I said, and I shook his hand, getting ready to leave. 'I just wanted to say thank you.'

We hugged. I'd banished a demon. I'd *become* a Demon.

And I walked back to Europe's tiniest hotel room, happy.

July 10th, 2006

Dear Andy

We now turn our attentions to your letter of March 8th, 1989, concerning your trip to the Isle of Man and your birthday gift of a 14-inch Sanyo remote control teletext colour television.

To start with, I will say how pleased I am that you enjoy switching the subtitles on and off, and indeed that you do it all day. It is vital to have interests and hobbies, and I trust you have brought these with you into adulthood.

Now, to me.

Guess what? You might remember Cameron, who went to our school. Well, he is now a Fijian chief who has his own village.

Also, I have just returned from a very successful trip to Berlin, during which Italy won the World Cup (if it is still 1989 where you are, you should put a bet on this straight away) and I managed to meet up with an old friend named Tarek. Tarek is now a rapper, which I think is quite an interesting job to have. I'd never considered it as a child, and now feel quite the fool. I hope you stuck with your plan to become a moon pilot.

I still haven't heard back from you, Andy – I hope my letters are finding you somewhere in space and time. You are nowhere to be found on the internet (a kind of futuristic phone book... but you probably know that by now). Please get in touch!

Daniel

P.S. In reference to **your** P.S., you've only got yourself to blame. Your mum **did** tell you not to pick at it.

Daniel

P.S. In reference to your P.S., you've only got yourself to blame.
You mustn't die till I've got to pick ...

Conked out!

DELAYED by other events, the annual conker championship at Holywell Primary School, Loughborough, between finalists Timothy Sismey and Daniel Wallace was declared a draw when, after 30 'strikes' each, both conkers were intact and both boys had registered the same number of hits.

Chapter Fourteen

In which we learn that hardcore rap is seldom romantic...

More than anything else, the 'thank you' moment with Tarek was what came to define my trip to Berlin. I hadn't planned that it would be such an important moment – I hadn't even planned to say it at all. But I was glad I did. No matter how trivial or small that day must've seemed to Tarek, it was important to me. And it seemed just as important that Tarek should know that, too.

I was happy as I rode the Heathrow Express back into London. And happy as I walked back into my house, to find Lizzie sitting in the garden. So happy that as I wandered up to her I started to serenade her with a song I'd learnt on my way home.

'*Do you love me for my* dough, *ho?*' I cheerfully sang.

Lizzie looked slightly alarmed.

'Sorry?'

'*Do you love me for my* clothes, *ho? Do you love me for my* shows, *ho?*'

'What *is* that you're singing?'

'I'm not sure what it's called,' I said, 'but it's by a man named Axl who seems to be very concerned that his ladyfriend might not be being totally honest with him.'

Lizzie now looked mildly shaken.

'He's just telling it like it is,' I said. 'Keeping it real.'

I continued: '*Do you love me for my* Rolls… *Royce?*'

I struggled with that bit, seeing as how none of it seemed to rhyme with the word 'ho', and I was beginning to quite enjoy rhyming things with the word 'ho'. But perhaps this line was based on fact, not rhyme. Maybe the song was from the perspective of an insecure baker with a girlfriend named Royce, desperate for praise for his Rolls. It would certainly explain his fascination with dough.

'You have a Nissan, not a Rolls-Royce,' said Lizzie, interrupting my analysis of modern music. 'A little green one.'

'I was singing!' I said. 'You motherbitcher!'

She just looked at me.

'I do apologise,' I said, and went and made her eggs on toast.

I'd been doing my best to convince myself I was entranced by the beauty of odd jobs for the last hour and a half. I'd fixed the garden hose with a rubber band (1MP), I'd started sanding down a door to make it close properly (2MP), I'd put a call in to Paul to see when he could start work on the small canopy (he couldn't talk now, he was giving a quote to someone), and I'd even experimented with a hole in the wall and some filler (another 1MP). This last job had started out fine, until I realised I'd been inadvertently dropping filler between the floorboards (-1MP).

All I was really doing was biding my time until Lizzie had to go to work. I'd promised to pop to the Post Office to pick up a form she needed, but the minute she was out the door, with only the slightest slither of guilt tapping me on the shoulder, I was back at the Box, tipping its contents onto the floor of the living room and diving straight in.

I was over halfway through the Book, now, with just five friends left to locate... Mikey, Anil, Simon, Cameron and Tarek all had shiny new addresses in my battered old book... Peter Gibson and Ben Ives were located and locked-in... meaning that now it was all about finding...

Akira!
When known: Loughborough, 1988
First memory: Michael Amodio's Deadly Crane Kick to his head.
Concerns: He returned to Japan. He could be anywhere now. Or, like Cameron, he could be *minutes* away.

Tom!
When known: Bath, 1991
First memory: Him claiming his dad invented the Sprite logo, when, in fact, he was a builder.
Concerns: I now know he was lying about the Sprite logo.

Lauren!
When known: Loughborough, 1985
First memory: Receiving her first pen pal letter, in which she told me she enjoyed shortbread and the works of A-Ha.
Concerns: How do you recreate the magic of a pen pal?

Andy!
When known: Loughborough, 1984-1990
First memory: Seeing his mother's bosoms by accident.
Concerns: Has he been receiving my letters? Is he annoyed at the sixteen years it took me to reply?

Chris!
When known: Dundee, 1984
First memory: First day at school. First best friend.
Concerns: He has disappeared. Completely. And utterly. Disappeared.

So they were the five I told myself to concentrate on. The last five of the Book.

But something Rapping Papo had said had struck a chord with me, too. Yes, so these people had a special place in my life. The Book had, after all, come to symbolise the best of my childhood. But there were other people involved, too. Why limit myself to those twelve? There was a renewed sense of freedom opening up inside me. My time with Cameron, Tarek and the others had shown me that it was possible to not only revisit those old friendships... but to *renew* them. Reinvigorate them. So what would be the harm in saying hello to a few other people, too?

I'd had a twinge of regret that Grisha, the Russian kid, wasn't on my list. That neither were Brian, or Amy, or any of the other guys from Berlin. Phoning Josh had been a delight, after all... so where were they?

I sat down at my computer and typed a name into Google.

Grisha Kozlov.

I pressed Search.

Nothing useful.

So I did what I'd tried with Cameron, and typed Grisha's dad's name in.

I pressed Search.

I found him. I fired off an email.

And then I wondered whether that might help with the Final Five, as well... Akira Matsui had proved elusive. The only clues I had for him were an old address, and a postcard, in which he'd said his dream was to become a medical doctor. Searches on the net for him proved fruitless... Akira Matsui seemed to be the Japanese equivalent of Brian Jones... rare enough that you'd probably only have one friend with that name... common enough that so would sixty million other people...

So what was Akira's dad's name again?

Isamu?

I checked his postcard. It was.

I tried it.

Up came a page...

An Investigation on the Influence of Vitreous Slag Powders on Rheological Properties of Fresh Concrete
Isamu Matsui

Table 1. X-ray diffraction (CuKa) shows that BFS and PS have similar XRD patterns, and...

I gulped. Reading about vitreous slag powders and fresh concrete wasn't really my forte. Another nail in the coffin of falling back on quarry manager as a trade. But I scanned through, right to the bottom, where I found a footnote, telling me that Mr Matsui had, in 1995 at least, been teaching at the College of Industrial Technology at Nihon University... a quick hop to their website and moments later...

I had his email...

I pressed Send & Receive and heard my email whoosh away, on its way to Japan... but as it set off, another arrived...

Hi Daniel,

So nice to hear from you after so many years!

I attach Grisha's email address at the bottom of my mail! He now lives in Tel Aviv, learning Electrical Engineering. In addition, he is working at Intel.

Bye!

M

P.S. You should know that he has recently changed his name to Ben Berlin.

I laughed, as much out of delight at the speed of the reconnection as at the fact that Grisha had apparently and inexplicably changed his name to 'Ben Berlin'. Oh, and I also liked the fact that he was now working in IT.

But Tel Aviv! How cool was that? It was incredible to me how my friends had travelled, and once again I wished I could map out a route of their movements over the years... a vast map with lines darting across the globe, like a map of airline routes from the seventies to today...

And so I typed in more names, almost at random... Many I could find nothing for, or just mere mentions that they'd been in a place or done a thing but after that the trail ran cold... but for others – so *many* others – I was tracking and tracing with great success. I was on fire. If I discovered a technique for finding one person, I'd try it with the others – and, crucially, for the Big Five.

A page on MySpace for someone I only barely knew at school linked me immediately to the page of someone I'd known very well, but had never seen again. Quickly, I made my own MySpace page, for the sole purpose of saying hello. And so I typed another name into the site – someone else I hadn't seen in around twenty-five years – Eilidh McLaughlin.

Eilidh was a little girl I used to hang around with in Dundee when I was four... we did everything together. When a kid down my road broke my arm, Eilidh made sure to break her arm by falling off a swing just a week later. And within minutes, thanks to MySpace, I knew where she was (Glasgow), what she was doing (translating Gaelic programmes for the BBC), and even what she looked like (the same, pretty much, and not much bigger). Underneath her photo was the word 'Online!', and I smiled in disbelief. Right now we were both online, both looking at a screen, *both on the same website*... literally connected to each other... I fired off a hello, and she wrote back, delighted...

I found a number for Big Al through my friend Little Dan, and sent out a text... Al was now apparently a policeman in Liverpool, and was probably on duty, so I held out no great hopes – but moments later, I had my reply...

Danny! Hey mate how are you? I saw you on some weird TV programme recently – what's all that about? What's your address?

I texted him back, and he said:

I'm getting married! Hope you can come to the wedding!

From never seeing the man to being invited to his wedding – re-introduced to the *bosom* of his friendship! – and with just the press of a few buttons in between. I swelled with pride, and texted back:

Wow! Of course!

This was what it was all about.

I pressed on. I found out that my mate Bob from university was now teaching English in Osaka. That my friend Rob from Bath – who I'd met while doing work experience at school – was now editing a magazine in Sydney. Brian from Berlin was a dad and working in Aurora. And Amy was in Washington.

I don't really need to tell you what Amy was doing.

Okay, then.

She was working in IT.

I fired off email after email, referring from time to time to the contents of the Box, finding clues, and titbits, and things I might try... I found a small note from Leanne Davis, a girl I'd been 'going out with' before moving to Berlin – when who you were going out with was decided by their friends and consisted of awkwardly drinking a milkshake at the Wimpy once a week. I looked at her name and realised that, technically, we'd never actually broken up. I'd just moved to Berlin and gradually the letters had stopped. I was horrified. We'd never ended it! For nearly two decades I'd been going out with a thirteen-year-old girl! Obviously, she may have grown up just as I had, but what if she hadn't? The scandal! A quick look around revealed not just her picture and her location, but her company's name and her position as head of corporate affairs!

And then I found Alex Chinyemba... Alex was a kid from Zimbabwe I'd known when I was about ten... we'd spent a childhood holiday together in a disused water mill up in the highlands of Scotland, and gone climbing and horse-riding and eaten sweets and burnt pizza. We'd also spent a day at a local water park, when we'd told girls he was an African prince and charged one of them 50p to touch his hair. He'd popped into my head, and within ten minutes I'd found a clue... one phone call to an East Midlands karate centre later, and I'd found out that he was now an estate agent with four kids and taught karate on the side. We talked and laughed, and six minutes later he texted me a photograph of himself with a large moustache. Four kids and a moustache! Here was a man comfortable with turning thirty.

Plus, he agreed to help me work on my block.

And it didn't stop there.

An inspirational moment had reminded me of a way of finding Tom... his dad, the builder that Tom had insisted had invented the Sprite logo, had founded his own company... could they possibly have a...

They did!

The website proudly proclaimed they were part of the Federation of Master Builders, but, more worryingly, also provided a definition of what a builder is...

> Builder n. One who builds; one engaged in the trade of construction

Just what kind of market was this website catering for? If someone doesn't know what a builder is, how did they even manage to turn the computer on? Actually, I thought, maybe I should show this to Paul.

There was a *Contact Us!* button, and I rushed out an email to Tom. The day was just getting better and better. I asked whoever got these emails to forward mine to Tom, saying it would be great to see him! That I'd been revisiting my childhood! That I wanted to update my address book! That we should meet up, hang out, finally get together! That I'd love to see him! That I hoped I wasn't coming on too strong! This could be another address updated!

The success was making me giddy, and as the sky outside my windows darkened, I found the clipping from the *Loughborough Echo* which mistakenly reported that both Tim Sismey and I had both won the conker championships of '87... and then found Tim Sismey's email address hidden away on a website about music... I wrote to him apologising for such a devious media cover-up, and he replied, saying:

> Thank you so much for your concern about the Echo article. I feel it's important that we, the people who make the news, do not let the people who report it use our lives to further their own causes and I applaud your honesty.
>
> And guess what? In clearing out a wardrobe in my mum's house a year ago, I discovered a Harrogate Toffee tin, which actually contained the remains of the winning conker from that brutal battle. How weird! Take care, Tim.

That *was* weird. A memory that I'd assumed was probably just mine had been remembered from a slightly different angle only a year before… how often do shared memories pop up around the world? What happens if two people have the same memory at the exact same moment? Are they connected for a split second? Does the memory get stronger, somehow?

This was all a little too philosophical for me, and my head had started to hurt, so I made a cup of tea and had a sit-down.

I ate a Hobnob and thought about the names that I'd tapped out on my keyboard today. I knew that – granted – it was fairly unlikely I'd ever get to recreate my conker battle with Tim Sismey again. Nor would I see Bob in Japan, or Grisha in Israel. But it suddenly hit me that with all the tools at my disposal – texts, MySpace, Facebook, Bebo, Google, email, iChat, Skype, *everything* – I had no excuse whatsoever for letting *any* of these friendships ever slide again.

And then I sat back down at my desk, and looked at all I had achieved with my day. It had been nine hours since I'd started. I decided I should probably think about lunch, and then I'd earn myself a few MPs. But then I heard Lizzie's key in the lock. It was evening.

'I'm sorry,' I said.

'Don't worry about it,' she said, not entirely brightly.

'But I'm sorry.'

'It's fine.'

We were eating our dinner in front of *The National Lottery*. Neither of us had bought a ticket but we'd both been pretending it was interesting all the same. Paul's ladder was now in the corner of the room, mocking my lack of manliness.

'It's *not* fine, baby. You asked me to do *one* thing.'

'Seriously, it's cool.'

'It's not *cool*, either. You asked me to get you that form from that Post Office and I didn't.'

'Relax.'

'But the Deal!'

'You can get it tomorrow.'

I looked at her.

'You're not making sticking to the Desperados Pact very easy. Perhaps if you were nastier I'd get more done. It's making me feel very guilty.'

'And that's exactly what I'm relying on,' she said, putting her fork down. 'So have you found Chris yet?'

I shook my head.

'Nope.'

'But he's the big prize, right?'

'Kind of. I mean, I want to see all twelve, but Chris was first, y'know?'

'You'll find him. And as for the Deal, you'll have all next weekend to work on that...'

'Will I?'

'Yup. Sarah's thirtieth, remember?'

Ah, yes. Sarah's thirtieth. Another brave twentysomething warrior stepping into the unknown. Another birthday closer to it being *mine*.

'She's booked a hotel in Brighton for the girls... is that cool?'

'Of course it's cool,' I said, feeling somehow more guilty than ever. 'And I'll get to work, really I will. I'll finish painting the shed. And also, Paul's coming round to sort out that canopy.'

Lizzie smiled. I made a mental note to ring Paul to get him round to sort out that canopy.

'The reason I can't sort out your canopy,' said Paul, very slowly, 'is due to the nature of the corrugated plastic which we all agreed would be the best material for the job...'

I waited for him to continue, but he didn't seem to have much more to say. And then I realised that I'd never actually talked about corrugated plastic with him before. I'd never talked about it with *anyone*. If anything, I find corrugated plastic to be a *boring* topic of discussion, but I do realise that's quite a controversial thing to say.

'But Paul – I don't even remember really *wanting* this canopy,' I said. 'I just wanted my *guttering* sorted. *She* was the problem!'

'Who was?'

I pointed.

'The guttering... lady!'

'The guttering will be sorted, Danny,' he said, very calmly. 'Leave it with me. But the canopy has to go up first, you see, and *then* I can begin work on the guttering.'

It made no sense to me, this builder logic. As far as I could see, the two jobs were entirely unrelated. It was like saying, 'I can't punch a tiger because my aunt likes ceramics.'

'Well... do you still need to leave your ladder here?' I asked.

'Yes,' he said.

And then he said he had to go because he said his daughter had been mugged.

'She wasn't mugged,' said Ian, shoving some bacon into his mouth.

We were at a small café off Poland Street and Ian had gone for the full English.

'I *know* she wasn't mugged,' I said. 'But how do you tell a man his daughter hasn't been mugged?'

'You could ask if you can meet the mugger.'

'Why would I ask to meet someone's mugger?'

'Just say you're interested.'

'I am not interested in meeting someone's fictional mugger.'

'So why have you asked me here, taking me so far away from the beauty of Chislehurst, if you've already decided *not* to meet someone's fictional mugger? I'm not dressing up as a bear again – I don't care how much Kung Po chicken you're offering...'

'I think I've done something stupid,' I said, and Ian looked thrilled.

'Brilliant!' he said, his mouth full of sausage.

Just hours after Paul had left, I'd been attempting to rack up some more MPs. The excitement of finding the names of those people not in the Book had died down somewhat, and their replies and hellos had stopped trickling in. I'd popped out to buy more filler as well as an electric screwdriver, which I thought might get me more excited about the prospect of screws and their driving. I'd decided to tidy up the shed, too, but it had started raining by the time I got home so I made a cup of tea and wandered around the house, working out what my priorities should be, and how many MPs I could expect to earn from each one. The problem, as I saw it, was that as far as MPs were concerned, I was flying blind. There was no *system* in place. What made one bit of DIY more valuable than another? And how much was an MP worth, anyway? A phone call? An email? A *trip*?

And then I'd heard the familiar bing-bong of New Mail…

There were two emails waiting for me.

The first was from – *joy!* – Akira's dad…

Dear Daniel

    Thank you for your mail.

    I remember clearly you and your family.

    I often remember our life at Loughborough.

    My son Akira became a medical doctor and works at the Yamanashi University Hospital now.

    I will tell Akira your email address and write his below.

Yours sincerely
Isamu Matsui

I sat back and smiled. So Akira had done it! He'd achieved his child-hood dream – the dream he'd told me about on his postcard. He was a medical doctor. And now I had his email address! His *direct* email address! I was one step closer to reconnecting with him.

I patted myself on the back, and then realised that was quite an odd thing to do.

The second email was from Ben Ives.

A rather *nervous* Ben Ives.

ManGriff (what's your real name, by the way?)

    Sorry, but I'm now guessing this is actually some kind of joke after all…

Shit! He *knew*!

    … in retribution for the article perhaps?

Ha! He still thought it was them! Even if it *was* a joke, he thought it was *ManGriff the Beast Warrior*'s joke – not mine!

I smiled, with relief. The trick was still on. But then... an ultimatum.

I also think that if we're going to meet it should be just the two of us, and not at the office. But next Friday is now the only day I can do. I am very busy at work and this is the only time I will be able to fit you in for the foreseeable. It will have to be very quick, I'm afraid.

Many thanks
Ben

I'd winced when I'd read the final paragraph.

Because I knew nothing more could now develop. I'd hoped to carry this on, to keep making him worried, perhaps cancelling the 21st and arranging more meetings for the future, each one more bizarre and more worrying, before finally phoning him up, and yelling, 'It was me all along!' But somehow, with this email, Ben had gained the upper hand. He'd forced me to quit early. He'd firmly told me that there was to be no more messing about – that this one date was the only one he'd be able to do, and the implication that this would be an end to things was clear. There would be no cancelling, no rearranging, no making things bigger or better – it was now, definitely, all about the 21st. In fact, I realised with a strange sensation in my tummy, it was all about *next Friday*.

'So what's the problem?' asked Ian. 'Have you lost your nerve?'

No. It wasn't that. Although I had slowly begun to feel a little unsure about what I'd been doing to Ben. I mean, yes, I owed him. And no, it wasn't malicious. But perhaps this was the wrong way to get him back. Was this really the best way of getting back in touch? Was this truly better than just turning up and saying hi, it's me, how are you, like I'd done with the others?

'Or,' said Ian, suddenly having an idea, 'is it that you think he knows it's you?'

'It's crossed my mind,' I said.

I'd started to think about my first proper job, when I'd been a journalist. Letters from members of the public were an occupational hazard, and those who did take the trouble to write, in order to proffer a correction or disagree with an opinion, were, more often than not, a little bit nutty. And then there were the letters from people like me and Ben, teenage hoaxers, giggling as we spewed out random opinions from made-up characters... which had started to make his at first blind acceptance of them all the more worrying...

'Nah,' said Ian, mopping up brown sauce with a slab of bread. 'It's LA. The fact that some people who enjoy dressing up as animals would take offence at an article making fun of people who enjoy dressing up as animals probably happens twenty or thirty times a day over there. And they're probably always turning up at journalists' offices all dressed up and waving their poetry about.'

And he was right. For about a quarter of a second.

Because this was *Ben Ives* we were talking about.

Was he actually, secretly, on to me? Was this an elaborate double bluff? You could never be sure with Ben. I thought back to my days at Argos, at the pristine, white A4 letter that had been pinned so carefully to the staffroom wall... the way he'd looked when he'd told me I'd never get him back... the way he'd always been one step ahead...

'So what *is* the problem?' asked Ian, sitting back, full of beans. *Literally* full of beans, I mean. 'Because I'm not being funny, Dan, but there's a *fete* on in Chislehurst today.'

'Well, I wrote back,' I said. 'And I arranged a meeting.'

'You'd *already* arranged a meeting,' said Ian. 'The made-up meeting.'

'No,' I said, slowly. 'I mean, I *arranged a meeting*...'

The fact was, this was Ben's fault. This was what I kept telling myself. This was Ben's fault for getting all jittery and precious and trying to force ManGriff the Beast Warrior's hand. Paw. Hand.

Had Ben not made it absolutely clear that this was ManGriff's one chance of a meeting for who knows how long, perhaps all that would've happened was, two or three minutes before the agreed meeting time, I would've phoned up and laughed down the phone at him.

But now, the way things had developed, I wanted more... I didn't want Ben calling the shots. *I* was in control. And I wanted to see Ben. Not in the same way as I'd wanted to see Tarek or Cameron, but in a more base and visceral way. Plainly speaking, I wanted to see Ben's face when he realised that it wasn't an annoyed group of Furries who'd come to see him after all. It was me. Danny Wallace. A wronged man. A wronged man finally wreaking his revenge. A wronged man who'd *never* had genital exfoliation, actually, and who'd—

'Hang on – *genital exfoliation?*' asked Ian. 'You didn't tell me you'd had genital exfoliation!'

'I have not had genital exfoliation!' I said, a little too loudly.

'Because if you've had genital exfoliation, you need to be very careful about—'

'I have *not* had *genital exfoliation*! That's just it! That was his clever trick!'

'And you let him off?'

'I didn't let him off – I just never got him back!'

'Well you should get him back!'

'That's what this is all about! Why do you think I've been pretending to be a variety of animal-obsessed poets?'

'Right!' said Ian, nodding, eyes closed. 'Got you.'

'Ben was trying to regain control of the situation, and I didn't want to let him,' I said.

And that was why, almost without thinking of the consequences, I'd gone to a website, checked a few details, and then tapped out my reply.

Ben,
  That's fine. We can meet alone – I'll clear it with my girl-friend. How about the Garden Bar, which isn't too far from your office, next Friday afternoon at 2pm?
ManGriff

'So you emailed him back?'

'Nearly,' I said, my finger pointing in the air.

'Why *nearly?*'

*

I'd been staring at the screen for a couple of minutes, my finger hovering over my mouse. And I just didn't know whether to press Send.

I'd been doing so well. That table was nearly all varnished and that rubber band had *really* sorted out my hosepipe. I'd been at a crossroads these past few months, and Ian knew that. Finding my old friends had been a handy way of coping with the prospect of turning thirty – of seeking reassurance that we were all going through the same things. Of making my leap into the world of the thirtysomething okay. Of calming myself down, and leaving stupid behaviour behind. But this was something else. If I was to fly to LA just because I wanted to redress a balance that had been off-kilter for the last sixteen years, I would have trouble justifying it to Lizzie. To me. To *anyone*.

And so I hadn't pressed Send.

Because I knew that, like all grown-up, responsible men in charge of their own destinies... I would require *permission*.

'So what do you need my help for?' said Ian, puzzled. 'Pressing your mouse down? Because I'm fairly sure you can do that yourself...'

'I need you to help me make my case to Lizzie,' I said. 'And also, I need you to help me put up a canopy.'

Ian and I had been working in the garden most of the afternoon, and by the time Lizzie got home we were sitting in the sun, feet up and enjoying a beer.

This was good. Sod Paul the builder. I had taken *control*!

'Hello, boys!' said Lizzie. 'Another one?'

We smiled and said thanks, and then looked at each other and smiled again. Lizzie had been standing under our excellent new canopy and not even noticed.

'You should varnish this,' said Ian, tapping the surface of the table.

'I *did* varnish it!' I said.

'Well, you should unvarnish it and then varnish it again.'

'I *did*!'

Lizzie came through the door again, brandishing fresh bottles of Stella, and studied our faces.

'Why are you two looking so proud of yourselves?' she asked.

We simply pointed and let our work speak for itself. Lizzie turned and looked, and said 'oh' in what I like to think was astonishment and wonder.

Now, granted, this was not the best canopy in the world. It was essentially a piece of corrugated plastic that we'd sawn up and smoothed down. And yeah, so the screws hadn't gone all the way in the wall, and we'd forgotten to remove the sticker from the plastic, and there was a crack in it, and the whole thing wasn't quite what you'd call 'straight'... but it was *our* canopy, and we were proud of it.

'That is...' said Lizzie, pausing so long that both Ian and I had time to hold our breath, exhale, and then breathe in and hold it again '...the most *beautiful* canopy I have ever seen!'

And then there'd been another pause, before we'd all sat about and laughed for a bit, because actually it was shit.

But it was what it *represented* that mattered. Things were getting *done*. Progress was being *made*. And it didn't stop there.

'We've made a list,' I said. 'A list of possible Man Points.'

'Aha,' said Lizzie. 'The Man Points thing...'

'I still wish to point out that this is an oppressive regime which removes the fundamental human rights of the adult male,' said Ian, as I held up a sheet of A4 paper.

'I realised that what we were lacking was a system, Lizzie, so with the help of an independent adjudicator, I have— '

'Independent adjudicator?' asked Lizzie. 'Doesn't Ian owe you fifty quid for that helmet?'

'Not any more!' said Ian, indicating the canopy.

'Now, I have attempted to put a system in place, by assigning a number of points to a specific task.'

Lizzie nodded me on.

'So – mowing the lawn, that's fairly easy, so that's a one-pointer. Tidying the shed, that's worth *three* points, we reckon...'

I looked up to see whether Lizzie was agreeing or not, but she was just sitting there, perfectly silent.

'Right – the canopy, that involves plastics, sawing and screws, so we were thinking...'

'That's a five-pointer right there,' said Ian.

Lizzie still wasn't saying anything. It was making me nervous. I cleared my throat.

'So… we thought you could take a look at all these jobs and see if you agree with the number of points we've allocated each one. In the meantime' – I reached for another piece of paper – 'here is a list of what you can buy with each Man Point.'

'Buy?'

'Well, not *buy*, exactly. But they're a little like Air Miles, I suppose.'

'Are you planning a trip?' she asked.

Ian's eyes widened. Mine did too.

'No! No! Not planning one, no. Not *planning*, exactly. Just… *thinking*. About planning. A trip.'

'Tell her what you've done today,' said Ian, thinking quick.

'Well, the canopy, obviously, then the shed – that's tidied. So that's 8MP in all…'

'8MP?'

'Eight Man Points,' said Ian. 'It's complicated but you'll get used to it.'

'I have also remown the lawn…'

'1MP,' said Ian, kindly.

'… put the blinds up in the bathroom…'

'2MP'

'… and bought four empty ketchup containers into which we can pour that big bottle of ketchup so as to make it more manageable.'

'That one's free.'

Lizzie picked up both sheets of paper and looked them up and down.

'Have you mended that broken socket?' she asked, calmly.

'No. Not yet,' I said. 'That's next.'

'How about the ladder?'

'Still in the hallway.'

I kicked myself. That was 1MP *easy*.

'And what are you saving up for?' she asked. 'With these Man Points?'

'I need... well, I'd *like*... to go to LA. I need to lay a ghost to rest.'

And then Lizzie looked at me, and looked at the list, and then said, 'Fine.'

'*Fine*?' I said.

'Fine,' she said.

Ian looked stunned.

'Just like that? Fine? But you don't even know why I want to go to LA,' I said, confused.

'You said you needed to lay a ghost to rest. That's good enough for me. Go lay your ghost to rest. Anyway, I'm going to Brighton with the girls at the weekend, and the last thing I want to have to do is start earning GPs.'

'Doctors?' said Ian.

'Girl Points,' said Lizzie. 'It's confusing but you'll get used to it.'

'But the Desperados Pact!' I said.

'The deadline stands!' she said. 'November 16th, okay?'

'Okay! And I promise I'll do even more stuff when I get back. I'll paint the spare room, and I'll repot those plants, and I'll move that ladder and mend that socket! I'll redouble my efforts!'

'You see, Ian?' said Lizzie, smiling. 'I've got him redoubling his efforts. I see your list and raise it...'

'GPs!' said Ian, clicking his fingers. '*Girl* Points!'

It was a beautiful sunny evening and I realised how lucky I was. The best relationships are supportive, even of the strangest things. The guilt I'd felt at even starting what I'm sure Hanne would have called a 'stupid boy project' faded as the three of us talked, and I showed them pictures of Tarek, and of Cameron, and spoke about how much I wanted to find Christopher Guirrean. I told them about the letters I'd written Andy Clements, and I told them stories about bellydancers, and the boy who lived at number 3 in Malaysia, and of days gone by. And Ian told me about his schooldays, and the time he fell out of a tree trying to look down a girl's top, and Lizzie joined in too, with stories of schools run by nuns and friends of the past, and as the beer brought its haze and the bright sunshine turned to tree-dappled beams, we sat in the garden, eating chilli and comparing stories in the warming way that thousands of other groups of friends were doing right then, right around the world.

'Jesus!' said Lizzie, looking round the house. 'You did all this?'

'Yup,' I said, proudly.

'All today?'

'Yup,' I said.

'Wow!'

The canopy still looked terrible, mind you. I'd already called Paul to tell him it was now sorted and whatever he had on special order could now be specially cancelled. He'd been in the pub. He'd told me it had been a very stressful few days, what with his daughter being rear-ended by that van, and all. Still, he generously said I could have the money I'd paid him not to build the canopy back, but that he was still determined to complete my guttering. It was his number one priority. And then I remembered something.

'I thought your daughter got *mugged*?'

'Yes,' he'd said. 'Terrible business.'

Ian wandered out of the toilet, shaking his hands dry and then clapping them together.

'Right then!' he said.

The three of us stood in front of the computer.

The email was still there. The cursor was winking at us, like it was in on the joke. I was about to update another address.

'But what *is* a Furry?' asked Lizzie.

'People who dress up as animals and then do all manner of unspeakable things,' said Ian, enthusiastically. 'Is... you know. What I've *heard*.'

I pressed Send.

I was going to LA.

Chapter Fifteen

In which we learn that sometimes secrets should stay secret...

I'm going to tell you a secret – something I have never told *anybody*.

It is this: for the last twenty years I haven't been able to have a bath without thinking of the Mexican guitarist Carlos Santana.

This is *terribly* annoying.

The problem is, somewhere around 1988, I happened to catch Carlos Santana on Radio 1 just as he was saying that the ideal temperature for bath water is the precise temperature which means you never even realise you're actually sliding into the bath. It should be neither too warm for you to notice, nor too cold for it to matter. That, said Carlos Santana proudly, is when you *know* you're in the ideal bath.

I was lying in the ideal bath in my hotel room in LA, late on the night of the 20th.

And I was thinking about Carlos Santana while eating a tiny packet of nuts. I'd taken them along with a couple of tiny cans of beer I'd nicked from the plane journey. I'd felt I had to hide them away, because the man next to me had been reading an article on addiction and had frowned at me every time I'd asked for another tiny Heineken (or tinyken). He'd shot me a look as if I'd belched and then ordered a bottle of Scotch and a straw.

Hey, I wonder if Carlos Santana drinks bottles of Scotch with a straw.

I really had to stop thinking about Carlos Santana.

And so I crushed my empty tinyken and I thought about the plan instead.

*

The plan was unnervingly simple.

Ben Ives would walk into the Garden Bar at 2pm and be looking around the room, trying to find a man who looked like he had something to get off his chest about life as an animal. He'd be wanting to sit down and get the whole thing over with as quickly as possible, but be confused by the fact that, instead, he had seemingly randomly bumped into an old friend he used to work with at Argos. Which is when I would reveal that ManGriff the Beast Warrior had been *me* all along. We'd then spend an hour or however long he could spare chatting and laughing, while he slapped his thighs and shook his head, and said, 'I can't believe you got me! I am a fool and you are a genius!' Maybe he'd cancel work and we'd hang out all afternoon. Maybe he'd show me LA by night.

Whatever we did, we would do it as friends. Friends reunited. It was the perfect plan.

But then… the inevitable paranoia…

It had all gone so well so far – Michael, Anil, Simon, Cameron and Tarek had all welcomed me back into their lives with open arms. But with Ben, there might always be *that thing* between us. Would getting him back lead to an entire life of one-upmanship and revenge? What if he took it badly? Would I have to keep looking over my shoulder for the rest of my life? Would I have to treat every email, letter or random phone call with suspicion, just in case it was him? Or would this bring an end to things? An evening-up? A balance?

I got out of the bath and convinced myself I was being stupid. I was on top of things. I was in charge. Ben had no idea whatsoever that I was ManGriff.

I opened the minibar and took out a tiny bottle of Scotch. It might help me sleep.

But then I couldn't find a straw, so I put it back in again.

In the morning I awoke bright and early and with what seemed like many hours of rest under my belt, and I wandered outside, and into LA.

I was staying near Robertson Boulevard, not a million miles away from Rodeo Drive, and took in the hipster boutiques with a Pretzel

Dog in my hand. A Pretzel Dog was a fairly new experience to me, and one I'm not at all concerned didn't come to me sooner, managing to fuse as it does a pretzel with a hot dog, while also managing to be nowhere near as nice as either a pretzel or a hot dog. I binned it, and looked around. I was outside a shop called Kitson. Through its vast windows I could see trainers, and jackets, and row upon row of vintage T-shirts.

I have a particular fondness for vintage American T-shirts – one I've had since I was a kid. I love the sense of unfamiliar history each shirt seems to have. Once worn to celebrate the achievements of a minor football team in some backwater town, or a Scout jamboree in North Carolina, or a spelling bee in Tennessee, or a mayoral announcement in Idaho, somehow they find their way from little-known towns and cities across the country to shops just like this. Each one meant something to someone at *some* stage of their life, but for whatever reason wound up out of fashion or out of favour, and discarded or donated or handed down, until there was no one left to hand it down to except a complete stranger in an unknown shop.

I don't know why, but I walked in. In front of me were towering piles of T-shirts, stretching the length of the shop. The ones I could see all seemed to have been modified in some way; updated somehow. Suddenly, I couldn't be bothered. There were too many of them. I was hot. The T-shirts smelled musty. I wanted to turn around and walk out, and find a breeze, and something to take away the taste of Pretzel Dog.

But for whatever reason, I persisted.

And this is when something utterly remarkable happened.

Remarkable to *me*, at any rate. I can only hope you feel the same.

Because I chose a pile at *random*.

And I knelt down.

And then I chose a T-shirt at *random*.

And I pulled it halfway out.

And I couldn't quite believe it.

Because I could see the word 'Loughborough'.

I froze, slightly, in disbelief.

Was there a Loughborough in America?

But that was only *half* of what was so remarkable.

I lifted the T-shirts above it and pulled it out the whole way.

And this is what it said...

4th Anniversary
McDonald's
Loughborough
1987 – 1991

And I just stared at it.

And I was stunned.

Absolutely, totally *stunned*.

4th Anniversary? McDonald's? Loughborough? *My* Loughborough? *My McDonald's*? A T-shirt celebrating *my McDonald's*?

A wise man once told me that coincidences do not exist. And in this moment, I couldn't help but think he might be right. I mean... what were the chances? What were the chances that the McDonald's of my childhood – the McDonald's which we'd been so excited about, the McDonald's I'd visited so many times with Mikey and Anil and Simon, the McDonald's which had caused me and Andy Clements to hug so ferociously on hearing of its arrival in our little town... what were the chances of that even *being* on a T-shirt? Much less being on a T-shirt I'm drawn to out of a thousand in a shop I hadn't planned on visiting in a city so far from home?

But, more importantly, there were other questions...

4th Anniversary? Who celebrates a *4th* Anniversary? And who makes *a T-shirt* to celebrate it? Why don't you wait till the *5th*? And who's *keeping* T-shirts celebrating the 4th Anniversaries of regional fast-food outlets? Why did *Loughborough's* McDonald's – out of the 31,000 of them in the world – decide to *make* them? Have you ever seen any *other* McDonald's celebrate four years of burger mayhem? And how in God's name did it get from Loughborough to *here*?

Was this a sign? A sign that what I was doing was... *right*, somehow? Was this just a billion-to-one coincidence... or was it something else?

I looked at the price tag. $58.

To me it seemed priceless.

The cab driver seemed very friendly, but I wasn't looking at him. I was still staring at my T-shirt.

'So why are you over here?' he said. 'Holiday?'

'Kind of,' I said.

4th Anniversary! Why 4th?!

'I'm here to surprise an old friend who thinks I'm an animal.'

'Cool,' said the driver. 'That's cool.'

I'd asked to be taken to the seaside, and we'd set off, driving down the Sunset Strip, with its bars and billboards and clubs. We passed the Chinese Theater, where I saw a man dressed as Spiderman having an argument with a man dressed as Charlie Chaplin, while Freddy Krueger smiled for the cameras and waved at passing children.

It was exciting being in LA. Just five minutes in a cab, and I'd already seen *three* celebrities – two of them fictional and one of them *dead*!

Finally, in the hot and battering sun, I arrived at Venice Beach, with its palm trees and sand and ocean sprawling out in front of me. I put the T-shirt away, got out and took in the view. It was the perfect LA cliché: there were people on rollerskates, a mass of cyclists, kids playing streetball. There were punks, and a Japanese rock band, and artists and psychics plying their trade. A little further down, a lone, pensionable musleman lifted weights far above his head in front of astonished children and a German with a camera. It suddenly dawned on me I'd been seeing these images since I was a kid. This was just a newer generation of the same people I'd watching doing the same things since childhood, on the same beach that had featured on *CHiPs*, or *The A-Team*, or – during those difficult teenage years – on *Baywatch*. I looked up to see a row of joggers approaching, sweat pouring out of them like they were being squeezed from the inside. I've never really understood jogging. And never really understood why anyone would jog in this kind of heat. What were they running from? But this was LA. And just as America would always be New York skyscrapers and hotdogs and steam billowing from manhole covers and shoot-outs in pool halls, it'd also be sun, and palm trees, and Venice Beach. I wondered if Ben Ives had felt the same when he'd first walked on this beach. I wondered how he'd ended up in America. What brought him here? A girl? The job? Or maybe as a kid he'd been just as impressed with the States as I was. Maybe this had been his dream. Maybe this had—

'WHOAREYOU WHATISTHIS?'

Eh?

I didn't quite know what to say. The old woman moved forwards, closer, and shouted it again.

'WHOAREYOU WHATISTHIS?'

And this time, only marginally less startled, I was able to say, '*Wha?*'

'THISISIT HERE!' she said, pointing at the floor, her long purple cloak swishing slightly as she did so.

Sometimes there is nothing more terrifying than a mad old woman in a long purple cloak.

'Is it?' I said, trying to remain polite in the face of some quite confusing information.

'THISISIT HERE!' she said, as if I hadn't understood her, which was fine, because it was true.

'Yup,' I said, attempting to sidle off. I had never sidled before, and didn't even know if I'd know *how* to sidle, but I turned out to be a natural and talented sidler.

'WHATISTHIS?' she shouted after me.

I shrugged and simply pointed at the floor.

'That's it there,' I said, still sidling.

She stared at me, looking very annoyed indeed.

I ditched the sidle and broke into a jog.

An hour later, feeling I'd exhausted all the points of interest to be had at Venice Beach – and mainly because I was a little scared I might bump into that old woman again – I found myself a cab, conveniently parked up on a pavement nearby.

I opened the door and stepped in to find a slightly thuggish-looking man sipping a can of Mountain Dew.

'Yeah, where you like?' he said, and I told him the name of my hotel.

The cab started up and we began to cruise down the street. American cabs have always impressed me. As wide as a train and as smooth as a slide. I was about to ask a very interesting question about the width of the cab to my driver, but noticed he'd just dialled a number on his phone…

'Yeah, I need you to do me a favour,' he said, into the phone, in a heavy Russian accent. 'Huh? I say I need you to do me a *favour*…'

Out of politeness, I pretended I couldn't hear him, but it was quite difficult, really, because he'd started to shout.

'I SAY I NEED YOU TO DO ME A FAVOUR' – he looked at me in the mirror apologetically – 'Yeah… I need you to call Central Casting.'

Central Casting?

'Central Casting, yes! Call Central Casting. Ask them if they need someone like me…'

The person on the other end must've asked what on earth that meant. Was he phoning on the off-chance that they'd need a cab? It seemed a laborious way of doing business.

'I mean, do they need like mafia, criminal, someone like that…'

Eh?

'Yeah… no, you call them, you tell them how I look, you say I am non-union… NON-UNION… tell them I have limo they can use too… Okay… bye.'

He hung up and shook his head.

'Are you an actor?' I asked, but what the subtitle in a film would've read is: 'Please say you're not in the Mafia.'

'I do little acting,' he said. 'I went into Beverly Hills drama course and learn to act emotions. I get diploma. I am in films.'

'Wow,' I said. 'What kind of films?'

'I don't know,' he said. 'I usually play driver. Or bad guy. Mafia, criminal, something like this. Sometimes cab driver, sometimes limo driver. I have limo, and I let film use it, if he can let me drive this. I meet many people who help me.'

'Really?' I said.

'Salma Hayek,' he said. 'She was very good with me. She is a nice lady. Ice T was also very nice man, but tall.'

I made a face which suggested sympathy towards the situation of meeting someone who was nice but tall.

'Worst one I have ever met... Hip-hop legend Rakim.'

'*Hip-hop legend Rakim*?' I repeated, wondering if that was his actual name, or just the way the newspapers described him. 'What was wrong with Hip-hop legend Rakim?'

'Ach,' he said, waving the question away. 'Ach.'

Oleg – for that was the name on his ID – didn't seem to want to discuss Hip-hop legend Rakim any more, which was a pity, because I was quite enjoying saying 'Hip-hop legend Rakim'. I made a mental note to warn Tarek about him next time I saw him. Oleg's phone rang. It was his friend, saying that Central Casting didn't need anyone like him today. Oleg looked annoyed.

'Here, look with this,' said Oleg, fiddling with his phone. We nearly hit the back of a truck while he turned to hand it to me.

'That is photo of me in my acting,' he said, and I looked at it. He looked exactly the same. There was literally no point in showing me this photo. He might as well have just pointed at his face and said, 'This is what my face looks like.'

'Oh,' I said, trying to sound impressed.

'Press for next one.'

I scrolled onto the next photo.

'That is also photo of me in my acting.'

He was wearing exactly the same clothes in this photo, too, except now he had a hat on.

'It's good, yes?'

'Yes,' I said, not really knowing what else to say. 'You look like a very good actor.'

To be honest, he looked like a cab driver with a hat on.

'I'm going to be in a film soon,' he said, and I sat forward to listen attentively, but suddenly and with a jolt he jammed on the brakes and raised his hands and yelled... My hand had slammed onto the back of his seat and I looked up to see a cyclist with a shocked face... he'd been innocently trying to cross the road but had wrongly assumed Oleg had seen him – Oleg had been too busy putting his phone away...

'Hey!' the cyclist had shouted, almost against his will.

'WHAT!' shouted Oleg, getting into character – the character in this case being an extremely angry cabbie. All he was missing was a hat. 'WHAT YOU SAY! WHY YOU HAVE BIKE? NO ONE HAVE BIKE IN THIS CITY!'

Uh-oh! I tried to make apologetic eye contact with the cyclist in my best and finest British way, but he was having none of it. I was just as much to blame for this travesty of traffic-based justice as Oleg. I didn't know what to do. Oleg did. He made a quick and rude gesture with his hand and stepped on the gas.

'Anyway, what I say?' asked Oleg, as we moved forward.

'Oh,' I said, a little shaken, 'you were saying you were going to be in a film, or something...'

'Yeah. B'dmutha.'

'*B'dmutha*?' I said.

'B'dmutha is name of film. About drug dealer. He is name of D'B'dmutha...'

'Oh!' I said, delighted. 'The Bad Mutha!'

'Badmutha, yes!' said Oleg. 'D'B'dmutha!'

'Are you the Bad Mutha in the film?' I asked.

'No,' said Oleg. 'I am the driver.'

The lights ahead turned red.

'*Bad Mutha!*' I said, as we slowed down. 'You know, that's quite a good name for a film. What's the—'

And then, through my window, and out of nowhere...

'*ASSHOLE!* WATCH YOUR DRIVING, MAN!'

It was the cyclist! He was *back*! Wild-eyed and curly-haired! He had a sweaty face, as red and round as a tiny Mars. Where had *he* come from? We'd left him back at the last set of lights!

'AH, GO LOSE YOURSELF!' shouted Oleg, obviously thinking he spoke for both of us, which I supported by maintaining a dignified silence. 'GO LOSE YOURSELF NOW!'

The cyclist was about to come back with something, but the lights were changing and Oleg stepped on it before he had a chance. I turned round and saw with horror that the cyclist hadn't decided to let this one go just yet.

'He's coming!' I shouted, worried. 'Oleg, he's coming after us!'

'Is fine!' said Oleg, his eyes darting between his mirror and the road. 'Is fine.'

'He's *chasing* us!' I said.

Oh my God. He was *chasing* us. This was a *car chase*! A car chase through the streets of LA! How much more textbook could my LA visit be? Spiderman, a mad woman, an actor *and* a car chase!

'We lose him, is fine,' said Oleg, but then, up ahead, I could see the lights changing to red again. We slowed to an embarrassing, painful halt and an agonising five seconds later the cyclist was at the window again.

'LEARN TO DRIVE, GUY!'

'LOSE YOURSELF!' said Oleg, looking straight ahead.

'YOU DRIVE LIKE SHIT!'

'YOU SHIT! YOU SHIT!'

I didn't quite know what to do with myself at this point. Usually in car chases, the drivers don't come face to face every couple of minutes. It can be a little embarrassing, especially if they've not actually got all that much to say to one another.

'FUCK YOU, MAN!'

'YEAH! YEAH! FUCK YOU! YOU LOSE YOURSELF!'

I didn't think I could really carry on the conversation about *Bad Mutha!* with Oleg at this point, given he was now engaged in his own conversation with the cyclist, so was pleased to notice an advert on the seat beside me, for a carpet sale which seemed to have ended the previous week. I suddenly decided it was the most interesting thing I could possibly have found.

Big time, once-only supersaver sale!!

'SHUT UP!'

'YOU SHUT UP! SHUT UP!'

Up to 25% off all carpet and laminate floors!!!

'YOU DRIVE LIKE SHIT, MAN!'

Vinyl floors!!

'HA! YOU LOSE! YOU SHIT!'

Natural stone!!

'YOU'RE A MORON!'

Oh my word, this was *awful*. I ran out of words to read, looked up and noticed something.

'Green light, Oleg! Go! Go!'

'BYE BYE!'

The wheels might have well have spun and plumes of smoke risen from the tyres, such was the speed Oleg managed to gather in just a second or two...

I turned in my seat and looked round, behind us.

'You should've just said you were sorry, Oleg! He's going mad!'

'I do nothing wrong. He is mad. He is very mad.'

'Maybe you should stop telling him he's a shit and so on...'

'He *is* a shit! He is a *terrible* shit!'

I didn't want to agree with Oleg in case somehow the cyclist could lipread or something, but he was getting smaller by the second, despite pedalling furiously...

'We have to lose him!' I said. 'He's still tailing us!'

'We lose him,' said Oleg, calmly. 'This is no problem. He go now.'

'He's still behind us!'

'Where?' said Oleg, his eyes scanning the mirror.

'By that sports shop!'

'*What* sport shop?'

'That one! The Merchant of Tennis! But now he's by the bank! He's *gaining*!'

'Because I have to stop...'

No! We were slowing down! More lights! This was *terrible*!

'YOU THINK YOU CAN JUST DRIVE OFF, MAN?' shouted our ruby-faced and nearly breathless friend.

'YOU THINK YOU CAN BICYCLE FOREVER? THIS IS A BIG CITY!'

'I'LL KEEP COMING, MAN, TILL YOU LEARN HOW TO DRIVE!'

The two men stared at each other, then looked away. I coughed politely in the back seat. There were a few seconds of silence, as both of them tried to think of something clever to say. There was nothing clever to say.

'So,' said Oleg, quietly. 'Why you in LA? Holiday?'

The cyclist was still there, still looking at us.

'I'm here to surprise an old friend who thinks I'm an animal,' I said.

'Oh,' said Oleg.

He didn't seem to think this was quite as cool as the last driver had.

The lights changed. We shot off again.

'Oleg, we have to turn off or something. He'll follow me all the way back to London if we don't.'

'We not turn off. I take you to hotel.'

'But we're taking *him* to my hotel as well!'

'We soon be fine. We soon be fine. We soon be fine.'

He'd started to say this under his breath, as if he was trying to convince himself as much as me.

The next set of lights were green, and we almost had to stop ourselves from cheering, united in our small victory over our cycle-stalker... but up ahead, cars were slowing right down...

'NO!' shouted Oleg. 'IT'S A BUSTY TOUR!'

I blinked a few times, confused.

I looked around. I could see no busty tour. Surely I would have *noticed* a busty tour. What the hell *was* a busty tour, anyway?

'A busty tour?' I said.

'Yeah,' said Oleg. 'They detour some bus.'

We slowed, annoyed and anxious, to a halt. A small fat boy looked at us from the window of one of the buses. We simply looked back at him, preparing for the inevitable.

It took the cyclist a little longer this time, but when he finally made it, he seemed a little more subdued. His hair was lank with sweat and he tried to catch his breath.

'I'll... just keep... coming, man...'

Oleg looked worried. I decided to take action.

'Um... excuse me,' I said.

'This is nothing to do with you, guy...' said the cyclist, putting up his hand and waving it a bit.

'But it is! You're chasing us, and that means you're chasing me home! Back to my hotel. And I'd rather you didn't, if that's all right by you.'

'This is nothing to do with you,' he said, pushing a pair of little round glasses up his nose. Up the *outside* of his nose, I mean, not the *inside*. He wasn't a *magician*. 'I suggest you step out of the cab if this is a problem for you and let me and this guy deal with this...'

'You can't just hijack my cab!' I said. 'And are you even going this way? You're going to be very late for whatever it is you're doing today. Just think about that for a moment!'

The cyclist just shrugged.

'I'm sure Oleg is sorry,' I said. 'He didn't mean to nearly hit you.'

Oleg said nothing. The cyclist looked at him, annoyed.

'Oleg, you didn't mean to nearly hit him, did you?' I said.

Oleg looked up. The lights were changing.

'Okay,' he said. 'I am sorry.'

I looked at the cyclist and smiled. Oleg started to move the car forward.

'I AM SORRY YOU'RE MORON!'

And then he stepped on the gas.

I looked behind me, horrified.

My heart sank as I saw the cyclist slowly and begrudgingly start up after us.

We managed to lose the cyclist thanks to a run of good luck and green lights. Oleg had clearly decided that we had bonded over this small adventure, and given me his card. I should give him a call when I needed to go back to the airport, he said. He'd bring his limo out for me. I said I'd look out for *Bad Mutha!*. In reality, I would never, ever do either.

As I walked back into the hotel I found myself jogging slightly, just in case the cyclist had somehow found a short cut. I now understood why people in LA like jogging.

I made my way to the Business Center in the hotel lobby. It's always made me feel quite important, using a hotel's Business Centre. Like I had Business to attend to, and nothing short of a Centre would help me do it. Sometimes I would ask a member of staff to direct me to the Business Centre, and then I would sit there and pretend I was Businessing, when in fact I was just checking my email and typing 'Funny Cats' into YouTube.

I logged in and checked my emails. First, my ManGriff the Beast Warrior account. There was nothing from Ben Ives – no cancellation, no query, no nothing. We were still on.

But... *were* we? I had to make sure. This was like planning a bank robbery. I needed to be meticulous.

Ben,
I landed in LA late last night in preparation for our meeting.
I'll see you at the bar at 2pm.

I looked down to check what I was wearing.

I'll be wearing a white shirt and reading a copy of LA Weekly.
See you then
M

And then I checked my normal emails. There was one from Peter Gibson!

Danny!
Hello mate. Are we still meeting up this weekend? I'm leaving work soon so let me know!
Peter

Bollocks. I'd forgotten to cancel Peter. But no worries. As soon as I was home, I'd hotfoot it round to Tooting to say hello, update his address in my book and notch up friend number 7. Besides, he'd understand – I had important business to attend to in an important Business Center in LA. *And* I'd just been in a car chase. Surely that topped every excuse ever. I tapped out my reply and promised to buy the first round as soon as I was home.

Things were working out nicely. But I was disappointed to see that there was still nothing from Akira in Japan. His dad had seemed to think that Akira would *love* to hear from me, and I'd written an excited and upbeat reintroduction, but so far: nothing. Maybe I'd written to the wrong address? I found his dad's email, and wrote another message.

Hello Isamu

It's Daniel Wallace here again. I wrote to Akira but have not heard back yet. I know he must be very busy indeed, but maybe I had the wrong email address for him?

Sorry to bother you with this,

Daniel

So. Nothing from Akira. And nothing, either, from Chris Guirrean. *Any* Chris Guirrean.

Before I'd left, I'd printed out a list of all the Chris Guirreans I could find in the UK. There were more than a dozen, spread around the UK from Colchester to Cardiff to Glasgow. I'd figured the Glaswegian Chris Guirrean would be the likeliest – he was closest to Dundee and our childhood home. But people could be anywhere. Literally *anywhere*. I'd written a standard letter, explaining who I was and what I was up to, and how vitally important it had become for me to meet my first-ever best friend again… and I'd not had a single reply from a single Chris Guirrean as yet. Oh well. There was time. It was still the beginning of September, and I wouldn't be thirty for a couple of months yet.

I logged back in as ManGriff the Beast Warrior and found a reply from Ben.

Sure.

I smiled, but then frowned.

What kind of 'sure' was that? Was it a *sure* sure, or was it a *sarcastic* sure? And if it was a *sarcastic* sure, was it sarcastic because he wasn't coming, or sarcastic because he knew this was a set-up? Or perhaps he thought that *I* wasn't coming? My levels of paranoia were reaching Woody Allen proportions.

There was only way to make certain.

I looked at my watch. It was 12.30pm. I would be meeting Ben in an hour and a half.

I decided to set off early.

*

'So, why are you in LA?' said the driver.

'Just keep your eyes on the road!' I said, pointing wildly in front of me. 'There might be a cyclist!'

'A *cyclist*? It's like four hundred degrees out there...'

'That just makes them angrier,' I said. 'They follow us!'

'So is this a holiday?' he said, implying, I think, that I might need one.

'I'm here to surprise an old friend who thinks I'm an animal,' I said.

And he stayed quite quiet after that.

We rode silently past the Chinese Theater again. Spiderman no longer seemed to be arguing with Charlie Chaplin. Marilyn Monroe was having her picture taken with a strange little man.

The cab driver put the radio on and for a few minutes we listened to Ryan Seacrest talking about Britney Spears, before all thoughts turned to Ben Ives. What would his reaction be? Would we get on? Would he find my little wind-up funny? Would it be worth the trip to LA? Worth the distance, worth the time? I hoped so. I leaned my head against the window and was about to drift off, when suddenly...

'Hang on – what was *that*?' I said, quickly craning round to see if the something I thought I'd seen was the thing I hoped it was...

'What?' said the driver.

'*That* – that shop back there...'

I had seen it for just a second. But a second was enough. In the window of a bright and colourful shop was something I now wanted more than anything. Something I knew I had to have. Something that would help me. Something *excellent*.

'Stop the cab...' I said.

I was sitting in a corner booth of the bar, hidden away from prying eyes, wearing a white shirt and carrying a copy of *LA Weekly*. I had a Budweiser in front of me, a great view of the doorway, and, crucially, a giant white rabbit head on my lap.

Yes. A giant white rabbit head on my lap.

It was brilliant.

It was huge, and furry, and had round friendly eyes and a big chuckling mouth. The lady at the costume shop who'd sold it to me told me that if I bought it, she'd also throw in a big plastic carrot for free – and that had really swung it. This was meant to be.

I wasn't wearing it yet, though. That would be insane. No. I was waiting. Waiting for Ben Ives. Waiting for him to walk through the door, before I'd pull it over my head and sit there, for the first time actually feeling like ManGriff the Beast Warrior, who today had chosen the stylings of a massive rabbit to fully embrace his Furry tendencies.

I giggled, and then sipped at my drink and looked nervously through the window. It was five to two, and there was no sign of him. The bar around me was reasonably empty and unnaturally dark. A couple by the window were chatting, and a middle-aged man was reading the paper and snorting to himself. I tried to read my copy of *LA Weekly*, but I couldn't concentrate, partly through excitement and partly through worry that people might think it was odd that I was balancing a giant white rabbit's head on my knees. But I needed it to hand – and it was perfect. It was another level to the joke; another layer Ben would have to bash through. I'd giggled when I'd walked out of the costume shop with it. I knew exactly what would happen. Ben would walk in and see a huge rabbit sitting in the corner, in a white shirt, reading *LA Weekly*. He'd realise with a sickening turn in his stomach that ManGriff was real, that ManGriff was a *proper* Furry, and that he'd have to spend an entire meeting placating a man in a giant rabbit head.

And that, friends, would be the moment I tore the mask off, and shouted, 'I NEVER HAD GENITAL EXFOLIATION! IT'S ME! DAVE CASEY! VERNON BODFISH! IT'S *DANNY WALLACE*! I TRICKED YOU! THAT WAS MY FRIEND IAN ALL DRESSED UP AS A BEAR! I WIN!!!!'

And then his eyes would register the truth, the fact that I'd got him back, the fact that after fifteen years, sweet revenge was mine. It was what the plan had been missing all along – the big reveal!

And that's what I was thinking about as a lone figure approached the doorway of the bar. I immediately pulled on the rabbit head, as subtly as I could under the circumstances. I raised my copy of *LA*

Weekly and sat, still and quiet, trying to make out from the corner of my eye whether the man who'd just walked in was, in fact, Ben Ives.

It wasn't.

Or, at least, I hoped it wasn't. Because the man had turned round and walked away again.

No! Had that been Ben Ives? Had he walked in expecting a chat with a man – a strange man, but a man nevertheless – and not with a rabbit? Had I pushed it too far? Should I take the mask off? Run after him? Explain?

But instantly, I knew it hadn't been Ben Ives. Because at that moment, another man walked in. And I could tell, almost just from his stature, and the way he walked, and the fact that he had just nervously glanced around the bar and spotted me – that this man was Ben Ives.

I stared straight ahead of me. Then pulled up my paper a little too quickly and pretended to read.

A moment later I heard the soft shuffle of damp and nervous feet. This was it!

A polite cough from somewhere next to me, and then, quietly, a man's voice...

'Uh... hi?'

I put my paper down, and looked at him.

For a split second, we were just a man and a giant rabbit, staring at each other in a bar, just as thousands of other men and giant rabbits were doing at that precise moment, all over the world. Through the mesh of my rabbit eyes, I could see it was unmistakeably Ben. Older. Bigger. But Ben. I paused as I took him in – not a big pause, a tiny pause, a paus*ette* – but it was enough for Ben to lose confidence, and become slightly embarrassed and unsure of himself, like maybe he'd got the details wrong and he was in the wrong bar with the wrong rabbit...

It was just a flinch of embarrassment, a scrap of a moment brushed across his eyes, but it was enough – enough to remind me of *my* embarrassment at *his* hands – enough to remind me *I had never got him back* – enough to remind me that *this* was why I was here...

He was still standing there, still looking at me, looking less certain by the microsecond. The hushed word 'hi?' hung tight in the air... I should have put him at his ease. I'd *wanted* to put him at his ease. To stand up, and rip my mask off, and shake his hand, and take my revenge by laughing in his face and saying, 'YES! I AM MANGRIFF THE BEAST WARRIOR!'

But I didn't.

I didn't do that.

I just looked at him. Something was forming in my head. An *idea*.

He cleared his throat.

'Um... I'm Ben... are you "ManGriff"?' he asked.

His eyes tried to find my own, somewhere behind the mask. He looked like a little boy – younger, even, than when I'd known him – and I crossed my legs and looked him full in the face.

'Am I ManGriff?' I said.

'Yes,' he said, nodding.

I shook my massive head.

'Nope,' I said, and went back to reading my paper.

In some ways, of course, I wish I could have left it at that. That would have been a *real* prank. A *better* prank. To have forced Ben to go to a bar to meet a man who enjoyed dressing up as animals, and then make him think he'd ended up apparently meeting the *wrong* man who enjoyed dressing up as animals. Part of me wanted to let him walk out the door, and return to his colleagues with his face a picture of confusion and embarrassment... but I couldn't. He was there. He was right *there* in front of me.

A moment has passed since I'd said 'nope'. All Ben had managed in reply was an 'oh'. And then, when it looked like he was about to turn around and walk away, I let out a small laugh, and I tore off my rabbit head, and I looked at him and I said, 'All right?'

And he looked at me, and he blinked a couple of times, and then a mixture of relief and happiness and annoyance flushed his face and buckled his knees, and he gave me a hug and he called me a wanker.

Chapter Sixteen

In which we learn that not everything
can go your way, all the time...

The homecoming was *superb*. Lizzie and Ian met me at the pub and I talked them through the whole thing.

'I think that's brilliant,' said Ian. 'You taught him a valuable lesson there.'

'It's a bit of a *strange* lesson,' said Lizzie.

'It's the type of lesson money can't buy,' said Ian. 'If you accuse someone of having had genital exfoliation, you should be prepared for them to turn up at a bar fifteen years later dressed as a rabbit.'

'Exactly!' I said. 'Exactly!'

'How do you spell "genital exfoliation"?' asked Lizzie.

'Shut up! I am an *excellent* speller!' I said. 'But check this out!'

I unravelled the T-shirt I'd brought out with me.

Ian and Lizzie stared at it.

'It's a T-shirt celebrating four years of McDonald's in Loughborough,' said Ian, flatly.

'Yup!' I said.

I don't think I need tell you how proud I was. But they didn't really say much after that. Sometimes they don't understand me like you do.

'So anyway,' said Ian, 'how many's that you've met?'

I counted them up.

'With Peter Gibson, who I'll meet next week, that's seven in the bag. Plus, I'm in touch with Akira's family, I've written to every Chris Guirrean in the land, and I'm hoping my letters to Andy are being forwarded on to him, wherever he now lives.'

'Yeah...' said Lizzie. 'Ah.'

'*Ah*?' I said.

Back at home, there they all were.

Bundled together with a red rubber band. My letters to Andy. Each of them returned, seemingly on the same day. Each of them with '*Not known at this address*' written on the front in dark blue biro.

I sighed.

This was a real setback. Just when I thought I was making such progress, with all the pieces starting to fall into place, I'd taken a large step back.

I'd just kind of assumed that with Loughborough being quite a small town, if Andy was still there, whoever was now living at his house would have forwarded it on. Or at least known where he was. Given me a clue; a tip-off; *anything*.

But no. They'd simply sent them all back.

I was back at square one with him. He didn't know I was looking for him. Didn't know I'd been replying to his letters. Didn't know the friendship was still there, if only he'd let me find him.

And the disappointing news didn't stop there.

I'd made myself a cup of tea and logged on. I was momentarily distracted by a bird apparently trying to fight itself in a tree outside, and when I turned back to the screen, I saw it. An email.

An email from Tom.

Tom, who I'd played football with. Tom, who I'd swapped Action Men with. Tom, who reckoned his dad had invented the Sprite logo, and who I'd emailed in a fit of excitement, proposing a meeting and demanding an audience.

It was a short email, but it wasn't sweet.

Hullo. Meeting up would be a bit weird! No thanks mate. Hope your well. Tom.

I stared at it.

In a sense it was quite friendly. He said hello. He called me mate. He said he hoped I was well.

But he was still saying No.

No matter how I read it, no matter how many ways I tried to make it sound better, he was *still* saying *No*!

The *bastard*!

But... why?

Had I been too forward? Did he always secretly hate me? I remembered lending him 20p so he could buy some Garbage Pail Kid stickers! I gave him my Koosh ball and we'd talked excitedly about the Chunnel, which no one *ever* calls the Chunnel any more! For his eleventh birthday, I'd bought him a bumbag! Bumbags don't grow on trees, you know! They grow in expensive Chinese sweatshops!

I couldn't work out what I'd done wrong. I went back and checked the email I'd sent him. It seemed *fine*. I wasn't being over-bearing, or overly keen, or a mad-eyed stalkerish freak... I was just saying it'd be great to see him! That I'd been revisiting my child-hood! That I wanted to update my address book! That we should meet up, hang out, finally get together! That I'd love to see him! I even said I hoped I wasn't coming on too strong!

Ah.

Finally get together.

Love to see him.

Coming on too strong.

I suddenly realised that, perhaps, in the cold light of day, and for a man not sharing my mood at the time, this may well have come across as a missive from someone attempting to realise their child-hood crush. And I did *not* have a childhood crush on Tom. If anything, I thought he had a strange walk and weird ears.

But what if he'd read my first-ever Friends Reunited entry? The one I'd been banned for? The one that said I'd been obsessed with the reader since school and was now standing behind them?

No. I was being paranoid. And anyway, so what if he did think that? I'm a metrosexual. I have a tub of moisturiser I got for Christmas in 2005. I always make sure my socks basically match.

What if, though, that was stopping him? What if he thought I was... *after* him?

I fired off an email, and tried to sound as casual as I could.

Hi again. Just to let you know, I'm not a gay man who's trying to come on to you. Not that that would be a bad thing if one did. You might be gay too. Anyway, I understand if you don't want to meet. Nice to hear from you.

I pressed Send.

I was disappointed at the brutally short email I'd had back from him. But annoyingly, most of me *did* understand why Tom didn't want to meet up. Maybe this *was* a bit weird for some people. Maybe I couldn't expect everyone to react in the same way. But part of me *couldn't* understand. The part of me that had so enjoyed meeting up again with rappers, and chiefs, and witches. I wanted to know what Tom was up to. I wanted to hang out, and remember times gone by. I wanted to be his *friend* again.

But Tom hadn't been on the same journey as me. He was probably very happy as he was. He probably had too *many* friends, and a hugely fulfilling job, and an ever-growing family. The *last* thing he needed was another drain on his time. Some bloke he used to know turning up and wasting his day.

But oh well. Maybe he'd write back, and say, 'Oh dear, I do apologise, I just thought it might get awkward if indeed you did have a crush on me, let's meet up!'

I'd just have to wait and see. I reread the email I'd just sent to make sure it was all as calm and understanding as I was beginning to feel again, and it certainly seemed to be... until my eyes stopped on a certain word.

Too.

Too?

I'd written 'you might be gay *too*'.

What I'd been trying to do was imply my indifference to sexuality – the fact that he might very well be gay, and that this would be as normal as the world can be... but somehow I'd managed to suggest that while I would initially *deny* my gayness, I would suddenly imply quite forcefully that I *was*...

I wanted to write to him again. I wanted to write, 'When I said you might be gay too, I meant as well as the fictional gay man coming on to you in the scenario which I outlined in my email, not as well as *me* – not that there would be anything wrong with that – but I am not and probably neither are you – but if you are then well done, that's great!'

And then I realised that might well make things worse.

How confused would Tom think I was? And what could I do now?

I decided the best thing I could do was wait.

He probably didn't think I was gay, anyway.

'Of *course* he thought you were gay!' said Hanne, with her latte in her hand. We were in the café near the radio station she works at. 'You said you wanted to finally get together with him! You asked if you were coming on too strong! I'm surprised more people haven't said they can't meet up with you.'

I thought about Akira. What had I written to him? Had I come on too strong there, too? Why hadn't *he* replied?

'Anyway,' continued Hanne, 'why do you have to *meet* them? If you'd just gone on Facebook, you could have done things more slowly, built something up first…'

'Why do you suddenly love Facebook so much? You're *obsessed*!'

'I have told you, it is a handy business tool!' she said.

'Yeah, right, you Facebook… face.'

As insults go, it wasn't brilliant.

'And anyway, that takes all the effort out.'

'And why is that a *bad* thing?' said Hanne, and I had to admit, she had a point. 'You wouldn't have had to go all the way to LA just to dress as a badger if you'd done things on Facebook.'

'A rabbit. And I'm just saying, there's something really special about rekindling the old flame of friendship. About looking into the eyes of an old friend. About…'

'You see?' she said, pointing her finger in the air. 'This is why Tom thought you were gay!'

'But what I'm doing is so much better than Facebook! I'm meeting face to face! I've invented Face-to-Facebook! And anyway, these are *real* friends! How many Facebook friends do you have?'

'About 142.'

'*142*? I bet you don't even know their names!'

'They are mainly business associates. Everyone in radio is on Facebook. And I'm not meeting these people. I'm... networking. You're *meeting* them!'

'I'm only after *twelve*! Plus, you told me you didn't understand this whole thing about the past – you said life was about moving forward, not looking back! Anyway, what do you mean, "mainly" business associates?'

'Well... I found someone on Facebook who was friends with someone I hadn't seen in years.'

'Aha! I *knew* it!'

'And we kind of got back in touch. And it was cool.'

'*You're* doing it too!'

'But I didn't set out to do it. It was just tapping into a network. Friends of friends. It seemed silly not to say hi.'

'You see? It seems silly *not* to!'

'But I'm not going to travel back to Norway just to see them! And then dress up as a...'

'As a rabbit.'

'As a rabbit, yes.'

'Well, *maybe you should*!' I said, although, on reflection, I am not entirely sure why.

On the way home, my BlackBerry went off. I had an email.

To: Danny Wallace
From: Ben Ives
Subject: GIT!!!!!!

Okay, so you got me and we're even. What annoys me most is I go back and look through my emails and I notice that one of the other recipients seemed to be called 'Fishbod' at Casey.com... right near someone whose address was Jennyt@lexfoliation.com...

You GIT! I'll be in the UK by Christmas, so how about we

meet up again? And if we do, leave the bloody rabbit head at home.

Ben
X

P.S. Forgot to ask: who the hell was the bear?

Ha! Here it was! The written confirmation of my revenge! And all taken in such good spirit! *That* was friendship. You see, Hanne? With just a few lines of friendly text, Ben had let me know that ours was a friendship which had been rightly reinvigorated. And all thanks to a bit of effort – a friend being worth a flight. Would that have happened on Facebook? No. I felt my actions were rejustified.

Although I did nevertheless make a mental note to keep my eyes peeled for any *revenge* revenge attacks in 2022.

But immediately I knew – I *would* meet up with Ben at Christmas. I'd travel to Bath, maybe on Boxing Day, or the day after. Because somehow, lately, this had become something *more* to me. I looked over at the sofa, and at the *McDonald's Loughborough* T-shirt that lay across it. I smiled. This wasn't just ticking names off a list. It wasn't just updating my address book. This was... *important*, somehow. I *cared* about this. These were my *friends*. This was my *history*.

My phone went off. It was Paul the builder.

'Hello, mate, just to say, I'm not going to be able to make it round today.'

'Fine,' I said.

'My van's broken down, see.'

'Fine.'

'I'll be in touch about another date.'

'Fine,' I said, and I hung up. I didn't care. I didn't care a *jot*.

There was still so much more to do.

I quickened my pace.

If *Tom* wouldn't meet with me, I had to make sure that the *others* did...

*

What was it Hanne had said about networking? It had given me an idea.

I only had three people left to actually locate. Chris. Lauren. And Andy. Maybe if I couldn't find these people *individually*, I could find them through people *they knew*. I could follow the human footprints until they led me to the foot I needed. And once I'd found the foot, I could look a bit higher up, and say hello to the face.

I got home and typed a name into Facebook.

Lauren Medcalfe.

Two people came up. Neither of them her.

Who did she know? She'd been a pen pal of mine. We moved in different circles. Knew different people. *Who did she know?*

We all have our own networks of friends. Each one of them is entirely unique to us. But there are crossovers – there *must* be crossovers.

I thought back. Who did Lauren used to talk about in her letters? Was there *anyone* we both knew?

I picked up my phone.

'Mum! It's me!'

'Who?'

'Let's not go through all that again – listen, do you remember when I was a kid, I had a penpal?'

'Yes! Natalia! The French girl! She liked pop music.'

'No! Not her – another one. Lauren?'

'Yes, of course. She was the daughter of a friend of Lorraine's.'

'Who was Lorraine?'

'A friend of Martha.'

'Are you still in touch with Martha?'

'Well, we send Christmas cards, and so on...'

'Can you ask Martha to ask Lorraine to ask her friend to give her daughter my number? Or my email?'

'Well... yes, of course... but why?'

'I'm updating my address book. I want to send her a Christmas card.'

'Oh, how *lovely*!'

'Thanks, Mum.'

'Bye, picklebear.'

Well, that was something. And I knew I could entrust this important mission to my mum. She throws nothing out. If she did, you wouldn't be reading this book.

Fired up, I thought about Andy.

Where would he be? How could I get to him?

I hit Facebook again.

Plenty of Andy Clements came up, most of them students in America. But only a handful of Brits, all of them either too young, a different colour or the wrong sex. So who else was there? Who had he hung out with? We'd been at different schools, spent our days with different people, but there'd always been a crossover *somewhere*... the days we'd spent kicking a football around on the patch of grass outside A. MISTRY's newsagents... the long afternoons at the park near the school, trying to catch sticklebacks but only ever coming home with tadpoles... the nights we'd spent at the annual fair, when for one week only the high street would be full of waltzers, and dodgems, and helterskelters and more... we'd buy toffee apples and candyfloss and throw inadequate balls at nailed-down coconuts...

All those days, and afternoons, and nights – they had *all* involved *other people*.

And then a name came to me.

Louisa.

Louisa had always been around. Andy had lived next door to her for a while, and their two families had spent a week in Blackpool together... Andy's friend, whose name I couldn't remember, had briefly gone out with Louisa's sister, and I'd always assumed that maybe Andy and Louisa would end up together, too...

Louisa was the *key* to finding Andy. Hey – maybe they'd be *married*!

But how would I find her? Would *she* be on Facebook? And what the hell was her last name? Maybe it was now the same as Andy's!

I suddenly really wanted Andy to be the next friend I met. Peter Gibson would just have to wait. I already had him, in a sense. He was fine. He was there. He'd agreed to meet. But the gauntlet had been thrown down the very moment Andy's letters had made their way back to my house...

I typed 'Louisa' into Facebook. It was a long shot, to be honest. *Too* long. I tried putting in keywords, like Loughborough, and 1989, and anything else I could think of that could *possibly*, on the *off-chance*, have *conceivably* been mentioned.

But wait – hadn't Louisa's dad run some kind of shop on the high street? A newsagent's, maybe? And wasn't it called something like... Robinsons? Wasn't that what we'd called it? Robinsons?

I scooted straight to Google and tapped it in... nothing. They must've shut up shop. Or perhaps local newsagents just don't see the need to be found on the internet. But now I had her last name...

Louisa *Robinson*.

I went back to Facebook, and tried it...

Fewer results this time... that was good...

I waded in... one of them looked faintly familiar... it wouldn't let me check her page unless we became friends, and I didn't have time for that... but it *did* say she lived in Brighton...

I typed Louisa AND Robinson AND Brighton into Google, and, in among the various names and places and people that came up... there was Louisa Robinson AND a job title AND a phone number...

I high-fived myself. Which made me look a little odd.

This could be it! *Why* hadn't I thought of this before?

I dialled the number and looked at my watch. It was 3pm. Louisa Robinson should really be at work now, and if she wasn't, I'd ask to speak to her boss and have her reprimanded.

It was ringing.

I held my breath and told myself not to worry. I was just an old friend of a friend, phoning to see if she could tell me where Andy was. Andy, who'd written to me so faithfully when I'd moved away. Andy, who I'd had such fun with. Andy, who...

'Hello?'

'Oh. Hi. Is that Louisa?'

'Speaking.'

'Louisa – listen, you probably won't remember me. I'm a friend of Andy Clements. Or I used to be.'

There was a silence on the other end, which I did my best to fill.

'My name's Danny Wallace. Well, Daniel Wallace. I used to live in Loughborough. Does the name ring any bells for you?'

A pause. And then...

'Daniel... yes... how are you?'

She sounded a little shocked that I'd phoned. I figured that was more than okay – I was asking her to think back quite a few years.

'I'm fine, I'm fine – and you?'

'Yes. I'm okay. Thank you. So why have you...'

'I'm basically ringing to ask a favour,' I said, picking up my treasured McDonald's T-shirt and stretching it out in front of me. 'Now I realise that's a bit of a big ask seeing as we haven't seen each other in so long, but I'm just wondering... after I left Loughborough, did you keep in touch with Andy?'

'Of course, yes,' she said. 'He was my neighbour...'

'Yeah, fair enough, that was a stupid question. Well, thing is, I'm kind of updating my address book, and I was hoping you might be able to put me back in touch with Andy?'

A silence.

'I promise I'm not a stalker,' I said. 'It's just I've been getting back in touch with people lately, and I'd really like to see how Andy's doing.'

Another silence, long enough for me to start to fold the T-shirt, but then broken by the words...

'Daniel... I'm not sure how to tell you this... but Andy passed away.'

And I sat down.

And I nearly dropped my phone.

Chapter Seventeen

In which we learn how to stop...

An unknown number of days had passed.

I'd done nothing. Seen no one. Been nowhere.

That's not to say I hadn't been busy. I'd kept myself *very* busy.

Work-wise, it was time to get on with things. I phoned my agent and told her I was ready to do stuff; that my summer holiday was finally over. She arranged some meetings.

At home, I'd painted three rooms, spending hours on my knees making sure the skirting boards were immaculate. I'd emptied the last of the boxes. Arranged all my books first in alphabetical order, then in order of theme, then back to alphabetical. I'd done the same with my DVDs, although not by theme, by sleeve colour. I'd sorted out the garden table at last, spending a long and arduous afternoon with some varnish remover and a scraper, and an early evening with a brush and a tin of matt black paint. I'd resecured the rickety canopy, wondering why on earth I'd ever deemed a canopy necessary, and I'd hung pictures, fixed blinds and taken down old and worn curtains. I'd done it all in near-silence.

Paul the builder had been supposed to come round to fix the guttering. Again. But he'd phoned half an hour before he was due to say that his van had broken down. Again. I'd suggested a cab, or the bus, but he said he really had to stay with his van.

'It's got my equipment in, see...'

'It's not got your bloody ladder, though, has it?' I said.

'Eh?'

'*I've* got your ladder. It's been here bloody *months*. But you haven't.'

'There have been complications, yes,' he said. 'But the screws have come in, now, and I can…'

'You're sacked, Paul. Come and get your bloody ladder.'

'What?' he said.

'Come round and get your bloody ladder. The ladder is clearly in on this. It's a conspiracy. It's the only one that knows about our appointments. Appointments you can never make, because your van breaks down, or your daughter gets mugged, or you can't find the "correct" screws even though you are a BUILDER and they are NORMAL SCREWS.'

Paul laughed, uneasily.

'Plus, I've done the canopy myself. And you know what? There was absolutely no reason to have a canopy. But I did it. Not you. Because I *can*.'

'I could probably be there about five thirty…' said Paul.

'I can't make that,' I said. 'My foot has fallen off and I've got all of Belgium coming round. I'll leave the ladder out the front.'

'Hang on…' said Paul.

'Nope. Sacked. Bye.'

And for the first time, I truly felt like a grown-up.

Lizzie's time on the big reality show had come to an end, and we'd half-heartedly celebrated with a night in a restaurant, but I'd been distracted and distant. She started a new job two days later, one that meant she'd be getting home earlier from now on, but I hardly noticed, busy as I was making myself busy.

Andrew James Clements had died in a car crash when he was just eighteen years old. And I really didn't know how to take it.

Eighteen.

Every single second that I'd been alive since I was eighteen was a second that Andy never had. And the more I thought about this, the less I knew how to react. For the past few months I'd been naively undertaking this small and personal quest. Travelling about, and knocking on doors, and turning up out of the blue. It had been a simple and happy way to spend my days. But now, I understood, it had also been *dangerous*. Blindly walking into other people's lives is a *stupid* thing to do. Because sooner or later, you're going to find out something you didn't want to know. That you *should* have known, but which you were better off not knowing. That sounds selfish, and stupid. But maybe I *was* selfish and stupid. Maybe I *deserved* this. Maybe this had been about mortality all along. Knowing that I was closer to my threescore and ten than I ever had been before. Knowing that tomorrow I'd be even closer than I was today. But *my* 'mortality' issues had been trivial and childish. I was turning thirty. So what? So bloody *what*? Now, mortality had shown me just how serious it can be. The fact that in real life, bad things happen. The fact that you have to be prepared that sometimes life is unfair. Unjust. Horrible.

Andy had been a good friend, and a good human being. Someone who was loyal, and upbeat, and funny. You think if you're not in touch with someone, everything is probably okay with them. Life just ticks along. They do the same things as you. They grow up. They meet a girl. Maybe they get married. They progress in their work. Perhaps they get into IT, or move abroad, or have a kid. Maybe they get rich, maybe they stay poor. But you never, ever think, that maybe they're dead. Because actually, the cold, hard truth is that you don't know *what* can happen to them. To you. To *anyone*. And actually, the cold, hard truth is that bad things *can* happen to good people. And if you rush in, unprepared, this is a horrible truth that becomes all the more horrible when it's so very unexpected.

And so I'd stopped looking for old friends. I'd met Cameron, and Anil, and Mikey, and Simon, and Tarek, and Ben. I'd nearly met Peter. I hadn't found Chris. I'd been rejected by Tom. And Akira had never found the time to write back. So what was the point in continuing? What had been the point all along? To make me feel better? To make me feel that everyone was going through the same things? To make me feel I was part of something – a random group of people about to start their thirties? Because Tom had made me realise that just because we went to school with people, ultimately, what does that mean? That means *nothing*. Yeah, we share a classroom. We learn about the water cycle and crop rotation and oxbow lakes and we learn about these things at about the same time. *And*?

There was no mystical reason for this, no destiny guiding us together. We had nothing in common, apart from the fact that we just *happened* to live in the same school catchment area, as decided by some faceless bloke in a cheap two-piece suit on the town council dozens of years before. Apart from the fact our parents just *happened* to have conceived around the same time, *happened* to take us with them, *happened* to have had us at all. And that was it. These were the two facts. Two facts which mean absolutely nothing in the world. Why *should* we get on, stay in touch, be friends? If any of this actually meant even a scrap of a hint of anything, then surely Tom, for one, would have felt the same way?

Tom had it right. I hadn't seen it at the time, but Tom had it right.

Yeah. So I'd had some fun. But fun isn't what life is about. Life is about growing up. Getting through. That's what you do. And that's what I'd been avoiding. So that's what I should now do.

Lizzie had been concerned for me. I'm not saying I was walking around with a dark and brooding face all the time. I wasn't. I'd accepted Andy was gone pretty quickly. But as one week turned into two, and two weeks threatened to become three, it was clear that something was missing. A little bit of joy cancelled out. A friendship finished, first and foremost. One that could've continued, and could've been great, but one that I'd ignored or lost sight of, and which I'd now never have again.

'Are you okay, baby?' she'd said, one night, as I'd pretended to watch *Life On Mars*.

'Yeah! Course. Yeah.'

'You're sure?'

'Sure I'm sure,' I'd smiled. But I was looking through her.

'How many left to track down?' she'd asked.

'Oh. You know. Not many. Though I think I'm kind of okay at the moment for all that stuff.'

'Really?'

'Yeah. I think I'm done for a while.'

And then I'd turned the volume up, and pretended I was watching some more.

I'd just wanted everyone to be okay. But at the time, that had meant happy, and healthy, and enjoying life. I'd never for a moment considered that for one of them life could have ended.

And so I'd cracked on with the house. This time for me. And for Lizzie. Not for childish Man Points. Not to buy me time. But just to do it. I was, after all, a man. Not a boy.

The earthquake, the one that had started its rumble that night in a friend's back garden – the one I'd been doing my best to put off or avoid or run away from – had finally, forcefully, hit home.

And as evening crept up, I didn't check my email. I turned my phone off. I watched some telly, and then, slowly, I went downstairs to bed.

And I lay there for an hour or so, staring at a dark and feature-less ceiling.

To: Danny Wallace
From: Peter Gibson
Subject: Hello!

Hey Dan – Just thought I'd remind you we STILL haven't met up!
Will have to be soon as I'm finishing work and moving on... would
be good to tell you all about it before I go. Am having leaving drinks
soon – do you want to come along?

Pete

To: Danny Wallace
From: Anil Tailor
Subject: London

Hiya mate

Me and Sunil are gonna be in London next week. Sunil is working
at a dojo in Docklands for a bit and then we thought we could grab
a beer. Can you make it?

Anil

To: Danny Wallace
From: Lauren Medcalfe
Subject: Blast from the past!

Daniel! (or should I call you Danny now??)

My mum tells me you are looking for me because you want to send
me a Christmas card! It's been a while – you owe me about seventeen of them! Funnily enough I have seen you on some strange TV
shows once or twice but didn't realise it was you!

Only just got the message as have been travelling through
Thailand, Australia, China etc having a whale of a time before I turn
30 (eek!). I'm moving to Dublin in the new year but am back in
Britain now. Would LOVE to meet up! When were you thinking? Lx

To: Danny Wallace
From: Cameron Dewa
Subject: Potato!

Potaaaaaaaaaaaaatooooooo!!!!!!!!

Wednesday 8Lth May

I have got a new bike.
But we have to fix it.
The chain is broken it is d
bit too big but I can ride it
and it is good

Chapter Eighteen

In which we learn that *no one* ever dreams about cabbage...

The phone was ringing. Why was the phone ringing?

I rubbed the sleep out of my eyes and tried to find my glasses.

'Hello?' I said.

But I was speaking into the telly remote. That would never work. The telly wasn't even *on*.

I found my glasses, and then the phone.

'Hello?'

'Pub!'

'Eh?'

'Pub!'

'It's... not even ten o'clock!'

'Pub at *eleven*, then!'

'Who *is* this?'

'Who do you think?'

'Ian?'

'No! The other one! I'm back off tour for a couple of days!'

'*Wag*!'

'So – pub?'

I thought about it.

'I *guess* so!'

It was great to see Wag again. A little bit of normality. He'd been away for what seemed like months now – and, in fact, *was* – but he was back in London for a few days R&R before jetting off again, to...

'Moscow!'

'*Moscow*?'

'Moscow!'

'Wow. I got all your postcards. Thanks for that.'

'S'all right. Cheaper than a text.'

'It really is *great* to see you again, Wag. What's been going on?'

'It's been wild. Sleeping on tour buses. Whisky and cigars. Great audiences.'

'That's brilliant.'

'And you?'

'Yeah. Pretty much the same.'

I didn't really want to tell Wag too much about what I'd been up to. Especially not lately. Because what I'd been up to lately wasn't too much.

'Come on – you must've been up to *something*. Any more TV stuff?'

'I've taken a sabbatical. Too many things I needed to do.'

'Like what?'

'I sacked a builder,' I said, and Wag made a very impressed face. 'And I've been sorting out the house. Ian and I made a canopy. That kind of thing.'

'How *is* Ian?'

'Um… I'm not sure. He's left a couple of messages and I've been meaning to call him back, but you know how it is.'

'Canopies to build?'

'That kind of thing.'

'And that's it, is it? That's all you've done?'

'Well, I'm nearly thirty, Wag. Time to sort things out. Get my affairs in order. I'm not a boy any more.'

'What? *Yes*, you are. We both are! We're… the *boys*!'

'We're a boy and a man, now.'

'What are you saying? That you're my father?'

'I am not saying I'm your father. I'm just saying there comes a time in a man's life when he has to stop sleeping on tour buses and buy himself a people carrier. And then not sleep in it.'

'I'm confused. Are you talking about you or me, here?'

'It'll come to you, too, Wag. You mark my words.'

I felt wise. But I also felt old. I may as well have had a pint of bitter in front of me.

'And why,' asked Wag, 'did you order that pint of bitter?'

'Forget that. Tell me tales of the road.'

And so he did.

'What are you doing tonight?' he said, after lunch. He was wiping food off his mouth with a serviette but he'd missed a bit.

'I don't know,' I said. 'I don't really know *what* I'm doing these days.'

'Well, Friday night, my friend – that's when the fun will re-enter your life. I'm having a few drinks to say hello and goodbye again. Ian's coming. You better be there!'

'Yup,' I said. 'Although it depends on whether there are any other canopies to build…'

I guess, in a sense, I'd been robbed of some purpose. I'd robbed *myself* of some purpose. The emails I'd received from Peter Gibson and Anil Tailor and Cameron Dewa I'd kind of batted away. Those asking me if I wanted to meet up, I'd replied to with non-committal non-answers, like 'yeah – I'll give you a bell!', or 'love to – bit snowed under right now'. This had kind of happened to me before, and I knew the best way to combat it was to do precisely the opposite, but I also knew I needed some time to myself right now. And maybe that was more important. Sometimes Mikey would pop up while I was absent-mindedly playing Call of Duty, being bashed on the back of the head by the Bald Assassin, which didn't even have the power to stir up anger or annoyance in me any more. Up the words would pop: *theblindsniper_1977 wants to play*. And I'd say hi, and maybe play half a game, and then most of the time I'd say I had to go off and do a thing.

And then there was Lauren's email.

So Lauren had got back in touch. I'd found her. Just a little too late. A pity. Perhaps if I'd met her sooner, things might've been different now. Perhaps it would have kept me going. Or perhaps it would've stopped things altogether.

I hadn't really known how to reply to her, so had just sent something generic back. Something along the lines of, 'Yes! Great to be back in touch! Maybe I'll see you in Dublin someday!' No plans, no promises, no real encouragement.

But Lauren hadn't left it there.

'I'm going to be in London quite a bit!' she'd say. 'I could come to you!' And she'd list dates, and I'd kind of look at them, and I'd feel rude and silly and awkward, and I'd write back and apologise, saying I wasn't around on those days.

And she'd joke, and say, 'You seemed a lot keener when you first got in touch', and she'd suggest more dates, and I wouldn't reply for a day or two.

And then, one day, and out of the blue, a phone call.

'Hello?'

'Daniel?'

'Yeah?'

'It's Lauren.'

And I was slightly shocked.

'Lauren? How did you...'

'I asked my mum to call Martha to get Lorraine to ask your mum for your number...'

'Well... how are you?'

And we talked.

And finally, and in the end, and because it's so much harder to avoid something when you can hear the person asking the actual question, we agreed to meet up.

Lauren Jessica Medcalfe was born in the same year as me: 1976. A year which anyone born before then would come to tell me – and, I imagine, her – was the summer of the Great British Heatwave. That nearly thirty years later people still boast of a particularly hot summer tells you more about Britain than it does about 1976. Plus, they're forgetting: I was still in the womb at that stage. How did they think *I* felt? To say it was a bit parky in there would be to do the babies of '76 a great disservice.

It was also the year Concorde made its first commercial flight.

The year Apple made its first computer, and the year Microsoft became a trademark. The year the first space shuttle was unveiled. The year Renee Richards won the US Women's Open, despite the fact that she'd been a man the year before. The year everyone thought they could see a face on Mars.

Among the many pretty hats, bonnets and teddy bears I received to welcome me into the world, a family friend in Dundee also presented my proud parents with *The World of Wonder Book 1976*. It seems to me now quite an optimistic gift to give to a baby. Bearing in mind I could hardly see, let alone read, I wonder now whether he'd really thought that gift through, or whether he'd simply decided that boys – no matter what age – would be fascinated by its educational chapters, such as 'The Story of Wool', 'Inside the Egg of a Fish', and 'The Moving Staircase! – The History of Escalators'.

Lauren and I had become pen pals through a mutual family friend. There was no rhyme or reason to it. People just thought that seeing as we were the same age, we'd probably have some of the same interests. We didn't, really. Lauren liked Bananarama, whereas I liked Huey Lewis and the News and Michael Jackson. Lauren liked *Pretty in Pink*, whereas you'd be hard pushed to make me admit that *anything* was better than *Ghostbusters*. I have often thought, in fact, that were I ever to be asked for my specialist chosen subject on Mastermind, I would go for *Ghostbusters*.

Well, that or *Teen Wolf*.

What made our friendship work was the distance. It meant that when we wrote to each other, it felt like we were sending our thoughts thousands of miles away, even though it would've taken just forty minutes in a car.

After we'd talked on the phone, I'd looked in the Box. I knew there were still some of the old letters there. I'd read them.

There had only ever been one rival in life for my pen pal attentions. A French girl named Natalia. Here is a typical letter:

Hello Daniel!
How are you? Me, I'mm fine.
Now! I'm 14 years (fourteen) – 3 april!

A cat
Do you like JIMMY SOMMERVILLE and ELTON JOHN?
Me, I like the pop singers. They're marvellous.
I hope than you have good!
(J'espere que tu vas bien)
Love from Natalia

I never really knew what to write back to Natalia. I suppose I could simply have written:

Hello back
I am well
Me too
An ostrich
No
You too
Daniel

... but that would've looked like a haiku, and I must *never* be accused of trying to write a haiku.

With Lauren it had been different. Precisely because we knew different people meant we could be honest with each other. And it helped that we had a language in common. We could be open, knowing that no one – not our friends, not our parents, not *anyone* – would ever read our letters. Mainly because 95 per cent of them were about Bananarama or Michael Jackson, and that's quite a boring thing for parents to have to read. My secrets were safe with her, and hers with me. It was a mutually beneficial arrangement, which these days, almost anyone can have, thanks to MySpace, and thanks to Facebook. But *we* had it on paper. And for some reason, that makes it more special.

I sat, in Bar Kick in Shoreditch, waiting for Lauren to arrive.

This had been my old stomping ground just a year before, and I looked around. Nothing had changed. There were still the same European-style table football tables, which, though fancy, will *never* be as good as the ones you find in the back of old men's pubs. Still the same men with interesting haircuts behind the bar, talking in Portuguese or Italian. Still the musty smell and the nostalgic pictures on the wall. I liked it here.

I ordered a Coke and sat near the back.

And maybe five minutes later, in she walked.

'I'm so sorry I'm late,' she said, putting a small rucksack down on the floor. 'You know what the tube's like.'

I hadn't known whether to shake her hand or hug her, so I did an awkward mix of the two. By which I don't mean I hugged her hand. I just kind of got a bit too close and *then* shook her hand. Was this because I wasn't into this any more, or because she was a girl? I couldn't tell.

'It's really great to see you!' she said, brightly. 'So tell me *everything*. Are you married? What do you do? Do you live round here?'

She seemed genuinely excited. In precisely the same way *I'd* been when meeting Simon, or Tarek, or Cameron. Full of questions, full of energy.

'I'm married,' I said. 'To an Australian girl. It's great.'

'Amazing! God, *I* nearly got married! Haven't yet, though, although I wouldn't say no to half these barmen...'

'They *do* have interesting haircuts,' I said. 'How about you? Married?'

She looked at me oddly.

'I just *said* I wasn't!' she said.

'God, yes, sorry, I know. Sorry,' I said.

There was an awkward pause, and then she laughed.

'I guess this was always going to be a bit weird. I haven't seen you in... how long?'

'Years,' I said, shaking my head. 'It must be *years*.'

'Well, it's not *months*,' she said, and laughed again.

I was really messing this up. I took a sip of my Coke, hoping the caffeine would make me feel myself again. At least until this was over. I tried again.

'So what do you do?' I asked. 'Nowadays, I mean?'

'Well, I've just come back from travelling the world. Or, at least,

South-East Asia. I never travelled, really, apart from to Spain and France, and that doesn't really count, because that's just an hour or two on the plane. So I decided to take some time out and spend a year on the road. I did Thailand, Australia, a bit of India. I spent some time in Nepal, before heading to…'

I'd started to zone out a little. I knew it was wrong. I knew I was being a twat. But for some reason, I was finding it hard to take in all the facts of someone's else's life. I'd had a real hunger for these facts before. A real interest. But I was tired, now, and finding out about Andy had knocked me for six. Maybe I just didn't have room in my head for any more things which…

'Daniel?'

Oops.

'Yeah!' I said.

'I was just asking if you'd been to Nepal?'

'No!' I said. 'Sorry. No. I haven't. But I'd like to. One day.'

'Are you okay?' she said, with a smile.

'I'm good.'

Her smile fell a little.

'Did you not want to meet with me?' she said.

And then I thought about it. And I realised that I *hadn't* wanted to meet with her. And I realised what an *idiot* that made me. And how *different* I was acting. And how *excited* I should be. And so I said…

'I'm so sorry. I've just had a weird time lately. Start again. Start at Thailand. Tell me everything.'

And this time, I made sure I listened.

'So what else?' I said, on the second beer. 'I mean I know you work in IT…'

'Only temporarily!' she said. 'God, didn't you think that *everyone* would work in IT?'

'I never doubted it,' I said. 'And what else? You have a cat?'

'Peewee,' she said. 'You?'

'No cats. Or Peewees. Although sometimes I steal next door's for an evening.'

'Your next door neighbour has a Peewee?'

'I have no idea what that means.'

We'd started to laugh. And have fun. It had taken a little while to get to. It had taken most of *South-East Asia* to get to. But now it was here, it was welcome.

'Do you remember, you were always writing to me about different hobbies you were starting?'

'Karate. Yup. That was one. I made it to a white-belt-with-red-tips. My friend Anil told me that was very impressive. And then there was autograph-hunting. I got *three*. There just weren't very many celebrities wandering around Leicestershire at the time.'

'What else?'

'Stamp collecting. Postcards of old planes. World Cup stickers.'

'Ha. Like every other lad.'

'Yeah. But that one I nearly *did*. Just needed a Hungarian. Otherwise I'd have *done* it.'

'Well, you *nearly* did it. You *tried*. There's always that.'

'Yeah. There's always that.'

Lauren smiled again.

'Do you remember, you used to be so into Michael Jackson?' she said. 'And you used to write me these letters detailing exactly what you thought each lyric of each song meant?'

I blushed slightly.

'You even thought he was speaking directly to you on the "Black Or White" single.'

'It wasn't necessarily about racism!' I said. 'It could *just* have easily been about little boys in Loughborough!'

And then we'd both laughed, because, actually, it *could*.

'Did I ever tell you about Cameron?' I asked. 'In any of my letters?'

'Cameron?' she said, tapping her lip with her finger.

'Doesn't matter. You probably didn't memorise my letters. Well, he's the guy who got me into Michael Jackson. A Fijian kid. Turns out he's a chief. He's got his own village!'

'What?'

'Seriously. And my mate Simon's solved time travel. A couple of them are architects, which is a great job, but given the choice I'd rather be a time traveller.'

'That's *incredible*,' she said. 'And here's me, working *temporarily* in IT for what seems like *five years*...'

'Well, Cameron works in IT, too... there's nothing wrong with IT...'

'Yeah, but... it just makes me sound a bit *boring*.'

'It does not! You have a cat named Peewee! *That's* not boring!'

'It's no Fijian chief, though.'

'Well... very few cats *are*,' I said, and then I laughed, because I thought that was quite a good joke, but Lauren didn't get it. It was embarrassing. I'd been expecting her to laugh, so now I was just a man laughing at a Fijian cat. But it seemed like Lauren was thinking of something else.

'Are you ever dissatisfied?' she said. 'As you approach thirty, I mean?'

'I wouldn't say dissatisfied. For me, it was more about turning into a man. Leaving my boyish ways behind.'

'It's a benchmark, though, isn't it?' she said.

'It *is* a benchmark,' I said, and for a moment, we just sat there, in silence.

'Can I tell you something?' I asked, and when she nodded, I told her *everything*.

'I'd *wondered* why you seemed so incredibly keen to meet up,' said Lauren, after I'd told her about Anil, about Simon, about LA car chases, giant rabbit heads, Berlin rappers... and Andy. 'I mean, usually people just turn up on Facebook, force you to be their friend, and you get one email from them saying they've got two kids and an interest in badminton.'

'This is face-to-Facebook,' I said, still quite proud of that.

'I guess it's nice that you still have hobbies,' she said.

'Hanne used to call them stupid boy projects. Being a girl, you may agree.'

Lauren thought about it.

'No. No, I don't. There's nothing stupid about wanting to see old friends. There's nothing stupid about *this*, is there? You and me sat here, catching up? So why did you stop?'

'Well, you know. After the whole Andy thing, I just kind of lost interest.'

'Out of respect for him?'

'I don't know. I guess so. In some way. I felt like I was intruding on something. On something private. Like I'd just been blundering about, thoughtlessly and selfishly, never considering for a moment that something like that could have happened to *anyone*. I mean, what if I'd phoned his house? What if I'd said something stupid? It just felt right to back off and leave things alone for a while.'

Lauren thought about it for a moment or two.

'You're wrong,' she said.

'Eh?'

'You're *wrong*. It's only my opinion, but you're wrong. If anything, this should have made you do it *more*. Because in some ways, it's precisely what your whole... "adventure"... has been about.'

I was about to ask her to elaborate, but I didn't need to...

'What I mean is, you've found out one of the great big secrets about life. That it can end. And instead of deciding to make the most of it, and do the things you want while you can, you've decided to... well, what?'

'Do some DIY and stuff.'

'Exactly. But, Daniel – *life is for living*. Listen, I'm not going to preach to you. I've only heard what you've just told me and I don't know any of the details and, to be fair, I haven't seen you in years. But it seems like maybe you shouldn't be *stopping* this because of Andy. But *starting* it.'

I looked at my bottle of Beck's.

'Let's talk about something else,' I said.

It was a few minutes later, and we'd moved on to more light-hearted conversation. What Lauren had said was still tingling at the back of my mind, though. It had been classic Lauren. Yeah, so our problems when we were kids weren't quite so dramatic. But Lauren had always been the one with the level-headed advice. She'd always been level-headed. But *she* thought that meant she was boring.

'You can't *really* think you're boring,' I said. 'There must be *something*.'

'I am! I'm boring! I'm the most boring person in this bar!'

'Something! A hobby! An interest! There is *no such thing* as a boring person…'

She thought about it.

'You'll think I'm odd.'

'Odd or boring – which would you prefer?'

She glanced at her rucksack.

'There is *one* thing,' she said.

'Okay?'

'You'll think I'm *odd*!' she said, again.

'I won't! What is it?'

She took a deep breath.

'I analyse dreams.'

Christ. What an *oddball*.

'That's good!' I said. 'That's… good!'

'I'm no expert,' she said. 'I picked up this book at a hostel. Someone had left it behind, and I got really into it. Want to see?'

'Yes!' I said, and so she got it out.

I looked at it. *The Dictionary of Dreams* by Gustavus Hindman Miller.

'So when you say you analyse dreams, you mean you look them up in an old book?' I said.

'Kind of,' she said. 'It's a starting point.'

'But this was published a million years ago! What if someone dreamt of an iPod?'

'I'd *improvise*!' she said.

'Give that to me,' I said, and took it. I flicked it open at random. '"*Cabbage*. It is bad to dream of cabbage. Disorders may run riot in all forms." Who dreams of cabbage?'

'*Some* people dream of cabbage!' she said. 'And if not cabbage, then lettuce.'

'*Mallet*!' I said, still reading. '"To dream of a mallet, denotes you will meet unkind treatment from friends on account of your ill health!"'

'Could happen!'

'"To dream of a bullfrog, denotes, for a woman, marriage to a wealthy widower, but there will be children with him to be cared for."'

I closed the book.

'They're quite *specific*,' I said.

'How about you?' she said, taking the book off me.

'How about me what?'

'Like, what was the last dream you had?'

I couldn't think.

'I'm not sure,' I said, and then: 'Oh! There *was* one the other night. I had a banjo at one point.'

'You see! People *do* dream of weird stuff!'

'Not cabbage, though!'

'*Banjo*,' she said. '"To dream of a banjo, denotes that pleasant amusement will be enjoyed..."'

'That sounds good,' I said.

'"To see a negro playing one..."'

'*Hang* on...'

'"... denotes that you will have slight worries, but no serious vexation for a season..."'

'Keep your voice down! Christ! When was that *written*?'

'Turn of the last century.'

'And you *believe* this?'

'I believe there's *something* in it. Dreams are our subconscious telling us what it thinks we need to know. Although I'm not sure about that banjo one. What else?'

'I remember my mate Dan telling me he was always dreaming of cows,' I said, flushed with embarrassment, and hoping *this* explanation might be a little more enlightened.

'"To dream of seeing cows waiting for the milking hour promises abundant fulfilment of hopes and desires."'

Lauren looked satisfied.

'Were they waiting for the milking hour?' she said.

'I have no idea!' I said. 'It was *Dan's* dream! And what does a cow look like when it's waiting? You don't *see* cows with watches...'

'Or babies. You never see a baby with a watch. I had a dream about that.'

And then she looked at me. And there was a beat. And I realised she was messing about. And we both started to laugh.

'So you *don't* believe that stuff?'

'Do I *bollocks*,' she said, chucking the book onto her bag. 'That's a birthday present for my weird aunt.'

'That was really good fun.'

Lauren's words. And I had to agree. We were standing on Kingsland Road waiting for her bus.

'It was really good to see you again, Lauren. I'm really glad I came out.'

'So when are you thirty?'

'Three weeks. The sixteenth.'

'Having a party?'

'I… don't know,' I said. 'I'll let you know.'

And then, in the distance, we could see her bus. And we shook hands, and *then* we hugged, and then we said goodnight.

And then she said, 'So are you going to see any of the others?'

'The others?'

'The final few?' she said.

And I shrugged, and I said, 'I don't know that either.'

'How about the one that's in London?' she said.

'Peter?'

'Seems like a good starting point,' she said. 'If he's only round the corner… treat it like you're just meeting a friend for a pint.'

I nodded.

'Just meeting a friend for a pint,' I said. 'We'll see.'

'Bye, then…'

'Wait!'

I'd forgotten something.

'I brought this. It's my old address book. You need to write your new address in it. The others all have…'

Lauren took it and did as I asked. She flicked through.

'The World of Michael Jackson?' she said.

'Yeah, let's not talk about that,' I said. 'I don't think it's likely I'll be seeing *him*, either.'

She handed the book back to me.

'You *nearly* did it,' she said. 'At least there's that.'

And I waved her goodbye as she boarded her bus.

Back at home, I thought about what Lauren had said. It *is* important to finish stuff. I knew that. As an adult, I'd always tried my hardest to finish my projects, finish my hobbies, achieve *something* – maybe as a result of rarely having managed it as a kid. It *did* feel good. And maybe there was something I *could* finish.

I made my way to eBay and typed a few words into the search box. And *bingo*. A man called Christian from somewhere in Germany had exactly what I needed.

A Panini World Cup Mexico 86 sticker album.

Completed.

Christian had managed to do what I hadn't. He'd even got the bloody Hungarian.

I didn't bid on it. I clicked on the *Buy It Now!* button and paid the asking price in full.

I went to bed, knowing that at least I'd finished *something*.

Friday.

Wag's welcome-home, bon-voyage party.

Ian was wearing a very odd shirt indeed.

'That's a very odd shirt indeed,' I said.

'Why do people keep *saying* that?' he said. 'This is what *everyone's* wearing in Chislehurst!'

'What do you *mean*? It's not a different country! It's just past the M25!'

'I happen to think it's quite a statement.'

'Dirty protests are quite a statement.'

'You'll *all* be wearing one of these come the winter,' he said. 'And *then* you'll be sorry.'

'Yes we will,' I said. 'So it's nice to see Wag again, eh?'

We both looked over at him. He was doing the big belly laugh he always does, and then he hugged yet another new arrival.

'Where's Lizzie?' asked Ian.

'On her way,' I said, and just like that, in she walked.

'It's rammed!' she said. 'So many people!'

There were indeed. It was great. They'd all turned up to say hello to a friend they hadn't seen in a while, and weren't likely to see again for quite some time. I couldn't help but think of Neil's thirtieth, those few months ago, before any of this had started.

An hour later, and the whole gang was round a table. Ian, Wag, me and Lizzie.

'Listen, I've got some bad news,' said Wag.

'What about?'

'Your birthday. I'm not going to be back in time. The tour's been extended. We're going to be in Australia on the sixteenth.'

'Oh, well, don't worry. We'll hang out when you get back.'

'But your party!' said Wag, outraged. 'I'll miss your party!'

'Yeah… I'm not really sure I'm going to have a party this year.'

'What?' said Lizzie. 'It's your thirtieth! You've *got* to have a party!'

'This is my party shirt, Dan!' said Ian. 'Don't retire my party shirt!'

'I'm just saying, maybe we can have a little thing. Just a couple of people. But I don't see what all the fuss is about. It's just another year. What's the difference, really, between twenty-nine and thirty?'

'A year,' said Ian, working it out on his fingers.

'I don't mean *mathematically*. I just mean in the grand scheme of things. Anyway, nothing will ever beat my sixth birthday, so there's no point even trying.'

'What was so good about your sixth birthday?' asked Lizzie.

'I got a bike and the bloke from Radio Tay read my name out on the radio. And even though it turned out the bike was a *girl's* bike, it would be very hard to top that…'

'But my shirt!' said Ian.

'We'll see…' I said, and then, looking at Lizzie: 'And I know what you're thinking. But I don't want a surprise party. So can we just leave that idea there?'

Lizzie bit her lip, and just nodded.

'Anyway, tonight's about me,' said Wag, raising his glass. 'To me!'

'To soon-to-be-absent friends!' said Ian.

And though I tried hard not to, I couldn't help but think about Andy.

Back at home, Lizzie was in bed. And I was in the living room, looking through the Box. It had been fun, this. I'd had a laugh. But maybe it was time to finally close the Box.

I started to pile everything back in. Pictures, and letters, and memories had been spread around it for weeks. Clues, and pointers, and stories waiting to happen, with them. I'd put Andy's letters at the top of the pile, along with my returned replies. But something made me want to have a last look at them.

Not all of Andy's letters I'd managed to reply to. There were still one or two left. I'd read them, of course, but not needed to think about what to write in reply. If I'm honest, the replies had just been a bit of fun. A way of reintroducing myself to Andy in an unusual way. A way of highlighting the fun we'd had – the friendship we'd had. But now it was like I'd been saying goodbye to him.

I opened one of his letters at random and began to read. It was the one telling me he'd got a new desk. Such a small event. Such a forgettable event. I'm sure, had we met, we'd never even have thought to mention it. But it was a peek into a life. Small moments of normality. And those small, lost moments – once remembered – can often mean more than you could ever guess. Like a forgotten joke, or a final hug, or a local restaurant's fourth anniversary.

In the past few months, I had a whole host of new moments to remember.

I thought back to what Lauren had said. *Life is for living*. A cliché, yeah, but a cliché, I now realised, for a *reason*. A cliché because it was absolutely *true*. And it summed up, in its four words, a million *other* things, all of which were *also* absolutely true.

I found another letter. A sentence jumped out. 'I'm having such a lot of fun!' Another sentence. 'I wish we can meet up again soon – that would be really good!'

Well, now we couldn't.

And suddenly, it hit me. I'd been down lately because yes, I'd uncovered an uncomfortable truth. But I'd reacted in the wrong way, and that had only served to make it worse. Lauren had been right. Reading these letters made me realise how alive Andy had been. I don't mean 'alive' in a singing-and-dancing, musical number kind of a way. Nor in the way people say 'I feel so *alive!*' after they've just done a bit of abseiling or jumped out of a plane. I mean alive in its most basic, normal, literal alive kind of a way. *Everyday* alive. Alive like we are right now. Me telling you some stuff. You listening.

Okay, so the events in question weren't the most exciting events ever put to paper. Moving rooms. Getting a new desk. Going to Leicester for some printer ribbon. But they were *life*. They *happened*. For a brief moment of however long, they *mattered*.

And that made realise that *my* days mattered. Whatever I was doing. Fixing a canopy. Walking about. Painting a shed.

So if even *that* stuff *matters* – what was *important*?

Family.

Health.

And *friends*.

I'd seen that tonight, with Wag. I'd seen it at Neil's thirtieth. I'd experienced it myself, not just with the friends around me, but with the ones that I'd let go and now found right back where they were – right back in my address book.

I suddenly realised that every moment of tedium, every disappointment, let-down and sadness I'd ever felt... every moment of depression or boredom or blues, every hung-over Sunday, every heartbroken Monday... each of those moments was one *trillion* times better than no moment at all. Life *was* for living.

Finding out about Andy shouldn't have stopped me from seeing people. It should have taught me that people are what life is all about. I should have been grabbing more chances in honour of Andy, doing more things that I was lucky to be able to do at all. Because one day is all it takes for lives to change. Every single second I'd had since I was eighteen was a second Andy had never had the chance to live. I shouldn't have stopped for him. Like Lauren said, I should've *started* for him.

There I'd been, bemoaning the fact that I was turning thirty, that perhaps youth was ending, and suddenly that me of then – that *former* me – felt like the most trivial and self-absorbed man alive. I am sure there are those of you who will agree. But I'm hoping that there are others of you who will think that now – *right* now – you've got an opportunity of your *own*.

As for me... there was a very simple way for me to get back on the horse.

I picked up a postcard.

Peter Gibson.

I fired up my computer, clicked on my email, frantically finding one from Peter.

He'd sent me his phone number. I *had* his phone number. Where?

I found it.

I tapped it into my phone, and sent him a text...

Peter! Where are you? It's Danny!

Moments later, I had a reply.

Just got up! Hello mate.

Just got up? It was after midnight! The people of Tooting must lead *very* exciting lives. I ignored it and urgently typed away...

Let's meet!

I waited for what seemed like an age. I paced about. Moved things on my desk around. Peter hadn't replied. Peter wasn't *replying*.

I picked up the Book and flicked through it. I just wanted to update his address. That's all I wanted to do. All I *needed* to do.

The page fell open on a random page.

A page which read: *Forever Friends.*

I stared at it.

A moment later, my phone buzzed. The reply was in.

Ah, it read.

My house. Grown-up. 2006.

Dear Andy,

Well, I suppose this will probably be my last letter to you. One that I won't even send. But one that's definitely worth writing.

I'm sorry I didn't reply to your letters more when I was a kid. I'm sorry I once 'borrowed' that Action Man with the beard that you had, without ever giving it back. And most of all, I'm sorry we never got to meet again.

Friendships are all too easy to let slide. I'm going to do my best never to let it happen again. Not with the important people.

I'm glad I at least got to read your letters again. I'm glad I was able to revisit times in my life, and people from those times, and remember the small and inconsequential events that suddenly don't seem quite as small, nor half as inconsequential.

I think you'd be pleased to know that I'm about to rekindle another friendship. A friendship that I could've rekindled at any time over the past few months, but always put off. Because there always seemed like there was something else I had to do first; somewhere else I had to be.

I'm going to find Peter Gibson. And if a friend is worth a flight, this friend must be worth a *lot*.

I'll tell him everything I've done, from start to finish. And maybe one day he'll get in touch with some people that mean something to him. Maybe one of them will then do the same.

It's been a blast, Andy. Thanks for being part of it, even if you never meant to be. I'll say hello to Peter for you.

Your friend,
Daniel

Chapter Nineteen

In which you may be surprised to learn that Daniel is not at home...

Soon after.

It was hot where I was.

Far hotter than London had been. Far hotter than I'd been expecting.

I was standing outside the arrivals lounge, my phone in my hand. It seemed just as confused as I was. I wanted to dial Peter's number, wanted to tell him I'd made it over. But my phone was still adjusting to the time difference, and still trying to find its new network for the week.

Finally, as I was fumbling with my sunglasses and trying to work out where I'd put my wallet, it went off.

A phone call.

I answered it.

'Hey, Dan...' said Hanne. 'Are you out?'

'Well, sort of,' I said.

'Whereabouts? In town?'

'I'm actually in Australia.'

A beat.

'You're... *what*? What are you doing *there*?'

I thought about it.

'I'm just meeting a friend for a pint.'

The moment I'd received Peter's 'Ah' text, I knew there was a problem. As we've already established, anything starting with an 'Ah' usually points in that general direction. I'd ended up phoning him.

'Where *are* you?' I'd said.

'I've moved to Melbourne,' he said, laughing, and my heart had dropped to my feet.

Melbourne.

'I hadn't been planning it long, but the time just seemed right. I told you I was leaving work!'

'Yeah, but I thought you'd maybe be moving to Swindon, or something...'

'Never mind. I'll be back in a year or two. We can meet then – we've waited *this* long. Or if you're ever out here. I mean, let's face it, we were never going to meet while we were both in London, were we? That would've been *far* too convenient...'

And now here I was.

I hadn't booked my ticket on a whim. I hadn't just upped and left London. I'd considered all the options very carefully.

But none of them seemed as attractive and *necessary* as seeing Peter again.

Plus, I'd had good news. *Excellent* news. Akira had finally written back. Okay, so it wasn't the heartfelt, I've-missed-you missive I'd been hoping for. If anything, it was quite 'professional'. But it was *something.*

Hello Daniel

I was in Sapporo Hokkaido, north in Japan, to partici-pate Digestive Disease Week -Japan 2006 from 13th to 15th October.

This is an academic meeting of the Japanese Society of Gastroenterology and the Japan Gastroenterological Endoscopy Society.

I am a member of these society, and I presented rare case of the familial adenomatous polyposis.

I will make a study of Colonic cancer from this November.

How about you, Daniel?

Akira

I hadn't really known how to respond. I couldn't exactly say 'me too', could I?

But check it out: not only was Akira a medical doctor, he was studying *cancer*, probably with a view to *eradicating* it altogether! Akira was helping solve cancer!

Receiving this email had made my mind up for me about visiting Peter – because a plan had started to form...

But a plan like this needed backing. Support. Permission.

Since finding out about Andy, I'd abandoned the idea of Man Points. There seemed to be little purpose to them any more. I'd simply undertaken the necessary works on the house because I'd wanted to – I'd needed something to occupy my mind and time. But now I'd realised maybe I needed something to fall back on. Especially if I was going to sell the idea to Lizzie.

Lizzie had, of course, been incredibly supportive of the whole endeavour. And she'd been there to quietly pick up the pieces when it had all gone wrong. But jetting off to Australia – to *her* home country, *without* her – had seemed a little too much to ask with no payback...

And so I'd found the list that Ian and I had made that sunny afternoon in the garden. And I'd studied our thoughts, and tried to work out what I'd need to do to make this happen...

I wandered around the house, reading it as I did so... but discovered that, strangely, most of the items on the list had already been done...

Painting the skirting boards (3MP)

Sorting the table (2MP)

Cleaning the...

Fixing the...

Replacing the...

... *all* done!

The only thing left over, in fact, was mending that broken socket. And that was only worth 1MP!

'I've done most of it,' I said, almost in awe. And then I realised what that meant.

I was a *man*.

I was still a man who needed to get permission to go away, but I was a man nevertheless.

'I've *done* most of it!' I said, again, shaking my head.

Who needed *Paul*?

'Done most of what?' said Lizzie, suddenly there. She was carrying a bag of shopping, and was sticking her headphones in her pocket.

'This!' I said, holding up the list.

'Ah!' she said. 'The List!'

'The Man Points list!' I said.

'Yes indeed.'

'So I was hoping I could trade these in. Because I need to go on another trip.'

'Another trip?' she said. 'To meet an old friend?'

'Yes,' I said, handing it to her.

'Peter?' she asked, casting her eye down the list. I could see her looking from left to right, taking in all the ticks I'd added.

'Hmm...' she said.

And then Lizzie looked at me, and looked again at the list. And then she did something remarkable. She tore it up.

'I agree with Ian,' she said. 'I think Man Points represent an oppressive regime which removes the fundamental human rights of the adult male.'

She hugged me.

'Go and see Peter. And say hello from me.'

It was 2pm and I was in Sydney with almost a day to kill.

In my nineteenth hour on the plane, cramped and pushed up against the window, with a baby crying behind me and a man next to me who'd annexed my foot space, I'd begun to lament the fact I hadn't pounced on Peter when he'd been in Tooting.

But now, here, in the blazing sunshine and with happy-faced Australians all around me, I was excited.

More so, since I'd had a text from Lizzie.

Off to bed. Call me in the morning, baby. PS. Some messages for you at home. One is from a guy named Chris saying you should call him... could it be?

Could it be?

It *had* to be! Christopher Guirrean had got my letter! You see? Everything was suddenly working out. And being here, in Australia, demonstrating my commitment to the cause, was all part of the fun.

Yeah, so me and Peter would have had a nice evening in a Tooting pub, talking about London, and living in London, and how different London is to where we'd grown up... but I now realised that *this* was where Peter's life was now. And I was here, right at the start of it. A whole new chapter in his life. Plus, he'd been right. Just as Londoners never see all the things that London has to offer precisely because they can, it'd been too easy to see Peter there. Now that there'd been the chance that we'd never meet again – with him as far away as it's possible to be without starting to come home again – I had to see him. It was an address which, more than ever, needed updating.

I grabbed a cab, and headed into town.

I love Sydney.

It's the way cities should be. Historic and futuristic, wide, bright and beautiful. The last time I'd been here I'd had a strange conversation with a girl who, because I wear glasses, thought I was perhaps more intelligent that I am, and attempted to get me to pontificate on her city in quite a poncey way.

'What's the first word that pops into your head when I say "Sydney"?' she'd said.

'Poitier,' I'd said, in response.

'Hmm,' she'd said, leaning forward onto the table, fascinated. 'And what would you say is particularly *poitier* about Sydney?'

Now, here I was again, down by the harbour, taking in the Opera House and sipping a frappacino, trying to convince my body not to give up the fight by using sunshine and caffeine.

I watched the news on a TV hanging outside the café.

'We'll be back after the break,' said the anchor.

The break started. A man shouted incredibly loudly about a new CD that was not available in the shops. 'BUY THE GREATEST BEER SONGS EVER!' he yelled. And then it was straight back to the news.

I headed towards George Street and the city centre, and began to walk around the shops. My flight wasn't until 7pm, and it would only take me about...

Hang on.

I turned around, and saw a man with a small entourage walking past me. One of them had a headset on, and there was a woman with a clipboard, looking nervous. And the man at the centre of it all, the man they were clearly all worried about, looked strangely familiar.

But no. It *couldn't* be.

You don't just turn up in Australia and immediately see...

Bloody hell. It *was.*

The man had been stopped by someone with a camera and obligingly had his photo taken with them. And then signed an autograph. And then someone else was upon him, apologising for the intrusion but immediately videoing him on his phone... was *that...?*

It was *Shane Warne!* Perhaps the most famous Australian in... well... in Australia. Even on a global basis, there are only a few more well known than him. Kylie. Jason. Mick Dundee. Dame Edna. Wolverine. And that's almost half the country.

Here he was – Australia's cricket captain. Media darling. Devil of the tabloids, with his sex scandals and his straight-talking and his blonde highlights. A sporting hero, right here in the middle of a shopping centre in Sydney. Surely he'd shop online? Surely he'd get everything for free, anyway? What was he *doing?*

Suddenly, I realised it was a pity I'd stopped collecting autographs as a kid. Getting Shane Warne's to go with my Barbara Windsor, Phillip Schofield and Emlyn Hughes would have been a real boost to my collection. My grandchildren would never have had to worry about money again.

But alas, I am not an autograph hunter. Not any more. I had my three, and that was fine by me. I decided to move on, but as I turned around, I saw a giant poster.

COME AND MEET SHANE WARNE!
Shane will be signing copies of his new book at 2pm at Angus &
Robertsons!

I looked at my watch. It was ten to two. I suppose I *could* get an autograph. I'd probably be first in the queue!

The queue stretched pretty much all the way back to Britain.

I'd decided I would get Shane's autograph, not for me, but for Peter Gibson. Because it had suddenly struck me what a fine gift that would be. A proper Australian gift. A welcome-to-your-new-life gift. If Shane Warne would agree to condone Peter's decision to move here, surely his stay in this fine country would be blessed forever more? It would be like being in a Travelodge in Reading, finding a copy of the Bible and seeing it had been signed, 'Enjoy the stay! Love, God!' You'd think, 'I've chosen the *right* hotel here.'

My fellow autograph hunters in the queue were an incredible mix of people. Old, young, couples, strange men in jumpers, the odd Brit – everyone. But the queue was incredibly slow-moving, and it was hot. Having come straight from the airport, I had my rucksack with me and I was a slightly dishevelled mess. I'd spent a moment in the arrivals lounge bathroom, attempting to make my hair not look like I'd been sleeping on it for a day, but then realised that's pretty much what it looks like anyway, so I just wiped some wax across it and hoped for the best. But this, I'm afraid, was to be to my detriment. The flies in Australia are big fans of the faint smell of sweat – particularly, it seems, when mixed with that of hair wax. I'd started to be bothered by six or seven of them, and they buzzed around me, sometimes landing on my face, sometimes just whizzing by, but all of them definitely interested in getting to know me at an unusually intimate level. I'd begun to furiously swat at them with a small leaflet a lady had given me about some kind of horse-racing event, but I realised my actions had begun to make me look mental. I couldn't walk off for fear of losing my place in the Shane Warne queue, so had to keep insanely and randomly hitting out with my leaflet, before coming across the perfect solution. Blowing. A sharp blow would panic the flies for a second, and off they'd go, before returning in force. All I could do was breathe in and then maintain a steady flow of air from my mouth, changing the angles every few seconds in order to discourage them from coming back by confounding them with unpredictable currents. It was working pretty well. Until the man in front of me turned around and give me quite an aggressive look, and I realised I'd essentially been blowing erotically on the back of his neck for the past few minutes. I decided to welcome the flies back into my life.

Up ahead, a lady with a microphone was interviewing people in the queue about what Shane Warne meant to them. Some talked of his being the first bowler to take 700 Test wickets. Others of his record for having the most Test runs without a century. And I just listened and looked a bit blank.

Because, I'll be honest, I didn't really know much about Shane Warne. The only thing I know less about is cricket. Shane Warne, to me, was the sportsman you'd see on the front cover of the *News of the World*, standing in his underpants with a couple of models, or being funny on telly, or advertising revolutionary hair loss treatments in the back of the Sunday papers. I knew he was big, and I knew he was important, but that was *all* I knew.

Still. It was enough to warrant an autograph. An autograph for Peter.

Suddenly, the microphone lady was right in front of me.

'And you, sir, you're here for Shane Warne too, aren't you?'

The logo on her microphone told me she was from one of Sydney's premiere radio stations. But what I couldn't tell was if we were live or not.

'Yes!' I said. 'I am here for Shane Warne. And his autograph.'

'And what is it you like so much about Shane Warne?'

I froze. And then unfroze.

'Er... you know. The things that the other people were saying about wickets and stuff. And his cricket. Ing. Abilities.'

She widened her eyes and nodded, encouraging me on.

'He's really good at it,' I said, swatting away at a fly that I'm not sure she could see. 'At cricket. And at... sport.'

'And are you looking forward to meeting him today?'

'Yes, I am,' I said. 'Looking forward to meeting him. Today.'

The lady was still looking at me. Still willing me on.

'It will be nice,' I said.

I could tell, now, from the look on her face, that this *must* be live, and I had just given one of the worst interviews of her professional career.

'Well...' she said.

I had to say something. *Something*! I had to help this woman out! She was dying here, live on the air! And then, out of the blue, and as surprising to me as to anyone around me, I said...

'I'vecomeallthewayfromEnglandtoseehim!'

The lady looked at me. I looked at her.

Finally my brain caught up and I heard what I'd just said.

The woman looked shocked, and then broke into a smile. This was good! I'd rescued it!

'All the way from England?' she said.

'Yep!' I said. 'Just to see old... Warny.'

'You heard about the book signing in England?'

'I like to keep my finger on the pulse,' I said, confidently. 'Of Australian... book signings...'

'So all the way from England? Where in England?'

I thought about it. I didn't want to get caught out.

'Bromsgrove,' I said.

And then I thought, *why did I say Bromsgrove?*

'Bromsgrove? Where's that?'

Christ. Where was Bromsgrove?

'It's in England,' I said, quietly.

'Well, that's very impressive indeed. And over here, who do we have...'

And she moved on down the line.

The man on whose neck I'd been blowing so erotically turned around and looked at me again.

'You know he *plays* in England, don't you?'

'Correct,' I said.

A fly landed on my face.

The man turned away.

Life in the queue was going well. We were moving forward slowly, and I'd made friends with both the neck man, and the elderly couple behind me.

'I'm actually just getting his autograph for a friend,' I told the neck man.

'Sure, mate. Me too.'

'I don't normally get autographs.'

'Or travel thousands of miles to get one,' he said.

'No.'

'So why are you here?'

'I'm just meeting a friend for a pint,' I said.

Up ahead, I could now see Shane Warne. He didn't look particularly bubbly. The queue was picking up pace now, as he lost interest in engaging people in long chats and just signed one book after the other. The book, now that I could see it up ahead, seemed to be called *Shane Warne: My Illustrated Career*. I couldn't help but worry he'd misspelled 'Illustrious' (I was very good at spelling at school – I am aware I may not have mentioned this), but it seemed like the book was all just pictures anyway, so I think he'll get away with it. But then, worryingly, I spotted the lady with the microphone. She seemed to be off-air now, and was relaxing with a bottle of water and chatting to Shane. And then she looked over at me, and pointed, and said something. I think she'd just told Shane Warne I'd travelled all the way from England to see him.

He looked at me with some concern.

'Could I have "To Peter", please?' I said to cricketing legend Shane Warne.

'Are you Peter?' he asked.

'No. Peter is my friend who I haven't seen in seventeen years.'

'Oh,' said Shane Warne.

'I'm going to give it to him as a special gift.'

'Oh,' said Shane Warne.

'He's just moved to Australia.'

'Has he?' said Shane Warne.

'I came all the way from England to see him.'

And then Shane Warne smiled, and realised I'd said 'him', and not 'you', and he said, 'Thank God.'

I flew from Sydney to Melbourne that night, as tired and as jetlagged as any man alive. I texted Peter.

I've made it!

In the morning, I'd find his response, sent just moments later, but not soon enough to catch me before I fell asleep.

Great! Let's meet in South Yarra! 3pm tomorrow!

3pm. South Yarra, Melbourne.

I walked into the pub, wondering if I'd recognise the man waiting for me. Just as I'd now done so many times before.

And, like every other time, the connection was instant.

'Peter!'

'Dan!'

'How are you?'

He looked *exactly* the same. *Exactly* the same.

And we hugged.

'So you're in Australia now!' I said, delighted.

'It seems you are too! What the hell?'

We sat down. He had a pint waiting for me.

'Did you at least get to see a bit of Sydney?' he asked.

'Well, you know what it's like. I was straight off the plane and then I bumped into bloody Shane Warne, so…'

Peter chuckled, thinking I was joking. And yes, it *was* a chuckle. That's what Peter does.

'I felt guilty I hadn't seen you in London,' I said. 'And I needed to update my address book. I've been doing that a lot lately…'

'How do you mean?' asked Peter.

And so I explained.

'I think that's great,' he said. 'You lose touch with people too often as you get older. It's too easy to do. The world's supposed to be smaller these days, but it still feels pretty big. Especially after twenty-four hours on a plane. But moving here has made me realise it's even more important to stay in touch with people. The time difference makes it harder to call people, and I guess email helps a lot, but there's no real substitute for – you know – hanging out.'

'So how did this happen?' I asked. 'One minute you were in Tooting, and the next…'

'Yeah. Well, I guess it had to do with turning thirty,' he said.

So. Another one. Another friend not comfortable with the leap out of his twenties. With growing up. Becoming a man. I put it to him.

'Well, no, not really... it was more of a legal thing... I had to get a work visa before I was thirty, and so I had to act fast. We decided, applied, and that was that.'

'We?'

'Me and my girlfriend, Clare. She's out here too. We left London with a rucksack, basically. And now we're looking for work.'

'So it was as quick as that?'

'Basically. We had a bit of cash saved up, so I quit my job and came over. Time was running out. We had to do it before we were thirty...'

'And when are you thirty?'

'I was thirty on Tuesday.'

'Tuesday? But it's... Thursday!'

'I am now a thirty-year-old man!'

I looked at Peter, proudly. He'd done it. He'd made it to thirty.

'What did you get for your birthday?' I asked, because that's probably what I'd have asked him when we were kids.

'A video game and a ride in a sports car.'

And I laughed. Because that was probably the *answer* he'd have given me when we were kids.

'So what are you going to do over here?'

'Experience it. This wasn't a work thing. In some ways it was an *anti*-work thing. But I'm not an idiot. We're renting out our place in London so we've got *some* security, and I've got a job offer back in London. But who knows what'll happen? If we like it, we'll try and get sponsored and stay. At the moment we're only allowed to work in any one place for three months, so we have to keep moving.'

'Like the bloke from *Highway to Heaven*!'

'Very much like the bloke from *Highway to Heaven*. Only not so angel-based. I actually feel a bit brave...'

I loved it. Peter was living his dream. He'd rebelled against what we're supposed to be doing at thirty. At being locked down, grown-up, mortgaged-to-the-hilt and nine-to-five.

'It's funny, though,' he said. 'Because I don't feel thirty. I think of my dad at my age. They'd already had me and my brother by the time they were in their early twenties. I mean – *that's* grown-up.

People getting married, having kids... they had so much more to worry about. And less money to do it on, probably. I feel guilty sometimes... if it's raining, I can get a taxi, if there's no food, I can get a takeaway... I've just got less responsibility. I guess we *all* do, compared to how our parents were at our age... I suppose it's just easier to worry about getting older now. Because we're doing it later. There's not as much structure. Personally, I think there should be a timetable, like at school. 25: Meet a girl. 27: Have a kid. 29: Buy a sports car...'

'Or a display cushion...'

'I'm not sure *any* man's old enough for that,' said Peter.

I smiled. And then his face lit up.

'Hey, so who else have you seen?'

'Well, Anil...'

'*Anil*?'

'... he's now an architect, just like you!'

'No way!'

'And Simon – he's a Toby Carvery bigwig with an interest in quantum physics...'

'What?'

'Remember Cameron Dewa?'

'The Fijian kid?'

'He lives in London now, but still keeps a small village in Fiji...'

'God, I'd love to see those guys again...'

'Why *don't* you?'

'You make it sound easy.'

'But it *is*. That's the thing. It's *really* easy. Why don't you do it?'

Peter gestured around him.

'I'm kind of in Australia now...'

'But one day – why don't you do it?'

Peter thought about it.

'I guess I could. I guess I *should*. Thing is, half the time, when you lose touch with people, you don't *mean* to... I mean, there are some people you *want* to lose touch with, some you can afford to, some you'd hate to, some it just happens with... and it's difficult to get back in touch. You have to break the silence. They could say, "I'm not really all that bothered..." Did that ever happen to you?'

'Yeah. Once. A guy called Tom.'

'What happened?'

'He just said he wasn't interested.'

'You see, that's what I'd be scared of. That rejection. I guess it's easier to email someone and if they don't reply you can always pretend they didn't get it. The reason I haven't done it is a fear of rejection.'

'But for every Tom, there's been a Cameron, a Mikey, a Lauren... a *you*...'

'I think it's difficult, though, to get in touch with the people you were a kid with... because you weren't formed people then. You could've changed in a million ways, either good or bad. From university on, I think it's different. You are more or less the same person. But it's difficult to reconnect with people who might not even be the same person you knew...'

I thought about what Peter was saying. He had a point. But, from experience, I knew it could work out. If only you'd give it a chance, it could work out. And I knew how to prove it to him.

'Let's try it!' I said.

'Eh?'

'Let's try it right now!'

I got my phone out.

'Who are you ringing?'

I found the number, and pressed Dial. Peter waited while I pressed the phone to my ear. It rang once, twice...

'... hullo?'

They sounded knackered.

'Anil?' I said, and Pete's face lit up.

'... I think so,' said Anil.

'What time is it over there?'

'It's... seven in the morning...'

'God – sorry, did I wake you?'

'Yeah...'

'What time do you get up?'

'Ten past seven.'

'Oh. Well. Anyway, guess where I am?'

'The Congo?'

'No! I'm in Australia.'

'Oh... what? *Why?*'

'I just popped over to see Pete!'

I'd never get bored of saying it. There was a pause.

'Peter *Gibson?* What're you... what's he...'

'Here!' I said, and handed the phone to Peter.

'Anil! Hello, mate! How you doing? I'm doing well! We're sitting here having a beer in Melbourne, talking about old times... yeah, I just quit my job... yeah...'

And I sat back, and I watched Peter reconnect with Anil. Again, this was like a human Facebook. Joining the dots. Connecting the networks. Updating addresses. And Peter and Anil chatted, and reminisced, and told each other of their lives now... just like they'd been hanging out for years.

'So you're an architect? Me too, mate, me too! What you doing? Your part three? Next year? Cool – I did my part three two years ago, so been in London for a while... hey, if you ever want to come and work in London, mate, send your CV in, we're looking for people all the time... about a hundred people, I'm sure there'd be something for you if you ever want to get out of Huddersfield...'

I smiled broadly. Wouldn't it be great if Anil and Peter, my two architect friends who I'd played keepy-uppy with and cheated on maths homework with and walked home from school with, ended up working together?

'You've got a northern accent now! Ha ha! Hey, I'm trying to remember the last time we met – I can remember going round to your house and doing some colouring-in... or maybe bowling for someone's birthday...'

I smiled. We were always going bowling for someone's birthday. And then I realised that there was something else about what Peter had just said that had struck a chord... something to do with something Anil had told me that night with Mikey and Simon in Loughborough... what *was* it?

'You should see the houses round here, mate, the one-off architect-designed ones... land is so cheap, not like in Britain, trying to get as many units into as small a space as possible... you should come and work in Melbourne! Maybe we can go into business!

Listen, I'll get your email off Danny and send you an email – let's definitely *definitely* stay in touch! Cool!'

And he handed the phone back to me.

'Anil!' I said.

He sounded wide-awake now.

'That was so great!' he said. 'And weird, too!'

'How so?'

'Remember the last time I saw you... I told you about the day that weird guy came up to me when I was in my car?'

I thought back.

'The one who could read your mind?'

'Yeah! Well, he said that I would meet up with an old friend soon and have a good time. That was you. And he also said that this could help me make a decision about whether to stay in Huddersfield, or do something else. He said it would lead to new opportunities.'

'Okay...' I said.

'And now Pete's just said I should send my CV in to his work! I'd *love* to live in London for a bit...'

I didn't want to get too carried away. Even though I'd just got a bit too carried away.

'But didn't that bloke also say you'd have some kind of important event with someone with the initials EJ?' I said. 'Your ex-girlfriend?'

'Well, that hasn't happened. I did get drunk and watch an Elton John special on MTV, though, so *that* could have been it... when are you back in London?'

'In a few days,' I said. 'I'll give you a call then...'

And we said goodbye.

'God, that brought back so many memories,' said Peter. 'About Holywell School, for one thing...'

'Ian Holmes taking his cycling proficiency test...'

'On a tricycle!' said Pete. 'The stuff of legends. And Mr Williams banning Wispa bars... do you remember his advice if you were getting bullied by bigger boys?'

'No.'

'Curl up into a little ball!'

'Sound advice. Remember that kid who'd been given a Casio

keyboard for Christmas and then insisted on playing it at the end of every assembly? He could only play "When The Saints Go Marching In..."'

'Remember Anil singing "He's Got The Whole World In His Pants"?'

And we laughed. And we got another Guinness in. And we talked about the old days, while the sun shone through a stained-glass window, colouring in all the black-and-whites, and making them real again...

'So, who else is left?' asked Peter, over noodles down the road. 'From your address book, I mean?'

'Well... you're number ten,' I said. 'There's just Chris Guirrean from Dundee, and Akira Matsui.'

'Akira! The Japanese kid!'

'Yeah – remember him?'

'He was so cool. I'd never met a real-life Japanese person before. I remember his first day at school.'

'Me too. I think that was the day Michael Amodio kicked him in the head and I counted up to five very loudly in his face.'

'Michael *Amodio*! How's he?'

'He's very well. Very well indeed. I'll put you back in touch with him if you like?'

'I'd love that. And who was the other guy?'

'Chris? My first-ever best friend from Dundee.'

'And where's he?'

'I have no idea. But I think I've got him. I wrote dozens of letters. Sent them all over Britain. And I've had a reply...'

'I hope it's him...'

'It must be him. I said in the letter that if they were my Chris, they should phone.'

But suddenly, Peter had made me feel unsure.

'You could always go up there if it's not, couldn't you?' he said. 'I mean, if it's someone phoning you up, and saying, "I'm not *that* Christopher Guirrean." You'd be like Columbo. Head for Dundee, ask around. Get a T-shirt done with his face on and say, "Have you seen this man?"'

'I don't even know what he looks like these days. And I'm not sure walking around with a small boy's face on my T-shirt is the done thing for a man who's nearly thirty. Nah – it's him. I can feel it in my bones.'

I shoved some more noodles into my face. And then I noticed something. Just behind Peter was a free newspaper. And face up, on a page somewhere towards the back, was a picture.

'Pass me that, will you?'

I looked at it. On a page marked Upcoming Gigs was a photograph. A photograph of Wag and his band!

'I don't believe it!' I said. 'That's my mate Wag! He's on tour at the moment – he's playing here on...'

'When?'

Oh. Oh yeah.

'On my birthday.'

Part of me had always hoped that Wag would find a way to be home for my thirtieth. It was a stupid hope, really, and one that was now dashed by a smudgy black-and-white photo.

'He's on at the Corner Hotel. Is that near here?'

'I'm not sure,' said Peter.

'Do you want to go and see him? Without me, I mean. I'm sure I could get you a couple of tickets...'

'Yeah,' said Pete, quite into the idea. 'That'd be cool. You know... *I* might do this. Look up a few people. Get in touch. Maybe even see them again. It's good, isn't it?'

'It *is* good,' I said. 'It's very good indeed.'

And then I looked up. And I noticed something else.

'Remember how when we were kids, there was the big birthday treat?'

'Well, if it was *your* mum sorting it, it was *Red Sonja*. I don't think I slept for a year.'

'I think I can make it up to you...'

I pointed behind him, at a huge sign with an arrow, and the word 'MEGA-SUPER-BOWL!' painted on it.

'What do you say?' I said. 'I missed your birthday. Let's have a birthday treat...'

And so Peter and I celebrated his thirtieth in fine style, with a jumbo Coke, some popcorn, and a lane of our own.

*

It was getting on for midnight.

Pete and I were now fully fledged friends again. Seventeen years had passed, but it was like they'd never happened at all.

'So what's next for you?' I asked, as we walked, happily and full of popcorn, to a taxi rank. 'In the next thirty years, I mean?'

Peter thought about it.

'I really want to design theatres,' he said. 'If I can do that, I'll be happy. But we'll meet again before we're sixty, won't we?'

'We definitely will,' I said, and I knew that definitely we would.

Then I remembered what I had in my bag.

'God, I almost forgot – I got you something. Something to welcome you to Australia.'

I handed him the package. He opened it.

'Ah!' he said. '*My Illustrated Career* by Shane Warne!'

'It gets better,' I said, which was lucky, because so far it was just a load of pictures of Shane Warne.

He opened it, and read aloud.

'*To Peter! WELCOME TO OZ! Shane Warne.*'

He smiled.

'It's like being welcomed to Britain by the Queen,' he said.

'I think he really liked me,' I said. 'He was ever so chatty.'

A taxi finally arrived.

'So,' he said. 'Is it straight back to London for you? Not by taxi, obviously, unless you're *really* scared of flying…'

'I'm getting a flight in the morning,' I said.

'Heathrow? Gatwick?'

'No.'

'Oh,' he said. 'Where, then?'

And I smiled.

Because I had one more stop to make.

Chapter Twenty

In which we learn that it is better to travel hopefully than to arrive disenchanted...

When I woke up, I was in the back of a small cab hurtling down a motorway with a strange blend of reggae-jazz causing the windows to vibrate and the driver to make involuntary noises.

I didn't really know what time it was. Darkness looked like it was on its way, and when I'd left Australia it had been light, but after twelve or thirteen hours on a plane I couldn't tell if it was night on its way or morning.

The blue neon digits on the dashboard clock said 18:32.

'Good morning!' said the driver when he saw I'd woken up. Which was nice, but only confused me more.

'Hi...' I said, and I looked out of the window.

There it was.

Tokyo.

I was here for one reason and one reason only. You know what that was. But you don't know how *important* it felt. Yes, I was here to meet Akira Matsui. But I was also here because I wanted to *finish* something.

If Chris *had* left a message for me at home, I was nearly *done*. Yeah, so Tom wouldn't meet me. So what? I would get Akira, and then I would get Chris, and then Tom would have to live with the fact that he hadn't been a part of this. A part of a regrouping of friends. Proof that in a society where everyone moves away, everyone moves on, where the internet can facilitate a thousand semi-friendships a second, *proof* that *real friendships* can *last*. That all it takes is a little effort. Effort that *I* was willing to go to, even if Tom wasn't.

Akira *had* to meet with me. And to make sure he did, I wasn't going to give him the option not to. I *had* to achieve this. Finishing a Panini sticker album wasn't enough.

But the fact that Akira's first-ever email to me had been... well... quite *formal*, meant that I *knew* I had to be careful with this one. If we'd *started* our renewed friendship by talking about the Gastroenterological Society of Japan, it could be *years* before we moved it on to talk of having dinner or a beer. And I wanted that now. Before I was thirty. Because November 16th was little over a week away.

So this was my plan. Go to Japan. Find him. Force him to meet me. End of plan.

Akira had literally no idea I was on my way. No idea that I was in Japan right this very second for the sole purpose of tracking him down. I had only one full day in the country to make my impact and achieve my goal. One day to locate him and meet him. But I had one ace up my sleeve.

When I'd been excitedly tapping new names into the internet that day – the day I'd emailed Tim Sismey about conkers and found the karate teacher estate agent Alex – I'd stumbled upon the fact that my friend Bob was now teaching English in Osaka. It stood to reason that he'd have a little Japanese under his belt. I'd emailed him and told him I was coming to Tokyo, and asked whether he'd like to show me around. He said yes, but warned me his Japanese 'needed work'. I told him that didn't matter, and that I was delighted he'd agreed to show me around. But little did he know that when he arrived at Shinjuku station at 9am tomorrow, I would have another task for him altogether...

I'd booked myself into a *ryokan* – a traditional Japanese hotel – on a strange and sparse street somewhere in the suburbs. The driver had had trouble finding it and we'd stopped to ask for directions. A man in a hat had his finger to his mouth, trying to work out where we'd need to turn off. He shouted out to a friend, who brought a map with him. They studied it together, and this brought the attentions of a passing cyclist, who stopped and asked if he could help. All three men and the driver were now studying the same map, huddled together, every now and again looking at me apologetically. I looked back, trying to look even *more* apologetic, and thankful for their attentions. It was like we were in some kind of etiquette-off, all trying to be as polite as we could possibly be. If there is anything that will bring the Japanese and the British to war, it will be over who is the most polite. But even if that happens, it'll never really come to blows, because we'll all spend so long insisting the other side take their shot first.

Finally, thankfully, I arrived at the *ryokan* – lit up from within like a lantern and as welcoming as you could imagine.

I opened the door and stumbled in to find the receptionist sitting right opposite me. At a cooker to my right, a man was frying some chicken and tossing bright green vegetables into a pan. At a table, a barefooted gent with a huge beard grinned at me, and poured some tea. It was a tiny room. But it was homely. In fact, it was so homely I was worried I'd inadvertently wandered into someone's home.

'Mr Wallace?' said the receptionist. 'We've been waiting for you!'

The bearded man nodded.

'Hi...' I said, turning to make sure I made eye contact with the chef and the bearded man, but forgetting I had my rucksack on and knocking something off a shelf. God. It was really small in here.

'Don't worry!' said the receptionist, as an orange plastic Buddha clattered around on the floor. 'Please don't worry!'

The bearded man found this inexplicably hilarious and nearly choked on his food.

'Please – you are in room four,' said the receptionist. 'I give you your key.'

She searched about in a drawer, trying to find the key to room four.

'You are on first floor,' she said. 'Bathrooms are on second floor.'

'Cool,' I said, taking the key. 'Thanks.'

A bathroom. That was a good idea. And food. I needed food. That chicken smelled amazing.

I knew my room didn't have en-suite facilities so I carried on up to the second floor, inching past an elderly couple on the very narrow stairs and apologising for knocking their elbows with my backpack. I found the toilets, and eased myself through the door. There was a sink in here, and, beyond, a separate cubicle. By now, the water I'd drunk in the taxi was tapping at my bladder, asking to be let out, and I squeezed my way into the cubicle, my backpack catching slightly on the lock of the door as I did so.

And then I simply let nature take its course, as I stood there, smiling blankly and thinking about chicken.

Finished and satisfied, I attempted to turn around and unlock the door.

But I couldn't. I tried, but I couldn't.

Why couldn't I turn around and unlock the door?

I tried once more, but my backpack only allowed me an inch or two of turning space. I turned right, but no. My backpack just softly baffed against the wall. So I tried turning left, as if that would make any difference whatsoever. If anything, it was worse. The toilet-roll holder made contact with an area that toilet-roll holders should never make contact with. So I tried turning right again.

God.

I was stuck! I was stuck in a Japanese cubicle!

Panicking slightly, I tried to reach up to the straps of my backpack and slide my arms through them – but there wasn't the space. My elbows couldn't get out far enough to get them through. I tried turning as far as I could and sliding – no luck. I tried simply leaning. I tried hopping up and down with my arms straight down but the backpack kept catching on my jacket and wouldn't budge. Eventually, I realised there was only one thing to do.

I looked at the key to room four. I got my phone out. I dialled the hotel receptionist. I waited while the call bounced via satellite from the toilet, to England, back to another satellite, and down to the receptionist, two floors below.

'Hello,' I said, when she answered. 'This is Mr Wallace. I'm afraid I'm stuck in your toilet.'

'You are *stuck* in the *toilet*?' she said.

In the background, I heard the bloke with the beard start choking again.

*

I decided, once I'd been freed, that maybe I'd better eat out tonight. The bearded bloke – whose name was Adriaan and who came from the Netherlands – still seemed some way off finishing his dinner, and I didn't really want to explain how I'd ended up stuck in a Japanese toilet. He, the chef and the receptionist all waved me off, and I strolled out to meet Tokyo for the very first time.

I could people-watch, I decided. Get to know the local culture. Get inside the mind of the Japanese. That way, when I finally managed to track Akira down, I'd have something to talk to him about. And so on I walked.

I walked down small streets and little alleyways, before finding myself on a large road twisting through tower blocks and past skyscrapers, under shopping malls and vast neon lights. I walked on, as a dark Tokyo evening began to blush under orange streetlights. The city was thriving. Cool kids with strange haircuts and risqué clothing hugged in the streets. Drunk businessmen staggered into bars, filling the air around them with sake fumes and belched laughter. My stomach rumbled as I watched people through windows, eating noodles or sushi or strange dark meats. I found everything fascinating. The people. The buildings. The street signs. The fact that their taxi drivers all seemed to wear small white gloves and drive cars called 'Cedric'. There was chatter everywhere; noise all around. There's nothing better, sometimes, than being somewhere where virtually nothing you see or hear is understandable – not a sign on a door, nor a symbol on a map, nor a single thing someone says. You're lost in a safe place. A strange mix of the alien and the totally familiar. And so on I walked, and when it looked for all the world like I was starting to get lost, there I saw it – a black, barely visible oval sign bearing the letters *NJA* – and the more welcome word 'Restaurant' beneath it. I was ready to eat. After a moment or two I found the door and pushed it, but nothing happened. There were no windows, no lights, and just as I decided it must be closed or non-existent, I heard a tiny, indefinable click. I pushed the door again, and this time it swung open, to reveal a small, dark room, with rocky walls and water features, and a girl dressed entirely in black standing behind a counter. It didn't look much like a restaurant to me. For a start, there was no... well... there was no *restaurant*.

'Hi...' I said, suddenly very unsure of myself. 'Is this... a restaurant?'

'Hello!' she said, clasping her hands together. 'Welcome!'

I stole another glance around. It still didn't look much like a restaurant.

'You are... alone?' she said.

I nodded. The girl looked slightly perplexed, but then shook it off and said...

'Please wait one moment. You will have wonderful evening. We have very nice food. Traditional Japan food. Please wait. Your ninja comes in one moment.'

I relaxed slightly. It *must* be a restaurant. I wasn't sure why she thought it was so unusual that I should be here on my own, though. Surely people in Japan sometimes ate on their own. I guess even in London, though, restaurants are for sharing, and...

Hang on.

My *what*?

'Sorry – *what* comes in one moment?'

The girl was now beaming at me.

'Your ninja will arrive in one moment!' she said.

'My *ninja*?' I said.

How jetlagged *was* I?

'Your ninja,' she said, and then, pointing one finger in the air, importantly. 'For ninja training!'

Ninja *training*? What *was* this place? When had I ordered ninja training? I hadn't even ordered a *starter*!

'But I didn't *order* a ninja!' I said, confused. 'Not even a little one!'

I tried to think right the way back through our conversation. Had I ordered a ninja? I was pretty sure all I'd said so far was, 'Is this a restaurant?'

'I'm not sure if this is the right kind of—'

But the girl put one finger to her lips.

And then I heard it.

But what *was* it?

And then there it was again...

A blood-curdling scream from a room somewhere far away.

Followed by a thump. And then a series of thumps. Like a toddler backflipping through a hallway. And then, totally without warning of any kind whatsoever, a hidden door was flung open and out leapt a small female ninja.

I realise I may sound mental at this moment, but I promise you it's true: out leapt a tiny ninja.

The ninja landed softly on the floor beside me, and crouched for just a moment, summing up in one split second the dangers the room held. But it didn't hold any dangers. It held a Danny. A rather confused and reasonably scared one. As odd as it may seem, I was very annoyed with myself. I'd only been in Tokyo a matter of hours, and already I'd let a ninja get me. *Why* had I come to Japan? Of *course* I was going to be got by a ninja!

There was another scream, and the ninja shot straight up, undertaking a number of rigorous hand movements and shouting various statements in Japanese, before turning to me, fixing me with the eyes of a killer and shouting, 'ARE YOU READY FOR NINJA TRAINING?'

I looked at the ninja. And then at the receptionist. The receptionist looked at me.

'And then will I get food?' I asked.

The receptionist closed her eyes and nodded. I looked back at the ninja. She raised her eyebrows.

'I am ready,' I said.

Like pirates, sharks, monkeys and ghosts, ninjas will never not be exciting. It was part of the reason why suddenly having a Japanese kid in school was so thrilling. Akira Matsui was our pathway to this mysterious and hidden culture. You can imagine our disappointment, then, when it turned out he neither knew any ninja magic, owned any ninja swords, nor even seemed to know what a ninja was. Michael Amodio and I put this down to a special ninja code of silence, and would often throw things at the back of his head to see if he would react with lightning speed. But he never did. He just turned around, looking hurt and confused. It was a shame, because the 1980s really was the decade of the ninja. The petrol station me and Michael used to stop at on the way home from swimming to buy packets of Revels and look at the videos bore testament to that.

These videos were brilliant. They were clearly pirated (which made them all the more exciting – *pirate ninjas*!), with photocopied sleeves and battered covers, but when we were able to get our hands on one, high production values weren't our concern. There was *The Nine Deaths of the Ninja*, of course, as well as *American Ninja* and *American Ninja 2: The Confrontation*, but Michael and I both found these simplistic portrayals of ninja culture too broad and Westernised in their scope. Plus, they didn't use nun-chuks anywhere *near* enough. There were nun-chuks galore in *Enter the Ninja*, which was also better because it ended with a freeze frame of the main character winking at the camera, which is a technique that I have now decided is how *every* film should end. Then you had *Revenge of the Ninja*, and *Ninja Resurrection*. *Mafia Versus Ninja* (imagine!), *Zombie Versus Ninja* (imagine!!!), *Chinese Super Ninja*, *Phantom Diamond Ninja*, and *Ninja Kids*, which was critically acclaimed, but rubbish.

Now, something tells me that very few of the classics listed above may have stood the test of time. But the unerring fact – the one thing these grainy, badly edited films showed us – was the absolute and unwavering dedication the simple ninja has to his training. They needed stealth, cunning, ruthlessness. Steely-eyed determination. They needed to be able to leap off speedboats, flying hundreds of feet in the air, to land on aeroplanes. They had to have complete mastery of their intuition. They had to feel their enemy's moves before their enemy had even thought about moving. It was training that went back thousands of years, treated with utter respect and reverence by all those who knew its dark and astounding secrets, and it was training that I now found myself undertaking in a small ante-chamber of a cave-like Tokyo building. And the only thing that took away from it? The fact that just above her authentic ninja-style shoes, I could clearly see that *my* ninja was wearing a pair of Garfield socks.

I was still ever-so-slightly confused as the ninja turned to me, suddenly, and said, 'Now we begin the training!'

She slapped me on the shoulder.

'You must always have awareness of your surrounding!'

I looked around the small room to show I was making myself aware of it. I watched as she pressed what looked like it was supposed to be a hidden button.

'Oh no!' she said, and a second or two later a small section of the floor fell away in front of me, with all the excitement and special-effects wizardry of a peanut. She widened her eyes dramatically and looked very worried indeed. 'What we do now?'

I had a think. We could always step over it, I thought. It was, after all, quite a small gap. But surely that wasn't the way of the ninja; that was just the way of the sensible.

'Quickly! WHAT WE DO!'

'Well, we mustn't rush into anything,' I said, quite calmly, given what was fast becoming quite a high-pressure situation.

'Quickly!' said the ninja, again. She seemed annoyed. Luckily, I spotted something.

'I notice that there's another button there,' I said. 'We could try pressing that?'

'Ah!' said the ninja, impressed. 'Very good!'

I felt quite proud. I was finally thinking like a ninja. She pressed the button and, sure enough, a small platform appeared from the wall, allowing us to step over the terrifying two-foot drop which had opened up before us. I was pleased I had passed the first stage of what was bound to be a rigorous and punishing period of training. The ninja clapped her hands together.

'So now you eat!' she said.

Maybe this was a test. Maybe this was supposed to relax me, and I was about to be jumped by dozens of furious ninjas. I tensed slightly as we stooped under a low ceiling to get out of a tunnel and into... well... into a restaurant. A ninja-themed restaurant. Which, if we're all going to be honest about this, is possibly the best theme any restaurant could ever have.

'Wow...' I said. Dim spotlights lit separated sections, where I could just about make out small groups of people sitting on the floor, being served by all manner of smiling ninjas. Now, *this* was what I wanted. Quality food in an authentic cave-like setting. Perhaps I should tell Simon about this, I thought. Perhaps it would make an interesting direction for the Toby Carvery, Colwick, to take. But the ninja had whet my appetite for far more than food…

'And what about my training?' I asked.

It couldn't be over yet!

'Yes! Training over! Food now!'

'My training's *over*?'

'All! Over! Yes!'

'It didn't seem like *much* training…' I said. And it didn't. All I'd done was press a small button. If that's all the modern ninja needs these days, it's remarkable you don't see more of them working in lifts.

'You eat now!' said the ninja, opening a small door for me into a private bamboo booth, and gesturing that I should take my shoes off and sit.

'So am I now a ninja?' I asked. 'Seeing as I sailed through my training?'

The ninja looked at me, a little sadly. She didn't say anything for a bit, and I took off my shoes as she thought about what to say. She had a small pad and pencil with her now, and to be honest, she just looked like a waitress all dressed up.

Then she just shrugged and said, 'Okay.'

Despite the disappointment of my training coming to an end, I was pleased to be able to sit and watch the ninjas in their natural environment. It was my first night in Tokyo, and this was precisely the way I had imagine it. And tomorrow, I would get up bright and early and attack the task at hand: finding Akira Matsui. Bob would be meeting me at Shinjuku station for what he thought would be a day of sightseeing and tourism. I would work out how to break the news to him later on.

I ordered some saki and some noodles from a ninja with a Swatch on, and laid out all the evidence I had before me. It was an intriguing set of clues.

The postcards. A picture of Akira. The email from his dad. The directions to Yamanashi.

The picture of Akira brought back the most memories. It was taken on the day we celebrated his twelfth birthday. His parents had taken us to see a steam train, and we'd gone on a short journey through the Leicestershire countryside. His mum had stopped off at McDonald's earlier that morning and whipped out some lukewarm Big Macs – which in those days seemed so impossibly big and mountainous that no human being could ever eat a whole one. We all did, that day. We were becoming men.

It was interesting to think about how much we'd all changed since then. I wondered what Akira would look like now. He'd be bigger, of course, but would he wear glasses? What kind of clothes would he wear? What was his style? Would I recognise him? And then something rather odd hit me. I wasn't sure if I *would*. We hadn't made plans. I was surprising him.

I'd come all this way in the vague hope of *possibly* recognising a man I once went to school with. A man I hadn't seen in twenty years. A man about whom all I knew was that he would have black hair and brown eyes.

And – at the risk of sounding politically incorrect – that's not really much to go on when you're in Japan. I'd basically narrowed it down to half the population.

'Sir?'

I looked up to see a ninja smiling down at me. He'd noticed that I was simply staring at a picture of a small boy.

'Your son?'

It was unlikely.

'An old friend,' I said, before, inexplicably: 'Do you know him? He's a man.'

I held it up, to prove one, if not the other.

'No,' said the ninja, placing my noodles in front of me. It turned out that this ninja was a Master Ninja.

'A *Master* Ninja? What does that mean?'

'I am expert in ancient Ninja magic!' he said, very mysteriously. 'I show you!'

He got out a pack of cards with classic cars on the back and I realised pretty quickly this magic probably *wasn't* all that ancient.

'You are in Japan on holiday?'

'Sort of,' I told the Master Ninja. 'I'm here to find *this* guy.'

I pointed at Akira's picture again.

'You know him well?' asked the ninja, shuffling the cards.

'Not really. Not any more.'

'When do you meet him?'

'I hope tomorrow.'

'You *hope*? You don't know?'

He was joking, but actually, he was right.

'Akira doesn't really know I'm here. In Japan.'

The Master Ninja considered this.

'A long way for hope,' he said. 'But it is better to travel hopefully than to arrive disenchanted.'

It was a remarkable statement. So remarkable I had to pause for a second and write it on my napkin.

'Are you *really* a Master Ninja?' I asked.

'Yes!' said the Master Ninja. 'But also, I am a student.'

'Oh.'

'Now for ancient magic!' he said, importantly. 'Pick a card...'

I left the ninja restaurant full of hope and enthusiasm. Especially when moments after wandering out of its door, thinking that my night of ninjas was over, I heard a shrill scream somewhere behind me and turned to see the same tiny ninja who had welcomed me to the restaurant now kneeling in the middle of the pavement and unravelling a giant scroll which read 'THANK YOU FOR COMING!' I waved at the ninja, and the ninja waved at me, and a middle-aged European couple in baseball caps stared at me like I'd just shouted out that I was going to stamp on some dogs.

'Ninjas,' I gently explained, and wandered off.

Later, as a Cedric I'd flagged down on the streets pulled in to my fun-size hotel, I considered the Master Ninja's words. He'd been right. It's better to go through life with optimism than be beaten before you even get where you're supposed to be going. It hit home.

Jetlag had sidled up on me and when I eventually managed to get my key in the door I was ready for bed. I wandered into reception and immediately knocked the small plastic Buddha off its shelf again. It bounced about on the floor, noisily. Upstairs, I could hear a muffled laugh. I think it was the Dutch bloke.

I tiptoed upstairs and fell to my mattress, exhausted.

This was it! I thought, the very second my eyes opened. *This was Akira Day*! The plan? Wash. Breakfast. And then Shinjuku station, where I would meet Bob and break the news that today would be a day of excitement and friendship and adventure!

First stop – the shower.

I opened the door of my very small, very basic room an optimistic man. I was revitalised and excited. I grabbed my towel and a toothbrush and walked upstairs, once again having to squeeze past some people on their way out, and found my way to the shower.

I looked at it. Somehow, the designers – if, indeed, there had *been* any – had managed to make the shower even smaller than the toilet cubicle of the day before. But no fear! Today I had no backpack to trap me. I stepped gingerly into the cubicle and turned the water on. Now, imagine standing in an upright coffin while someone three inches away fires an erratic but powerful hosepipe off in your face. This was fast becoming my Japanese shower experience. I tried to reach again for the taps, but such was the pressure of the water I had to lean down while doing it, meaning my head soon smacked against the wall and, as I rose in shock, thwacked the back of it on the shower head.

There must have been some *problem* with the water pressure, too, because the effect was like those garden sprinklers you see in American films – very fast, then virtually nothing, then incredibly fast again – and to cope meant not only managing the timing element, but being braced for temperatures which would suddenly soar from the mildly comforting to the impossibly hot. Not just that – but the closeness of the shower head to my own meant that not only was I feeling the full force of Japanese water power, but that every four or five seconds I was blinded and had a mouth full of water. But I was determined not to be beaten by my new aqua-nemesis. I would try and quickly rub my bar of soap wherever I could, timing it so I could have my eyes open while I did so. It was an excellent plan, but the size of the cubicle meant that each time I attempted to use the soap, one of my elbows would connect with a wall and I'd let out a small, involuntary yelp. This happened what felt like nine hundred times. Bruised, blinded and boiling, I stepped out of the cubicle, managing somehow to pull the doorknob off the door and stub my toe on the step.

I was not built for Japan.

Downstairs, the Dutchman was eating breakfast. He looked freshly showered, and not in the least bit bruised.

'Good shower?' he said.

I decided to go out for breakfast.

I was standing outside Shinjuku station at ten minutes to nine holding the last remaining breakfast item the little shop nearby had had to offer.

It didn't really look all that breakfasty. It didn't really look like it should exist at all. I'd had to look twice at it, and then a third time to make sure I could actually cope with it. There was a small caption in English underneath where the sandwiches had been. *To start well and finish is delights! Eat for humans to taste lustful and union!* I stared at it for a moment and then decided I was convinced. Which is why for breakfast I was now eating a spaghetti sandwich with a dollop of egg mayonnaise on the top.

Quite who invented pasta in a bap I'm not sure. Why they'd thought that tomato sauce and egg mayonnaise might be happy bedfellows is even more of a mystery. But I suppose it *did* taste lust-ful and union, and of course that's what humans taste to eat.

But I had to put all such thoughts aside. Because I had Akira to concentrate on.

Bob would be turning up here at nine o'clock, when I'd have to break the news of my quest. I figured Bob would be okay with it. He must've been up the Tokyo Tower before, and seen the parks and shops and sights. Going to an obscure hospital somewhere in the countryside to meet someone I hadn't seen since the late 1980s and was of no actual consequence to Bob would probably be a little treat for him.

I giggled to myself as I munched on my pasta bap. How surprised would Akira be to see me again, after all these years? And then I had a troubling thought. Hospitals are busy places. Busy places full of busy people. Bob could guide me through the Japanese train system and make sure I turned up at the right place – but as he'd said himself, his Japanese was 'a bit rubbish'. What if this meant we couldn't communicate with people? What if this meant that at the crucial moment, when I'd asked Bob to explain to Akira about turning thirty, and finding the Book, and tracking down my friends from my past, what Bob was *actually* saying was, '*To start well and finish is delights! Eat for humans to taste lustful and union!*'

I needed an insurance policy.

And then I remembered something Peter had said...

'What the hell are you wearing?' said Bob, looking slightly concerned.

'Hello, Bob!' I said, giving him a hug and then stepping back, proudly. 'This is my Akira Matsui T-shirt!'

'Who's Akira Matsui?' he said. 'How old is he?'

'I went to school with him,' I said. 'He's about twenty-nine.'

A man on a bike rolled by, staring at my chest as he did so.

'He looks a little younger than that...'

'In this picture, he is twelve years old, yes. In fact, this very picture was taken to commemorate the day of his twelfth birthday. I had this made across the road.'

'But... why?' he said.

'I'll tell you,' I said. 'But first, let's get this tour under way.'

'Okay,' said Bob, clapping his hands together. 'So what do you want to see first? There's Tokyo Tower. The National Museum. The Imperial Palace. The Science Museum is *amazing*. Or we could check out the Olympic Stadium. Or the National Park for Nature Study...'

'Well,' I said, cutting him and trying hard to give the impression that I was considering this very carefully. 'What I'd *really* like to see is Yamanashi University Hospital.'

And Bob looked a little confused.

'This is *exciting*!' said Bob, as we boarded the train. 'This is like an *adventure*! I have never been to Yamanashi or to its university hospital!'

'Me neither!' I said, happily.

'So he's got no idea you're coming?'

We sat down.

'Nope. I'm just going to turn up and *force* him to meet me.'

'Any particular reason?'

'He's not very good at replying to emails. And I can't risk him saying no. I have to get him, because when I get home, I'll only have one friend left from the Book. And *he's* left me a message, so *he's* in the bag. Which means that, come November 16th, I'll have completed my project. And then I can grow up happily and buy display cushions.'

'I don't understand,' said Bob.

I opened up my rucksack and brought out my address book.

'This is the Book,' I said. 'Twelve names, all of them representing a key part of my childhood. And Akira is number eleven…'

'I still don't understand,' said Bob.

And as we entered a tunnel, I filled him in.

Bob was fascinated by the photos, as he scrolled through my phone. We were shooting through Japan at the speed of light, on a clean and sleek, whispering train.

Bob and I had met at university, ten years earlier, when we'd started an underground student magazine which we'd sneak into the official university magazines and then pretend had nothing to do with us. It had been a great bonding experience, with late nights, stupid jokes and early-morning reconnaissance missions using fake IDs and people 'on the inside' to get our magazine out there. There had been controversial issues, obviously. Once, in a rush to get the magazine finished, I had tried to headline an article – BRUCE SPRINGSTEEN: ONE LEGEND, ONE STAGE. But in the rush it had appeared as BRUCE SPRINGSTEEN: ONE LEGGED ON STAGE. Don't tell Lizzie – remember, my spelling is *excellent*.

Bob had gone on to become a photographer, a journalist for a Marxist newspaper (despite no Marxist tendencies whatsoever) and now an English teacher. He'd met a girl in Osaka – Tomoko – and life was good.

We were scheduled to arrive in Yamanashi city sometime around twelve, meaning we'd have the whole afternoon to spend with Akira before hopping back on for the two-hour journey back to Tokyo, where I planned to celebrate in style.

Bob found another photo.

'And who's *that*?' he asked

'Peter Gibson,' I said. 'I met him in Melbourne a couple of days ago. He's an architect who once had a paper round. We ate noodles and went bowling.'

'And this one?'

'That's Anil. He's the first one I got back in contact with, really. His mum made me eat more curries than is technically legal. He showed me my old house but then the people inside thought we were going to rob them.'

Bob kept flicking through.

'And... this?'

'That's me in LA.'

'Why are you dressed as a rabbit?'

'It's very complicated.'

He handed the phone back and smiled.

'I think this is great,' he said. 'Getting back to basics. Seeing the people who saw you grow up.'

'Ever considered it?'

'Well... I've googled people. But never taken it much further than that. I kind of suspect that most of my old mates are still in the same place, and all working in IT...'

'You'd be surprised,' I said.

'I think we're arriving...'

The train slowed to a halt, and there was the sign. YAMANASHI-SHI. We were here.

'Are you hungry?' asked Bob.

'I had a pasta bap,' I explained.

'I'm hungry,' said Bob. 'Or maybe I'm just excited.'

It was sweet, Bob's excitement. He reached into his bag and brought out a jam sandwich and a small flask of juice. I looked at him, and swelled with pride. We were two friends, on a mission.

A mission of great import. Striding out into the unknown, with jam sandwiches and orange juice, and nothing but a dream. It felt like we were two of the Famous Five, or something, on the trail of a lost friendship.

'Right!' said Bob, realising he was now in charge. 'There's a map!'

I looked around the station platform while Bob studied the map on the wall. A small child with a balloon was staring at me. I smiled at him. He smiled at me. A train pulled in and out got a samurai.

'Bob…' I said, tapping him on the shoulder but not taking my eyes off the ancient warrior.

'Hmm?' he said, still engrossed in the map.

'There's a samurai over there,' I said.

'Is there?' he said, still not turning round.

'He's got a sword and armour and everything.'

'Oh.'

'I thought samurais were from… you know… the seventh century.'

'Yeah,' said Bob. 'It's probably just a ghost.'

I stopped tapping his shoulder.

I started again.

'He's stopping at that vending machine, Bob. The samurai is buying some crisps, Bob.'

Bob didn't seem all that interested in samurais buying crisps. The small boy with the balloon did, though. He turned and looked at me. We raised our eyebrows at each other and made impressed faces.

'Right!' said Bob. 'I think I know what to do.'

Upstairs, there were more samurais, just milling about, chatting.

'Is this normal, Bob?' I asked. 'Because there do seem to be an *awful lot* of samurais in Japan.'

'Samurais are actually a *Japanese* invention,' said Bob, wisely.

'Yeah, but they're not supposed to be just wandering about,' I said. 'Who's let all these samurais out? It's not like you arrive at Heathrow and you're immediately overwhelmed by Beefeaters, is it?'

'I suppose so,' said Bob, and he stopped, and took in the samurais. 'There must be some kind of show on.'

'Something that appeals to samurais?' I asked.

'Or that involves people dressing up as them,' said Bob, and actually that made more sense.

'There's one eating a hamburger!' I said. 'Look at his axe! Are you *allowed* to take an axe into a restaurant here?'

'Samurais are not generally allowed in restaurants,' said Bob, with a real and impressive sense of authority.

'Not like ninjas, then,' I said. 'I couldn't bloody *move* for them last night.'

Bob laughed. I think he thought I was joking.

'Let's walk up that street there,' he said, brightly, and we followed a samurai who was pushing his bike.

'So all we have to do is find the university,' said Bob, as we stopped on a gentle incline and studied the map. 'It should be straight up this road...'

'Excellent work, Bob,' I said, patting him on the back, and noticing a sign in the window of the beauty shop opposite advertising 'EXTENSION LIPS'.

'We're lost, aren't we?' I said, ten minutes later.

'We're not lost,' said Bob. 'It's just that I had the map upside down. I'm not very good at reading Japanese letters yet.'

'Okay...'

'And also, that was a map of Tokyo.'

We walked back past the EXTENSION LIPS shop again.

'This it it!' said Bob. 'This is Yamanashi University!'

I took it in. So this was where I would finally meet Akira Matsui. Somewhere within these large, sunlit walls I would find the man I'd travelled halfway across the world to see. Well, all the way across, and then halfway back.

We strode up to the guard manning the small security cabin at the gates.

'Hello!' I said, loudly, and then, realising I had nowhere else to take this, handed over to Bob.

'You handle this,' I said.

'My Japanese isn't brilliant,' he said.

'Don't you worry. It's better than mine.'

Bob looked nervous, and then, from somewhere deep within, managed to summon up the words: 'MEDICAL! UNIVERSITY?'

The guard just stared at us.

'MEDICAL! UNIVERSITY?' said Bob, again, even louder this time.

'Ah!' said the guard, and then he nodded.

'You see?' I said. 'Your Japanese is *brilliant*!'

But then the guard frowned, and started to speak very quickly indeed. He pointed from time to time at the map and then down the street. Wherever he pointed, we looked, as if there might be a small sign there translating what he was saying. Neither of us understood a word. But we raised our eyebrows and made encouraging faces and nodded and then, when he'd stopped talking and pointing, Bob held up the map again, and said, 'MEDICAL! UNIVERSITY?'

I stood outside the beauty shop and considered having my lips extended.

Bob was inside, pointing at his map and saying the words 'MEDICAL! UNIVERSITY?' to a confused receptionist.

I wandered to the little restaurant that sat next door and looked through the window. It was empty, save for an elderly man mopping the concrete floor. A sign on the window said, '10% OFF ON MONDAYS! MEAL FOR TWO PARSONS ONLY!'

This struck me as a distinctly odd offer. I mean, a 10 per cent discount is never to be sniffed at, but why limit your customer base to parsons? And what was the likelihood of a couple of parsons happening to be hungry in Yamanashi and wandering past this restaurant? It seemed like a con to me.

'No good,' said Bob, wandering out. 'She didn't understand me.'

'If we were religious men, we'd get ten per cent off here on Monday,' I said, pointing at the sign.

'Hang on... that's in *English*,' said Bob.

'So was "Extension Lips",' I said.

'But this is *proper*. Maybe that man in there speaks English...'

And so in we walked. And it was then that we discovered that Yamanashi University Hospital... is not in Yamanashi.

'So where now?' I asked, horrified, as we bounded up the stairs of the train station. 'Where *is* Yamanashi University Hospital?'

'Well,' said Bob, studying his map, and sidestepping a samurai. 'According to that old man, we've got to get to Kofu.'

'Kofu?' I said.

'It's a completely different town.'

'A different *town*?'

'That's where the university is...'

'I thought we'd *been* to the university,' I said.

'No. It turns out that was a spectacles factory. At least, I *think* that's what he said. I don't really know what the word for "spectacles" is. Anyway, we'd better get a move on...'

We found our train and sat down next to a samurai eating an apple.

I looked at my watch. It was already 2pm. *This is fine*, I told myself.

I broke into a sweat.

'Right,' said Bob, as I stood outside a shop in Kofu. This one sold designer T-shirts with well-known Western sayings on them. You know the kind of things. 'Swarms of Winter Gnats Run High!' was one. 'Give Me Strength! Are You Serious? Pise Myself Laughing!' was another. Pretty standard stuff.

'Right what?' I said, glancing at my watch. It was twenty to three. Time felt like it was slipping away from me. I had to get back to Tokyo tonight so I could get my flight in the morning. I *had* to get my flight in the morning. And I *had* to meet Akira before I did that.

'I said the words "Medical" and "University" really loudly again, and this woman started nodding loads. Mark my words, Dan, we're going to *find* you Akira Matsui!'

'This is *brilliant*,' I said. 'So where's the hospital?'

'Well... it's actually in a completely different town from Kofu,' said Bob. 'But don't worry – they have a train station. Let's go!'

*

The train was painfully slow.

Really, truly, *painfully* slow.

We were rumbling gradually towards a place called Joieu, some-where deep in the heart of the Japanese countryside. Around us were ancient Japanese women, all of whom looked like they'd probably seen samurais the first time round, and who carried old and tattered bags of strange foods. I looked out of the window to see us being overtaken by an old man on a bike. My tummy grumbled. It'd been *hours* since my pasta bap, and Bob had long-since finished his sand-wiches and squash.

'Okay,' said Bob. 'Joieu should be the next stop.'

'It's nearly four o'clock,' I said. 'We're going to have to work fast.'

'Don't you worry,' said Bob. 'According to the map, there's a road that'll take us right there...'

'You had the map upside down again, didn't you?' I said, as we stood, in the middle of a field, surrounded by mountains and beaten down by the sun.

'Pretty much, yeah,' said Bob.

Somehow I'd managed to get mud all over my jeans, and Bob had a leaf in his hair. I stood outside myself and imagined how we must appear. For a second, everything was silent. Because there are moments in life when you come to question your actions. Moments of outstanding clarity and purest thought, when you look around you, you take in your environment, you work out what brought you here, and you decide that something is wrong.

For me, it was happening right now.

Right now, right this very *second*, in the middle of a harsh and sparse Japanese countryside, a little over a week before my thirtieth birthday, past a town I couldn't remember the name of, full of people whose names I couldn't pronounce.

It was now four o'clock and I looked around me. I took in my environment. I worked out what brought me here. And I decided that something was wrong.

Here I was, standing in a rice field under a mountain in the after-noon sun, a Westerner in the far, far East, wearing grubby trainers, mud-flecked jeans and a T-shirt with the face of a small Japanese boy on it.

And I was lost.

I dug into my pocket and pulled out the document I'd brought with me.

I looked at it.

An Investigation on the Influence of Vitreous Slag Powders on Rheological Properties of Fresh Concrete

I stared at it for a moment, then put it away again. It wasn't helping.

But there – there, in the distance, just beyond a scattering of houses and a girl on a bike, I saw something. A vast, bright white block. This was what I needed. *This* was what I had come for.

'There, Bob – what's that?'

'What?'

'That building! That building there! That looks like... a hospital!'

Bob studied the map. Worked out the direction we'd been going. Turned the map around a couple of times. And then said, 'It *is*... that's Yamanashi University Hospital...'

And now all we had to do was find Akira...

'I'm trying to find Akira Matsui,' I said, to the first student I saw. 'Akira Matsui? He has this face, only older...'

I pointed desperately at my T-shirt. The student smiled and then moved away quickly.

'Does anyone here speak English?'

I was in a crowded courtyard outside the hospital. It had taken longer to walk to the hospital than we'd thought. It never seemed to get any bigger, always taunting us from a distance, never quite being in reach. But now, red-faced and thirsty, here we were, and there was some kind of celebration going on. A Japanese heavy metal band was thrashing about on a stage. Food was being cooked and sold. Everyone was laughing and happy. Everyone except me. I was getting increasingly desperate.

'Maybe we should ask inside?' said Bob, chewing on a hotdog and then offering me some. I waved it away. I had no time for food.

'They might have a staff list,' he said. 'Or a special area where all the doctors sit?'

It was a good idea. I barrelled through the double doors and immediately saw a noticeboard.

'There!' I said.

Bob and I ran up to it and simply stared at it. Everything was in Japanese. It wasn't surprising. We were in Japan.

'Any ideas?' I said, while Bob tried his best to decipher the code.

'Mah-ts-oo-eh...' he said, tracing his finger down a sheet of A4. 'Can't see anything...'

'Excuse me,' I said, to a passing student. 'Do you speak any English?'

He smiled apologetically and moved on.

'Does *anybody* know this man?' I said, loudly, and pointing at my chest. 'Akira Matsui? Anyone? Akira *Matsui*!'

But I got nothing back except embarrassed looks.

And then...

'Matsui?'

There was a thin and wiry student with a kind face looking back at me.

'*Matsui sensei?*'

Sensei! Hang on – that meant... teacher! I *knew* it did! I'd seen it on the Karate Kid! Akira must be teaching here as well as being a medical doctor! It made perfect sense!

'Yes! *Sensei*! Yes!' I said. '*Sensei*, Bob, *sensei*!'

Bob gave me a double thumbs-up and looked excited.

'I know him,' said the stranger.

'You do? Can you take me to him? I'm an old friend!'

He shrugged.

'I *think* yes...'

I shot Bob a look. This was it!

'You come with me,' said our new friend, whose name was Kyohei. 'I can try to help you...'

'This is very kind of you,' I told Kyohei. 'I haven't seen Akira in many years...'

'This is chance for me practise English,' he said. 'One day I wish to be a doctor in a foreign land.'

'Is Akira teaching you well?'

'Matsui sensei is good teacher. Good man.'

I smiled. I knew he would be.

'Come, we find his room…'

Kyohei, Bob and I marched down a dark corridor. A flickering striplight briefly lit the olive green floors and drab beige walls, and I stole quick glances into offices as we walked. I'd never have found my way here without Kyohei. And I'd never have found my way to Kyohei without Bob. I was filled with gratitude for the kindness of friends, and the kindness of strangers. Without these two, I'd still be trying to break into a spectacles factory in Yamanashi, possibly with greatly extended lips.

Finally, after what seemed like a thousand double doors and faceless corridors, we arrived at a room.

'This his office,' said Kyohei.

'Here?' I said, and Kyohei nodded.

I listened at the door. There was someone in there! Akira Matsui was in there! And before I could gather my thoughts, Kyohei had knocked on the door. A voice said something in Japanese. Kyohei opened the door wide open. A man sat in a chair.

'Akira!' I said. 'It's me! Daniel Wallace!'

He looked absolutely stunned to see me. Absolutely *stunned*. Well, wouldn't you be? A friend you haven't seen in twenty years – a friend you barely recognise – standing in your office in the middle of the countryside after flying thousands of miles to see you?

'I've got your face on my T-shirt!' I shouted, proudly.

And the man muttered something, which was probably about how happy he was to see me, and how much I had also changed over the years.

And then Kyohei quietly shut the door.

'That was not him,' he said, and we all tiptoed away, very quickly indeed.

'So where could he be?' I asked, increasingly worried that we were running out of time. 'Is he *definitely* here?'

'I do not know,' said Kyohei. 'Perhaps he is in the laboratory.'

We walked down a flight of stairs and through some more double doors. In one of the laboratories, several men were chatting quietly over a microscope. Kyohei approached them and spoke to them softly while Bob and I hung back.

'I'm worried, Bob,' I whispered. 'None of them is Akira Matsui. He's not in his office. We've checked the staffroom... what time's the last train to Tokyo?'

'We've got about an hour if we don't want to get stuck in the countryside,' said Bob. 'We've got to get that slow train, then the train to Yamanashi, and *then* the train to Tokyo...'

We looked back at Kyohei, who was approaching us.

'They told me they have not seen him. Perhaps he is in conference. Conference finishes only in two hours.'

I looked at my watch.

'That's too late... can we interrupt it?' I said.

Kyohei looked appalled.

'No – absolute no. Only when it finish can we see who is inside. But also – one of these men says he has not seen Matsui sensei today. Perhaps he has holiday.'

'*What*?' I said. 'He might be on *holiday*? He's just *been*! He went to a gastroenteritis convention, or something!'

Bob looked as distraught as I felt. But then he had an idea.

'His *house*!' said Bob. 'He must live around here! Maybe he even lives on *campus*!'

Of course! This place was miles from anywhere. If someone worked out here, chances are they'd have to *live* out here as well...

'Kyohei – how could we find his home?' I asked. 'How could we find Akira's *house*?'

Kyohei said, 'Hmmm.'

'This is it!' I said. 'This is the street!'

Kyohei had piled me and Bob into his tiny red car and driven us a couple of miles away to a street which a man with a clipboard had assured us was Akira's. Kyohei now seemed as excited at the prospect of meeting Akira as Bob and I did.

'Second house,' said Kyohei. 'Black door.'

'Okay, let's do this…'

The three of us, looking like the strangest gang in the world, stepped out of the car and approached the door.

'Definitely this one?' I asked, and Kyohei said, 'Yes. Definitely.'

I took a deep breath and knocked twice, hard, on the door.

I looked at Bob. Bob looked at me. We both looked at Kyohei, whose eyes darted between us. We all looked at the door.

Nothing.

'Maybe he's asleep,' I said, and then banged on the door, louder this time.

I pressed my ear to the door. I flipped open the letterbox and peered in. It was dark in there. Curtains drawn. No noise whatsoever.

I stood up and shook my head.

And then I banged on the door again. Three times. And then I paused for a second and a second only and I banged again.

'I'm not sure he's in…' said Bob, but I didn't hear the rest of the sentence because I was banging again. I kept banging, and I tried banging the letterbox, and I caught sight of a concerned Kyohei, and then there was a hand on my shoulder and Bob was saying, 'Let it go…'

'I can't let it go,' I said, stopping, and turning to him.

'He's not there…' said Bob. 'He's gone…'

And in that moment, I knew he had.

It was no good. I would not be meeting Akira today. Maybe, I realised, I would never meet him again.

We sat in silence in Kyohei's little red car and drove down a smooth, stark street. Kyohei had offered to drive us back to the station, and anything was better than giving Bob a map.

And then his phone rang. He took the call while Bob tried to make me feel better.

'Well, at least you tried,' said Bob. 'That's something. Who needed all twelve anyway? You've done very well indeed.'

I sighed. I supposed he was right.

And then Kyohei stopped the car.

I looked at Bob. What was going on?

Kyohei put the car in reverse, backed into someone's drive and turned the car round.

'What's up?' I asked.

'Conference about to have break,' said Kyohei. 'We drive fast, we get there...'

Kyohei sped into the car park, stopped the car at an awkward angle and all three of us got out and ran.

'Into elevator!' yelled Kyohei, who I now loved more than any Japanese medical student I have ever met before.

The three us jammed ourselves in and Kyohei pressed 5.

We rode in nervous silence, and when the doors finally pinged open, we could hear talking. Chitter-chatter. Voices, dozens of them, and all coming from behind one door...

We pushed it open.

Inside, various doctors and delegates were holding small cups of coffee and juice, and nibbling on foreign biscuits.

'Do you see him?' asked Bob.

'I don't know – hang on...'

My eyes scoured the room. He had to be here. Dr Akira Matsui *had* to be here...

'I can't see him...' I said. 'I can't...'

And then my eyes came to rest on someone. Someone whose eyes had come to rest on me.

It wasn't Akira.

It was a short, jolly woman, who was now smiling at me, with a curious expression.

She was pointing at me, now, and telling someone else to look.

I smiled and raised my hand in a friendly wave.

And then she pointed at my T-shirt, and she said...

'Akira?'

My eyes widened and my heart leapt.

The T-shirt had worked.

The T-shirt had bloody *worked*!

'Yes!' I said. 'Akira! Akira Matsui!'

This seemed to delight her, and she called for someone else to take a look at my shirt, and he found it as curious as she did.

'Kyohei – can you explain?'

And Kyohei did his best.

'What are they saying?' I asked Bob.

'Something about Akira... something about you travelling a long way to find him... something about his house...'

'Do they know him, then? Do they know where he is?'

'Hang on...'

And then, with no warning whatsoever, the small, jolly woman jabbed her finger in the air and shouted, 'Ah!' And then she turned on her heel and ran away.

'What's happened?' I said, mildly panicked. 'Where's that small jolly woman going?'

She returned a moment or two later with something orange in her hand. A phone. She found a number. Pressed Dial. And then handed me the phone.

'Is this...?' I said. 'Kyohei, is *this*...?'

Kyohei nodded. Bob gave me another double thumbs-up.

I put the phone to my ear.

It was ringing.

A male voice answered.

'... Akira?' I tried.

'Hai,' said the voice.

'Akira Matsui?'

'...'

'This is... Daniel Wallace, from Loughborough... I knew you when you were little...'

'... Daniel?' he said.

'Yes! Me! I've come all the way from England to say hello! And then I couldn't find you and I'd been looking for everyone else and I'd found lots of them and then I was in Australia and then I came to find you and I was in Tokyo and I came here but couldn't find you and then this lady gave me the phone how are you?'

And then I realised that all of that had come out in pretty much two seconds, and I decided to start again.

'Akira. Where are you?'

'... I... am... with my mother and father... in Tokyo...'

He was struggling to find his words. Struggling to speak English again after all these years.

'I... am...'

He trailed off. It was okay. I knew what I had to say next.

'Akira. I have come a long way to see you. Will you meet with me?'

And then there was a pause.

And Akira collected his thoughts.

And he weighed up what I'd said. And he made his decision. And he said...

'Daniel. I am very sorry... I can *not* meet with you...'

Huh?

I looked up to see my small crowd of friends new and old. Bob smiling. Kyohei genuinely excited. The small jolly woman positively beaming. And I didn't know what to say. Had he *really* said that? *Why?*

'Sorry, did you...'

'I am *sorry*, Daniel...'

This was too much. This was *not* acceptable. This was just not *acceptable*.

'Akira, I've travelled from London. From London, Akira. All the way just to say hello to you. For the past few months I've been doing it a lot. I've been back to Loughborough, where we met. I've been to Berlin, and to LA, and to Melbourne. And now I'm here in Japan – and it's all for you! Please, you *have* to meet with me...'

A silence.

An uncomfortable silence.

Was this really so weird? For me, turning up and saying hi wherever an old friend might be had just become natural. Normal. But for Akira, oblivious to my actions of the past few months and just trying to get on with his life, this would be strange. Why *should* he meet up with me? The fact that I'd travelled so far just added to the pressure. For me it was a reason he should meet me. For him, it could very well be a reason not to.

Part of me had always hoped I could rely on the past to help secure the future. That I could remind people how close we had been. Hope that that would be enough to convince them that reconnecting would be okay.

But people move on. They grow up. They don't *need* their past.

Tom, for example. Tom who didn't want to meet. Didn't need to meet. Thought meeting would be *weird*.

Was that what Akira was thinking right now?

And, more importantly, could I let that change things? Could I allow him not to meet up? Could I let a fear of awkwardness spoil an experience which, in its own small way – and for me, at least – had become something of a small but rich beauty?

No.

I had a decision to make.

The people around me had realised something was up. I'd been silent too long. Staring, sad-eyed, too long. The jolly woman looked less jolly. Kyohei and Bob had let their smiles drift.

I knew what to do.

I spoke swiftly and confidently.

'Akira, I'm coming back to Tokyo now. I'm going to get on the next train from Joieu and I'll be at Shinjuku station by nine pm. You *have* to meet me there. I will see you at Shinjuku station at nine pm.'

And I hung up the phone.

Kyohei stopped the car with a slight skid. He'd gone miles out of his way, driving me and Bob all the way to Kofu to save time.

'Good luck!' he said, and I shook his hand, warmly and firmly.

'You don't know what this means to me,' I said, but, actually, I think he did.

'We should make the 7.15 train,' said Bob, studying a schedule Kyohei had found in his glovebox. We ran up the stairs and tried to find our platform. 'It'll get us there after nine, though...'

'Here it is...' I said.

It was a long and nervy journey.

On the one hand, I was pleased. I'd talked to Akira. We'd made contact. Maybe, if he wasn't there, waiting for me on the platform, this might still be the start of something. Maybe it was an ice-breaker. Maybe he'd be more open to the idea of meeting up in the future. But I knew how busy he was. I knew how unlikely it was he'd ever make his way to London. This was where his life was. And I knew how unlikely it was I'd make it back to Japan any time soon.

On the other hand, I was sad. Sad he'd said no to meeting. Sad he hadn't jumped at the chance. Bob knew how I felt. He kept quiet on the train, as nervous as I was, but as full of hope as I dared to let myself be. I felt full of warmth for my friend. Glad that he'd been willing to share in this. Grateful that he'd thrown himself into it, when really what he'd been expecting was a day of sightseeing and photos. If I didn't get Akira, getting to know Bob again was a brilliant by-product.

'I've been thinking,' he said, suddenly. 'I'm going to get in touch with a few old friends. You know? See how they're doing. It's weird how we say we "used" to know people. Why "used to"? There was never any agreement to stop. It just happened. So maybe starting again can be just as easy... friendship is kind of what it's all about, really, isn't it?'

I smiled.

I'd discovered that very same thing, in a roundabout way. This had started because I'd been uncomfortable with the way my life was changing. But actually, life changes all the time. It doesn't change once you hit thirty, or once you start feeling like a grown-up. It doesn't change because of any one thing you do. It changes constantly, sometimes in small ways, and sometimes in seismic shifts. And the way you feel depends entirely on the way you deal with those changes.

Friends are a marker of time. And the friendships you make are a marker of life. We're proud of our friends. We're proud of the unwritten contract – we've chosen them, and they've chosen us. No one *had* to. We all *wanted* to. Friends define us, and we walk or trip or stumble through life just as they do. When a good friendship ends... maybe it wasn't a good friendship. Or maybe it can be started up again just as easily.

I reached into my backpack and pulled out my address book. Whatever was to happen next, I could at least do this. I could at *least* update it.

'We're here,' said Bob, and I looked up to see the bright lights of Tokyo; streetlights whizzing by the window, trailing like shooting stars.

The train slowed to a halt and Bob and I stood up.

'Well, here we go…' I said.

The platform was half empty as we stepped off the train. I glanced nervously around. I couldn't see Akira. I looked at my watch. It was nine twenty-eight. It had been more or less twelve full hours and Bob and I were at the same place we'd started our journey.

'He might be on a different platform,' said Bob. 'I'm sure he'd have waited.'

I turned to check what other platforms I could make out. A lone man sat on a bench, reading a newspaper and sipping something. Closer, a young couple were giggling about something. He was tickling her, playfully, and she was batting him away. In the distance, a station guard was pointing out the toilets to an elderly lady in a hat.

Our train moved off, signalling, somehow, the end of something.

'He's not here,' I said, and Bob didn't know what to say.

We stood in silence for a moment.

'Unless…' said Bob.

'What?'

'Unless we call him?'

'I don't have his number,' I said. 'I didn't know how to ask the jolly woman for it… *shit*, I should have *asked* for his number…'

'*I've* got his number.'

'Eh?'

'Kyohei got it off the woman. He wrote it down and slipped it to me when we were running to the car. Let's call him…'

He handed me his phone. The number was already in there, ready to go.

Thank God for Bob. Thank *God* for Kyohei.

I hit Dial.

It rang.

A pause. Then…

'Hello?'

'Akira?'

'Daniel! Where are you?'

'I'm at Shinjuku station. I'm on platform four! Where are *you*?'

'I am here too!'

'Where?'

But I didn't need to ask. I turned round and there, the man who'd been reading his paper and sipping something stood up and waved.

It was Akira Matsui.

Instantly, all weirdness had vanished.

Akira was *delighted* that I'd been standing outside his house that afternoon. *Delighted* that I'd been wandering around his workplace, seeing his office, bothering his colleagues. He even seemed delighted I was wearing his face on my T-shirt.

His English had lapsed slightly, but Bob and I took him off for a Coke in the nearest hotel bar. There we sat, the three of us, forty floors up and admiring the view. Tokyo's urban lightshow and vast towers. The people far down below, each one of them off on an adventure of their own. Each one off to see a friend, or have some fun, or who knows what. It seemed, suddenly, like a city in which *anything* could happen.

And we talked. And we caught up. And I told him about how important it was that he'd met me. How I'd been tracking people down and making sense of life. How to look forward you sometimes have to look back. How friends are the very definition of your life. How the people who've seen you grow up are the people who sometimes know you best. And he nodded, and he understood, and by the end, we were fine and fixed old friends again. He told me of his ambitions, of his hopes. He told me about turning thirty, and how it had made him think about life too. He told me things I'd forgotten about growing up. The things we'd done, the places we'd gone. I apologised on behalf of Michael Amodio for the day he'd done the crane kick from *The Karate Kid* on Akira's head. Akira laughed, and said he remembered that, and he'd thought everyone in Britain was a karate master. And Bob made him promise to give Kyohei very good marks in everything he did from now on.

Our meeting only lasted an hour. But it was a great hour. An hour that meant something to me, and, I hope, a little something to him. We took him back down to the train station, where I waved goodbye to Akira Matsui – friend number eleven.

And then, laughing like high little boys, Bob and I hit Tokyo to celebrate.

This was it. Just Chris to get. And I was thankful. Because I was *so* tired.

But not tonight. Bob and I sang loud and ridiculous karaoke in a small booth in Roppongi Hills. We drank sake in a strange bar in Akasaka. We high-fived confused strangers as we crossed the road before the Rainbow Bridge. We studied weird Japanese toys and a twenty-foot Godzilla in a shopping mall. We declined a foot rub by a fourteen-year-old girl dressed as a French maid. We stood at the foot of the Tokyo Tower, and wondered what it must be like to stand at the top.

But I already felt like I was.

And, when hunger finally set in, and Bob decided we needed to do something about it, I said, 'I know just the place.'

'Where?' he said.

'You'll love it,' I said. 'I know a master ninja who gives great advice…'

Heee eeHop

Wednesday 16th November

It is my Birthday To day Jamie
and Chris and Alic and Elie To
day   (are coming

Chapter Twenty-one

In which we meet someone unexpected...

The trip had been an unmitigated success. An *unmitigated* success.

I had *done* it! Peter and Akira. Numbers ten and eleven. Updated. In the book. Friends again.

Now, I thought, again, stepping off the Heathrow Express, there was just number twelve. Chris Guirrean. And he was virtually in the bag. He'd called. Left a message. I *had* him.

This had been quite a journey. From Loughborough, to Berlin, to LA, to Melbourne, to Tokyo, to London... and all in the name of friendship. And I'd come a long way in other ways, too. I would meet Christopher by November 16th. I would meet him by the time I was thirty. And then I would be ready. Ready to accept my fate – no, *not* fate: destiny – as one of the walking thirtysomethings.

At Paddington, I hopped in a taxi and cheerfully headed for home. Lizzie would be at home today. I texted her telling her to put the kettle on in anticipation.

Oh yeah. Because this was a *celebration*.

'How was it?' she said, and I got my digital camera out.

'That's Peter relaxing with a Guinness!' I said, pointing him out. 'We went bowling and ate noodles!'

'Brilliant!' she said. 'And Akira?'

'That's him there! I got trained by ninjas and traipsed around the Japanese countryside! If Bob hadn't been there I'd *never* have found him...'

'Who's Bob?' she asked.

'He's an old friend.'

'Of course he is.'

I hugged her.

'Tea?' she said.

'Yes! But no! First, give me Chris's message!'

And, like a dutiful wife, off she ran.

'I wrote it down,' she said. 'All he'd said on the message was, "This is Chris calling for Danny Wallace, can he call me back," and then his number.'

'Ace,' I said. 'Did he seem pleased to hear from me?'

'Well, it was a very short message, and he—'

'Hang on – what?'

'It was a really short message. I wasn't—'

'No, before that. What did he say? What did you say he said?'

Something wasn't right here.

'He said, "This is Chris calling, can he..."'

'No – you missed a bit. Did he say my name?'

'Oh – yeah. "This is Chris calling for Danny Wallace..."'

My heart sank.

'Danny, or Daniel?'

'*Danny*, I think...'

'Is the message still on there?'

'No – I – I don't know...'

I picked up the phone and checked. No messages. It'd been *deleted*.

'What's going on?' said Lizzie.

'Was it Danny, or was it Daniel?' I asked, frantically. 'Did he leave a surname? Did he say it was Chris *Guirrean*?'

'I'm nearly *positive* it was Danny,' she said. 'Is that bad?'

It *was* bad. Chris would not have known me as Danny. He'd have known me as Daniel. That's why I'd been so careful with the letters. That's why I'd signed them *all* Daniel.

'Maybe he found you on the internet,' she said. 'Or maybe he knows someone who knows you. Maybe when you've been on telly, or...'

'What's this number?'

'That's just what he left on the machine...'

'It's... *foreign*...'

And it was. But *familiarly* so. Was that good or bad?

'Is it him?' she said.

I picked up the phone and dialled.

One ring.

Two.

A man answered, saying something incomprehensible.

'Hello?' I said, cautiously.

He had an accent. Not a Scottish one. And he didn't say hello. He said h*a*llo.

'Is that Chris?'

'This is Chris.'

'Chris... *Guirrean*?'

It didn't *sound* like him.

'Who is this, please?'

'My name is Danny Wallace. *Daniel* Wallace. I'm calling from London. I got this message, saying that I should—'

'Aha! Yes!' said the man. 'Here is Christian Zimmerman!'

'Here is Christian Zimmerman?' I said. 'Where?'

'I am Christian Zimmerman!'

I didn't know what any of this meant.

'Sorry – you're *who*?'

'You had bought from me something from eBay. The World Cup 1986 book. It was just courtesy call to say I had sent the item and you should expect it. Has it been?'

Oh... oh, no...

I looked towards the stairs. There was a package. My eyes fell to my feet.

'Ja,' I said, and put the phone down.

I looked at Lizzie.

'It wasn't him, was it?' she said.

'Never mind,' I said.

And she gave me a hug.

*

I was tired. All my leads had gone. I'd done my absolute best, but I was *tired* and *all my leads had gone*. Chris Guirrean had simply disappeared. It happens. I could only hope that wherever he was, he was okay. And hey – maybe *one* day we'd meet up. I knew I couldn't do this forever. Eventually, I'd have to move on. Because moving on – growing up – had been the point of this all along.

'Why don't you go up to Dundee?' said Lizzie. 'Just for the day? See if you can find any leads?'

'Peter suggested the same thing when I was in Melbourne. I don't know. I'm not sure I have the energy. He's disappeared.'

'You should, you know. Just for your own peace of mind. You never know. He could be there.'

'Virtually everyone's moved on,' I said. 'It's unlikely.'

'Just for your own peace of mind,' she said again, softly.

And one day, just three or four days before my thirtieth, I'd decided I would. I had no expectations. It just felt right to do it. Complete the journey. See my first house, my first view, my first *home*. At least finish the *tour*.

The plane flew low over Magdalene Green – the green I'd grown up playing football on with Ross and Leslie from next door. The same green with the same bandstand. The hill my dad pushed me down on the girl's bike he gave me when I was six, letting me go without stabilisers for the first time, and watching me as I disappeared into a ditch at the end. And there was my house – number 1 Richmond Terrace, a grand and imposing Victorian house facing out towards the River Tay, the house I'd stood outside and had my picture taken on my first day at school.

As soon as I'd landed, I'd made my way back there, and sat in the bandstand in the middle of the green. I'd sat here with Christopher Guirrean nearly twenty-five years before, on the day the big Pickfords van came to take our stuff down to Loughborough. I stood up, and walked towards my old house.

Outside the house next door was a man bringing some shopping bags in from a bright red car. He looked at me for a second, and then looked away. But I couldn't stop looking at him. He looked so *familiar*.

'Leslie?' I said.

If it *was* Leslie, it was the same Leslie I'd always played football with all those years before. The Leslie that had accidentally let me watch *Blade Runner* with him and caused me endless sleepless nights as a result. The Leslie that used to make tapes of The Monkees and The Police for me and slip them through the letterbox.

'Yes?'

It was!

'I used to live next door to you!' I said. 'Well – *there*!'

I pointed at the house next door. *My* house.

'Daniel!' he said.

Leslie had bought the house from his parents some years before, and was now raising his own kids in it. One of them was about as old as I'd been when I'd left Dundee. We drank tea, and I met his lovely wife, and then he said, 'Do you want to see your old house?'

And he went and asked the neighbours, and in we went, and the memories came flooding back. They'd done a lot to the place, but the one room that remained untouched was my old bedroom...

I looked at the walls... they'd been wood-chip, and I'd loved picking bits of it away, despite being constantly told not to. I cast my eyes around. Incredibly, my damage remained. I didn't know whether to be proud or ashamed.

'I feel like I owe you a fiver,' I told the new owners. 'All those bits missing from the wall – that was me...'

It was a memory I didn't know I had, brought back into vivid colour right there and then. Just as so many memories had been these past few months.

I thanked Leslie, and we took a picture together, sitting on the same bench in my old front garden that we'd had our picture taken on so many years before. And then I walked down the road, to Strawberry Bank, the street on which Chris had lived, and on which we'd done so much playing. His house was still there. But there was a different name on the door.

And so I turned around, and, after a last walk across the green, I headed back to the airport, and back to my life.

*

I had officially given up, I decided, two days later, on my way to the corner shop to buy some milk.

But I wasn't too sad about it. After all – let's look at the evidence. Tom had said no. Andy I couldn't meet. And Chris was who knows where. But I'd managed to find and meet nine out of twelve of the names in the Book. And that's a score of 75 per cent. That's an *A*.

Plus, there were the bonus balls. I'd be going to Big Al's wedding soon – and that wouldn't have happened if I hadn't sent him a text on a whim. I could hop on a train and see Alex Chinyemba, the karate-teacher-turned-estate-agent, and his many children. There was Eilidh, the Gaelic translator, living in Glasgow. But all this was, I knew, for another time. Maybe next year. Or the year after. Because – you know – life *begins* at thirty.

I picked up the milk and wandered to the counter. And then I thought what the hell – and bought a packet of Wotsits. Just because I'm nearly thirty doesn't mean I can't buy a packet of Wotsits.

And then I made a mental note to pick up some hummus later on.

I was fumbling around in my pocket, though, when I noticed something absolutely extraordinary. Something you will not believe, but something which I promise you is true, and is easily verifiable, should you ever find yourself in the British Library with a few moments to spare...

On the front page of the Evening Standard – the *front page*! – was a picture. A picture of someone *very* familiar. Someone from my childhood. Someone in the Book. And what's more, it was someone I hadn't yet met...

I bought the paper and literally *ran* home.

And then I literally ran back again because I'd forgotten the milk and Wotsits.

'Cameron! It's Danny! What are you doing tomorrow night?'

'I don't know! Nothing! Why?'

'Meet me at the Richmond, on Earls Court Road, 7pm, tomorrow. Do. Not. Be. Late.'

*

It was the night before my thirtieth birthday. November 15th, 2006. 6.59pm. Cameron Dewa walked through the doors of the Richmond on Earls Court Road.

'What's going on?' he said.

'We have to meet a man,' I said. 'A man who's going to meet us round the corner.'

'Who? Why?'

'History requires it,' I said. 'It's to do with a man from our past.'

We walked round the corner and met the man. Cameron didn't recognise him. Nor did I. Because he wasn't the man from our past. He was the man I'd paid money to in order to *see* the man from our past.

I handed a small brown envelope over.

He handed me one in return.

I turned to Cameron.

'What date is it?'

'November the fifteenth.'

'Remember this date,' I said. 'Because this is the date we do what we always said we were going to do.'

Cameron looked at me blankly.

I took a deep breath.

I opened the envelope.

I took out the tickets. The tickets I'd paid for on eBay.

'We're going to see Michael Jackson,' I said.

Cameron's face lit up like I have never seen a face light up before.

'WHAT?'

'Yeah!'

'AMAZING!'

'Definitely.'

'INCREDIBLE!'

'Okay, people are *looking* at us now...'

And that is how Cameron Dewa and myself got to achieve our only childhood dream, the night before my thirtieth birthday, in Earls Court, London.

Michael Jackson was closing the show at the 2006 World Music

Awards, in front of Lindsay Lohan, Usher, Paris Hilton, Beyoncé, a few thousand people, and – right at the very front, just eight feet away – me and Cameron Dewa.

It was *brilliant*.

Michael Jackson even nearly sang his songs. He spent most of the time waving, and being surrounded by tiny, jumping dancers. But he was there. The thirteenth name in my book. The extra, added, unofficial member.

Next to me, a burly Asian lad with a single white satin glove was in tears.

'What are you crying for?' I said. 'He's right *there*!'

'He's just so amazing,' the lad said, and one of his mates pissed himself laughing.

'I don't suppose you know the current address of the Michael Jackson fan club?' I asked, as the opening chords of 'Thriller' sent the crowd into a frenzy.

'Eh?' he said, wiping away another tear.

'Do you know the current address for the World of Michael Jackson?'

'Oh – yeah. It's michaeljackson.com...'

Of course it was. Times had changed.

'Why?' he said, and I put my pen away.

'I'm just updating my address book,' I said.

Cameron and I jumped into a black cab at 11.15pm. If we timed it right, we could be back home, with Lizzie, by midnight. We tore through the streets of London by moonlight. The river looked amazing. Big Ben was bright, the Millennium Wheel lit up, and we crossed the bridge. I'd been over this bridge thousands of times before. Turning right at the end would take me to the East End, the place I'd lived throughout my twenties. But things were different now, in a dozen different ways. We turned left.

'That was so cool,' said Cameron. 'That was like being a kid again.'

'What time is it?' I asked.

'11.43,' he said.

'We're going to make it.'

And at 11.57, me, Lizzie, and my childhood friend Cameron were standing in my kitchen, back at home, holding a bottle of champagne and counting down the seconds.

And at twelve midnight, I, Danny Wallace, turned thirty.

The next morning, Lizzie woke me bright and early with my birthday cup of tea.

'Come on, old man!' she said. 'Come with me! Close your eyes!'

I did as she said and followed her into the hallway.

'Keep them closed! Now… open them!'

I opened my eyes.

And there, before me, *another* childhood ambition realised.

'It's a Chopper!' I said. 'You got me a bloody *Chopper*!'

It *was* a bloody Chopper. Beautiful, sparkling and fire-engine red. The bright yellow word CHOPPER down its side. The low-rise seat. It was *everything* I'd ever wanted as a kid. If it had come with an Evel Knievel suit I would've probably exploded.

'Do they still *make* these?' I said, gazing at its wonder.

'Special edition!' said Lizzie.

'Special *edition*!' I said. The two words lent it such glamour.

I hugged her, tight.

'I have to go to work,' she said. 'You'll get your *real* present, tonight…'

I raised my eyebrows.

'Are you being saucy?' I said.

'No', she said. 'I'm being literal.'

And with that, she went to work.

I lay back down in bed and turned my phone on.

The text messages started immediately.

HAPPY BIRTHDAY MATE. It was from Peter Gibson.

HAPPY BIRTHDAY! Lauren.

HAPPY BIRTHDAY BROTHER! AND THANKS FOR THE MARS BAR YOU LEFT AT THE CORNER HOTEL! That one was from Wag in Australia.

SEE YOU AT THE PARTY MATE! Ian.

And then the phone rang.

'Are you near a radio?' said Hanne.

'Yeah – I'm still in bed.'

'Lucky you – I'm at work. Turn it on right now!'

I turned it on and heard Hanne give some kind of signal.

Nick Ferrari on LBC took a deep breath.

'And a very happy birthday to a very lucky young man indeed – Danny Wallace turns thirty this very morning! Happy birthday from all of London, Danny!'

I smiled.

My sixth birthday had just been topped.

That night, on the top floor of a bar in Islington, they arrived.

My friends.

New, and old, and much older than I'd ever have dared hope for.

Ben Ives was still in LA, of course, but I'd sent him an invite anyway, and he'd sent me a birthday email in return. Tarek had recording commitments in Berlin. And Akira... well... Akira was in Japan, solving cancer.

But as I stood there, at the door, welcoming people in, I watched, honoured, as Michael Amodio and his girlfriend Nikol entered the room...

'We're *engaged*!' he said. 'You've *got* to come to the wedding!'

'I will!' I said. 'I promise!'

And then Cameron Dewa, still high after seeing Michael Jackson the night before, walked in with *his* wife, Nadine.

'Potaaatoooo!' he said, and then spent a few minutes explaining to Nadine precisely *why* he'd been saying 'Potato' so much lately.

Anil Tailor arrived, and moments later, Lauren walked in.

Timelord Simon Gibson had sent his apologies – he was busy opening up a new Toby Carvery and probably solving more mysteries of the universe while he was at it. But then, just as I was handed a pint by someone at the bar, in walked Neil Findlay.

'We only seem to meet at thirtieth-birthday parties,' he said. 'But happy birthday!'

'Happy birthday, mate!' I said, before realising that was quite a strange thing to say, as it was *my* birthday. I wanted to tell Neil what an effect his party had had on me. How it had come at just the right time. But suddenly there was a tap on my shoulder.

'I'm wearing my shirt again!' said Ian, proudly.

'It's brilliant,' I said, happily. 'It is a *brilliant* shirt! The people of Chislehurst should be proud!'

'Yeah – though – I *am* thinking about moving back to London,' he said. 'Even *they've* started turning on the shirt…'

'Get a drink. This is Neil…'

And as Neil and Ian walked off together, I turned and bumped into Hanne…

'Happy birthday,' she said, hugging me. 'Old man…'

She handed me her present. I opened it. It was a display cushion.

'Ian said you *loved* these…'

'Love is a strong word,' I said. 'But I'm ready for one now, I think…'

'You actually sit on them?'

'They're not for bottoms,' I said.

She smiled.

'I also got you some Wotsits,' she said, and I stood back, and I looked around the room, and I saw all my friends, and I felt so *lucky*.

'Having a nice night?' said Lizzie, putting her arm round me.

'The best,' I said.

'Good. By the way, this is Tom…'

I looked at the man with her.

'Hi, Tom…' I said, and then slowly, I realised *which* Tom it was…

'Your wife's been pestering me to show up,' he said. 'Email after email. A quite considerable marketing campaign. So I showed up… how are you, Dan?'

I looked at Lizzie. Because this wasn't about meeting Tom again, as nice as it was. It was about what she'd done for me. What this *meant* to me. She'd joined in. Seen something that was wrong. Made it *right*.

'It's really good to see you, Tom…' I said. '*Really* good.'

Another address updated. Not counting Michael Jackson, that was ten out of twelve. That wasn't an A any more. That was *first-class honours*.

And then Tom and I began to talk about the old days. And I introduced him to Cameron, and to Anil, and to Mikey.

'One thing, though, Tom – your dad *didn't* invent the Sprite logo, *did* he?'

'No,' said Tom, shaking his head. 'Of course he bloody didn't.'

And we all raised our glasses and laughed. And just like that, we were a gang again.

'That was the best present *ever*,' I said, to Lizzie, a little later on.

'That? That wasn't your present. That was just me harassing a man and convincing him you weren't a gay stalker *or* after his money. I told him everything you'd been doing. He was actually rather sweet about the whole thing…'

'So what's my *real* present?' I asked, confused.

She reached into her pocket and pulled out a slip of paper.

'This…' she said.

I looked at it, unsurely, and then unfolded it.

It was an address.

It was *Chris Guirrean*'s address.

'But… *how*? I tried *everything*!'

'I phoned your mum. We spent an age trying to find Chris's dad's address. Turned out he still works up in Scotland. We found an email address for him, and when she was spelling it out on the phone to me, it turned out that he wasn't a Guirrean.'

'How do you mean? He'd changed his name?'

Was this common? Was that little Russian kid grown up to become 'Ben Berlin' just one of *many*?

'No… I mean he was a Guirron. Not a Guirrean.'

'A Guirron? But he's a *Guirrean*. That's what it says in the Book…'

'Yeah. And when did you write his name in the Book?'

'When I was… six.'

Lizzie just looked at me.

'But I was an *excellent* speller!' I said.

'So anyway, I didn't email his dad. I used the information to find Christopher's address, instead.'

'Well… where is he?' I said, looking at the slip of paper.

'He's still in Dundee,' she said. 'I haven't made contact. You can go and meet him. I reckon we can extend this past your birthday, seeing as he's your best friend, and all…'

And I looked at Lizzie.

And I was filled with warmth and love.

And I said, 'No, he isn't,' and she looked at me, confused.

'*You're* my best friend,' I said.

And the next day, when the party had long finished, and before the sun had even risen, I got up, and I wandered into the spare room, and I *finally* mended that broken socket.

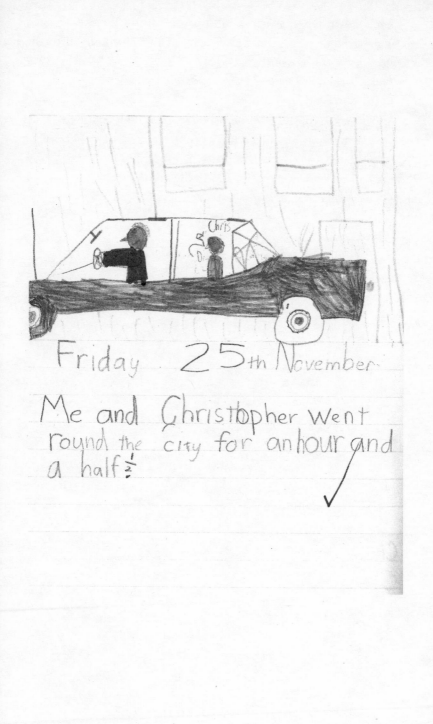

Friday 25th November

Me and Christopher went
round the city for an hour and
a half ½

November 19th, 2006

Dear Andy,

I did it. I found them.

Daniel

Epilogue

Well, there you go.

The story of a summer turning into a winter. And, in some ways, of a winter turning into a summer.

I didn't manage to meet all twelve of the Twelve by November 16th, 2006. Bearing in mind I only got Chris's address at around 10pm that night, it would have been a bit of a tall order. But, and I hope this still counts, in January of 2007, on a dark and brooding Scottish evening, I did indeed manage to finally meet up with him, in Dundee, after nearly twenty-five years apart.

It was excellent.

Chris is in insurance now, and we spent a long and warm evening talking about days gone by, and walking around Dundee. We happened past our old school, Park Place Primary, where we'd first met, in 1980, and where he was surprised to hear I had vomited on Scott Butcher's lap. To make it even better, with us was Jamie Maddox – now *Dr* Jamie Maddox – another great friend from those years gone by, and the three of us agreed never to lose touch again.

And so far, we haven't.

Later that year, I travelled to the small town of Teplice in the Czech Republic, to watch my old friend Michael Amodio get married to the bellydancing granddaughter of a white witch. It was a lovely day, attended by more old friends I'd lost touch with over the years.

Michael's brother – formerly of dance troupe Natural Born Thrillers – was also there, but managed to avoid any bellydancing.

Anil Tailor is about to finish his final exams before becoming a fully fledged architect. He never again saw the mysterious stranger he saw that day in his car... but it did make him think. He's currently deciding where in the world he'd like to go. He still thinks he might give Peter a call.

Simon Gibson has made no new scientific discoveries this year, but *has* just opened up a new Toby Carvery in Banbury. Check it out. You will love the adequate parking facilities, though you will find it annoying that you can't go back for seconds.

A builder called Greg has now replaced the guttering (despite being a man now, that was still a little too much for me). Plus, it took him about an hour, on the exact day he said he'd turn up. The canopy fell off during particularly high winds in April 2007. I have realised I have no use for a canopy. That socket broke again. But I fixed it straight away. It made me feel like a *man*.

In September of 2007, Lizzie and I travelled back to Berlin, where we met up with Tarek, his wife Anna (also a rapper) and their small daughter Naliyah (who does not rap). Tarek continues to produce some of Germany's finest hip-hop, and is an adoring and doting father.

BRD is, by all accounts, *still* the Bester Rapper Deutschlands. Papo is still demolishing whole concert halls with the strength of a hurricane.

Lauren is very worried you'll find her boring. I've told her you won't. She's also worried you'll find her odd. I've told her you will.

Akira, Tom, and Ben are all doing very well indeed, and all say hello. Cameron doesn't – he says 'Potatoo!'

But that's Cameron for you.

Peter Gibson returned from Australia after 357 hugely enjoyable days. He's back in London now, and I was finally able to have that pint with him in Tooting. He's expecting Anil's call any day now...

Michael Jackson recently bought a twenty-acre estate in County Wicklow, Ireland, and is currently working on a new comeback album, which is as yet untitled.

Hanne recently met up with an old friend she'd made contact with through Facebook. She grudgingly admitted, 'It was pretty great, actually,' and hasn't ruled out doing it again. Although she wants you to know that she sees it as a business utility, first and foremost.

Ian has joined the Neighbourhood Watch scheme in Chislehurst. He says it has given him a 'real sense of purpose about life'. He no longer wears that shirt, as he feels it does not fit in with the 'image of authority' that the Neighbourhood Watch requires of him.

I have suggested he roam the streets dressed as a bear, as if there's one thing that's bound to put burglars off, it's a burly, roaming bear.

Ian says I'm a tit for thinking this.

Wag is on tour again, with a second album in the shops, and I am now so good at Call of Duty 2 that the Bald Assassin refuses to play against me.

Ben Ives and I had a Christmas drink in Bath.

He turned up wearing a small dog mask on his head.

I wasn't tricked for a *second*.

Therefore I *win*.

Bad Mutha! is yet to hit cinemas anywhere.

Weirdly, ten days after my thirtieth birthday, the 1980s and early 1990s began to tap on my shoulder.

By Christmas, Take That had reformed and enjoyed their first number one in ten years. The Spice Girls weren't far behind. Even A-ha got in on the act. And Dirk Benedict from the *A-Team* went on *Celebrity Big Brother*, meaning that, thanks to Lizzie and her reality TV connections, I got to say hello.

Apparently, he never *got* my *Jim'll Fix It* letter.

A few months later, defying Mr Williams's ban, Cadbury's announced the return of the Wispa bar. As if in reaction to this, The Police announced they would be reforming.

Soon after *Transformers: The Movie* became Britain's number one film, and *Indiana Jones 4* made us all feel so happy, Steven Spielberg declared production on the film of *The Goonies 2* would finally begin this year. It is not known whether Tarek will be involved in the German version.

Plus, marvellously, in October of 2007, I was asked to appear on BBC1's *Mastermind*. My specialist chosen subject?

Ghostbusters.

Man Points are now a thing of the past.

Thank God.

I returned to Dundee towards the end of 2007 to attend the wedding of Christopher Guirron to his new wife Louise. I was the only man not in a kilt. They were married at a church in Broughty Ferry, and the reception was held on the River Tay, with the same view as I'd grown up seeing every single day without any thought as to how lucky I was.

It's funny, sometimes, how life works out, if you give it the chance.

I haven't stopped, either, by the way. Just because I'm thirty doesn't mean I can't still have fun. It just means I have to have display cushions.

Give it a go.

Look someone up.

Danny would like to thank...

My friends. Ian. Hanne. Wag.

Anil Tailor. Michael Amodio. Simon Gibson. Cameron Dewa. Tarek Helmy. Lauren 'Not Boring' Medcalfe. Tom Bain. Ben Ives. Akira Matsui. Peter Gibson. Chris Guirron. And Andy Clements.

Massive, massive thanks to Jake Lingwood, to Simon Trewin, to Jago Irwin, to Lisa Thomas, and, in advance, to Ed Griffiths.

Huge thanks to Tokyo Bob, Tomoko, Kyohei, and Jamie Maddox. Stefan and Georgia, my goddaughter Poppy (is that her name?) and near-goddaughter Daisy.

Thanks to Peter McInnes, Nadine Beatty, and Zairul (the kid who lived at number 3, Malaysia) for randomly getting in touch before the publication of this book and just before their thirtieth birthdays – after twenty-five years apart. Here's to meeting up. And to Elliot, who I hadn't seen in just as long, and who turned out, bizarrely, to be living in the building opposite my old flat.

Thanks to close friends from kidulthood who for whatever random reason weren't mentioned in The Book... Amy, Josh, Brian, Espen, Erik, Jonas, Ian, Helen, Anna, Ross, Alec (thanks for the wedding!) and everyone else.

Thanks to the waiter at Desperados who gave Lizzie and me free beer when we explained that we'd started an entire pact in his place of work.

Well done and thanks to Rich Glover and Natalie Byfield. To Ben Frost, Ken Barlow, Karl Pilkington, Mike Gayle, Phil Hilton, The Friday Fun Club's Richard Bacon and Marc Haynes, Mrs Tailor, and conker champion Tim Sismey. Bald Assassin – you suck. And no thanks to Paul the builder (but no hard feelings, either... plus, I still have your ladder).

And thanks to Mum and Dad, for sending me The Box out of the blue, and of course (especially) to Lizzie, who didn't mind me opening it.

This book was written on Great Barrier Island, New Zealand, in Berlin, Germany, and in my back garden, in London, with a cup of tea and a sandwich.

And then I sat outside The Crown in Islington, and made it all a bit better.

Thanks to you for reading it.

www.dannywallace.com

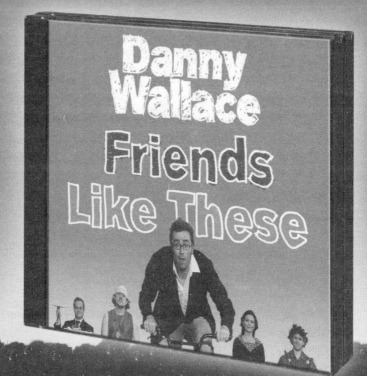